RESULTS WITHOUT AUTHORITY

RESULTS WITHOUT AUTHORITY

Controlling a Project When the Team Doesn't Report to You

TOM KENDRICK

American Management Association

New York • Atlanta • Brussels • Chicago • Mexico City • San Francisco
Shanghai • Tokyo • Toronto • Washington, D.C.

This publication is designed to provide accurate and authoritative
information in regard to the subject matter covered. It is sold with the
understanding that the publisher is not engaged in rendering legal,
accounting, or other professional service. If legal advice or other expert
assistance is required, the services of a competent professional person
should be sought.

"PMI" and the PMI logo are service and trademarks registered in the
United States and other nations; "PMP" and the PMP logo are
certification marks registered in the United States and other nations;
"PMBOK," "PM Network," and "PMI Today" are trademarks registered
in the United States and other nations; and "Project Management
Journal" and "Building professionalism in project management" are
trademarks of the Project Management Institute, Inc.

Library of Congress Cataloging-in-Publication Data

Kendrick, Tom.
    Results without authority : controlling a project when the team doesn't report to you /
Tom Kendrick.
        p.   cm.
    Includes bibliographical references and index.
    ISBN-10: 0-8144-7343-1
    ISBN-13: 978-0-8144-7343-6
    1. Project management.   I. Title.

HD69.P75.K463   2006
658.4'04–dc22   2006006937

Printing number

10   9   8   7   6   5   4   3   2

Contents

Acknowledgments

RESULTS WITHOUT AUTHORITY benefits from the hard-earned experience of dozens, if not hundreds, of excellent project leaders and managers who have shared with me so generously of their experiences over the years. In particular, I need to thank Terry Ash, Ron Askeland, Scott Beth, Karel de Bakker, Al DeLucia, Tom Fader, Bob Gudz, Esteri Hinman, Denis Lambert, Nancy McDonald, Revathi Muruvanda Muthanna, Joe Podolsky, Patrick Schmid, Richard Simonds, Arun Swamy, Peter Vogel-Dittrich, J. D. Watson, and Ashok Waran, who provided examples, feedback, and encouragement throughout the process of pulling this book together. I also want to thank my long-suffering spouse, Barbara Kendrick, who repeatedly read and reread the text of this book, attacking the confusion and untangling the knots.

Although these friends (and many others) deserve a great measure of the credit for what is in this book, any errors, omissions, or unnecessary complexity are all my responsibility. If you find any, or just want to provide feedback, please let me know.

Getting results without authority involves more than a little luck. Yet luck is what happens when preparation meets opportunity. I hope in this book you find ample guidance for your preparations, and all of your opportunities result in successful projects.

—TOM KENDRICK (TKENDRICK@FAILUREPROOFPROJECTS.COM)
SAN CARLOS, CALIFORNIA

CHAPTER 1

Control of Projects

PROJECTS ARE EVERYWHERE. Some projects we attempt succeed, and others do not. Many projects that fail do so because the project leader lacks sufficient control to keep things moving toward a successful conclusion. Insufficient project control is a result of many factors: lack of authority, geographically distributed teams, excessive project change, competing priorities, and inadequate planning, just to name a few.

Today's projects are increasingly undertaken in environments where the project leader has little formal authority. Even for project managers who do have formal authority, significant portions of project work are done by contributors who work for other managers, often in a separate company. Projects where no one is in charge are almost certain to fail. As leader of your project, you must assume control, whether you possess organizational authority or not. As unlikely as it may seem, there is much that any project leader can do to establish and maintain project control. This book has many ideas for achieving project success using techniques that do not depend on organizational position or formal authority.

▪ Who's in Charge Here?

In classes, workshops, and informal discussions of project management that I've been a part of, one of the most common questions is always, "How can I manage my project if I have no power or authority?" This issue comes up so often that I developed a list of things that project leaders can (and should) take control of, regardless of their position or power in an organization. None of these things requires any authority beyond what is implicit when you are delegated responsibility for a project, and some don't even rely on that.

Factors that Any Project Leader Can Control
- Measurement
- Reporting cycles
- Milestones
- Communication
- Project reviews
- Change management
- Rewards and recognition
- Constructive criticism
- Reciprocity and exchange
- Risk monitoring

Project leaders can use these ideas, along with many others you will find in this book, to enhance their control in *any* project environment. The techniques outlined in the next several chapters don't rely on the "command and control" authority of the project leader, so they are effective in cross-functional, matrix, heavily outsourced, virtual, volunteer, and other challenging environments. In fact, even project managers who do have substantial authority will benefit from the practices described in this book because they avoid the potential resentment and demotivation that can follow "pulling rank."

▪ Structure of This Book

The first half of this book explores three elements of project control: process, influence, and measurement. This introductory chapter introduces the three elements, and subsequent chapters (specifically, Chapters 2 through 4) dig into the details and show how to apply them in your project environment.

The second half of the book shows you when to use these three elements for control throughout the life of a typical project. The *Guide to the Project Management Body of Knowledge* (PMBOK Guide) from the Project Management Institute identifies five process groups: initiating, planning, executing, controlling, and closing. Chapters 5 through 9 map to these topics, describing how to make the ideas work for your project from its beginning to its end. Where the PMBOK Guide tends to assume that a project manager has formal power, the discussion throughout this book focuses on controlling project work even if you do not have much direct authority.

Each chapter begins by outlining the principal concepts for that chapter, then explores each idea in detail using examples. Chapters 2 through 9 conclude with a summary of key ideas, and Chapter 10 summarizes the fundamental ideas of the book and offers some final thoughts on applying them to your projects.

This book contains a lot of detail, far more than any single project will ever find need for. The advice here ranges from tips useful on small projects to ideas for dealing with the complexity of large, multiteam programs. Read through the book using your own judgment to determine which ideas will be most effective and helpful for your specific situation. To get started, pick an idea or two out of each section that you think will help you better deal with your project. When you encounter a problem, use the table of contents to locate pointers to deal with it, and adapt the practices outlined there to move things back under control. Never overcomplicate your project with processes that aren't needed; if there are two ways to approach a project issue that are equally effective, always choose the simplest one.

▪ Elements of Project Control

Every project leader has a number of levers available that increase project control. Three principal elements of control are:

1. Project processes
2. Influence
3. Metrics

Processes provide the structure necessary for control and can serve as an effective substitute for organizational authority. There are many ways to build influence, and the more you are able to sway, encourage, or win over those you are working with, the better you will be able to control your project. Measurement quantifies results and drives behavior, so metrics are useful for both understanding the status of your project and encouraging cooperation. With these three techniques, you can control and be successful with projects of any type.

Project Processes

Not long ago, a good friend celebrated a fiftieth birthday at a bowling alley with about a hundred friends. (Names are withheld here to shield the guilty.) As most of us in attendance were of roughly the same age and few had bowled more than once within the previous three decades, the initial frames we bowled were spectacularly pathetic. The gutters on either side of the lanes seemed to have developed an almost magnetic attraction for bowling balls in the intervening years. Some people were halfway through their first game and still trying to knock down their first pin.

Fortunately, the alleys had "bumpers" on either side, which in short order we flipped into position on almost all of our lanes. These bumpers ran the length of the lane over the gutters, so balls that would have otherwise fallen out of play were bounced back onto the lane. With more balls rolling toward the pins (if not exactly in the center of the alleys), scoring improved dramatically.

Good processes for projects are analogous to bumpers in bowling. Well-defined processes, properly applied, keep projects from wandering off into the gutter. Project processes are a source of substantial control, and they are usually owned by project leaders, because much of the work is their personal responsibility.

Even project processes that are owned by others can be easily influenced by the project leader when they are being established early in a new project. At the start of a project, most people will recall the unpleasant results caused on projects that lacked sufficiently defined processes. Your team members, stakeholders, managers, and sponsors are all likely to agree to process discipline that will address past problems and inefficiencies. Work to get all processes that will affect your project team defined and accepted by everyone in advance when initiating your overall project infrastructure.

Processes permeate the project life cycle. Some are related to specific phases of project work, such as those for requirements definition, scope freeze, baseline planning, risk identification, and project review. Other processes apply throughout a project, such as those for communication and change management. Whatever their timing, clearly defined processes are the backstop that enables the project leader to keep the ball rolling toward the final objective. Project processes are the main topic of Chapter 2.

Influence

In projects, as in most situations, people will work on activities that they want to work on. Even when a leader's authority is absolute, ordering people to do something is unlikely to result in them really *wanting* to do it. Using command-and-control authority to force people to do things that they don't want to do results in resentment and demotivation. Malicious compliance is also a risk; people may find ways to appear to cooperate while actually harming the project. In extreme cases, some people will fail to do as they are asked even when the personal consequences of noncompliance are severe. If generals and admirals cannot always expect automatic obedience, what chance does a project leader have?

Well, it turns out that as project leader, you have a fairly good chance of gaining cooperation if you approach it correctly. Gaining cooperation is much easier when you have a two-way relationship of trust and respect with your team members. Team-building activities, formal group events such as project start-up workshops, and informal one-on-one interactions are essential for establishing a foundation for influence.

Another way to enlist willing cooperation is to build on "what they want to work on." When project work is something that a team member is enthusiastic about, there's no trick to it; the project leader has to do little more than assign ownership and stay out of the way. When project work does not appeal to the members of your project team, however, you must work to create interest in it. The principal technique begins with an understanding that everyone's favorite call letters are "WII FM"—What's in it for me? Leaders in any field invest the time to understand what the people they are working with really care about. Effective project leaders identify opportunities to align what the project needs with what the individuals want to do, and they assign responsibility for project activities accordingly. The tools of influence rely on reciprocity—an exchange of something that the individual wants for the commitment to complete work that the project requires.

Another key to influence is effective communication. Project leaders are either good communicators or they are not project leaders for long. Communication is the one absolutely undisputed responsibility owned by the project leader, regardless of project type, other responsibilities, or authority. To succeed and retain control, you must manage information and communicate effectively.

Formal project communication includes written documentation for your project, such as plans and progress reports. Using the power of your pen, you can control your project through filtering and summarizing, and deciding how best to distribute information and when.

Informal communication is also an essential component of project control. Influence and relationship building depend on frequent conversations and other casual interactions. Often you will learn much earlier about project problems through informal discussions than you will by collecting project status formally. The earlier you can detect problems, the more options you will have. Control depends on quick resolution of issues and problems. You can also influence others by asking revealing (and sometimes embarrassing) questions. When your authority is insufficient to avoid situations that could harm your project, asking a pointed question or two at the right time can have the same effect. The perspective that you have as project leader—understanding the work, the capacities of your team, and the project's priorities—will give you the ability to guide people to rational conclusions that are consistent with project success.

Establishing and using influence for project control is explored in detail in Chapter 3.

Metrics

Control in any environment relies on measurements. Without clearly defined limits, the very concept of control lacks meaning. In addition to the obvious role of metrics in determining overall project performance, the metrics you select will also affect behavior of the project team. As Bill Hewlett, founder of The Hewlett-Packard Company, was fond of saying, "What gets measured gets done." Measuring a few key things on a project and publishing the results will powerfully affect your project's progress.

A small set of well-defined project metrics gives the project leader a powerful tool for managing project initiation, execution, and closure. Effectively using project measurement for project control is the topic of Chapter 4.

▪ No One Ever Said that Projects Are Easy

One analogy I like to use is that running a project is like driving a vehicle downhill. Control of a moving vehicle primarily involves the steering wheel, the accelerator, and the brake. Having all three is nice, but with a project, someone else's foot is on the accelerator, and if you brake you will be late. You do have both hands on the steering wheel, though. You steer with process, influence, and metrics, keeping your trajectory as true as you can. With adequate preparation, diligence, and attention to detail, you can reach your destination, exhausted but exhilarated, with no casualties and only a few minor dents here and there. Project control starts at project initiation, and it will require your full attention all the way through to the end. Applying the concepts you find in this book will carry you safely to your destination—project success.

CHAPTER 2

Control Through Process

MOST PROJECTS ARE DIFFICULT. Without adequate processes there will be chaos and they are certain to fail. Regardless of the formal authority of the project leader, projects undertaken using effective processes will have much better chances for success.

The foundations of project management are well established, and your ability to control your project will be significantly enhanced by clearly outlining project processes and gaining willing cooperation from your whole project team to apply them. When contributors understand what to do and how to do it, the project leader's job is far more straightforward, and keeping things moving in the right direction requires little formal authority.

This chapter outlines a number of important processes as well as the related topics of your project infrastructure and the project office.

▪ Project Management Processes

Successfully managing a project involves at least three separate activities: achieving project objectives, managing the project processes, and leading the team. The overall objective is the most visible of the three, but it depends heavily on processes and leadership. Project leaders, particularly those with less experience, tend to focus only on the work, often assigning significant (and difficult) portions of it to themselves. But ignoring the other responsibilities leaves the project vulnerable to frequent, serious problems. Successful project leaders spend much, if not most, of their time dealing with people, and the topic of productive team leadership is addressed in Chapter 3, "Control Through Influence." The focus of this chapter is the management of the processes you will use for your project. Some processes are "built in"—that is, your organization does things in a certain way and you must conform. A few processes in any project belong solely to the project leader and the effort required is all your responsibility. Still other project processes involve your team and may have impact on project stakeholders. Adopting new project processes, or improving existing ones, may require persuasion on your part to gain buy-in and commitment. This effort is more than justified, though, because these processes could be the difference between a project that you are able to keep on track and one that veers off into chaos. Broadly defined, project processes include:

- Life cycles and methodologies
- Project definition
- Contract and procurement management
- Project planning, execution, and tracking
- Change management
- Risk management
- Quality management
- Issue management
- Decision making
- Information management

Before doing a lot of work defining or redefining processes, assess where your organization stands on project management generally. Project management processes are far more effective for project control in organizations that place value in developing and applying project management skills and methods. High-performing project management organizations have:

- Easy access to project management training, mentoring, and support
- A process for project manager/leader selection that is orderly and creates few "accidental" project managers
- Programs that reward project achievements and teamwork over individual heroism
- Strong standards for project documentation, with periodic meaningful review of project information
- Ongoing support and sponsorship by higher-level managers throughout projects, not just at the start

If your environment lacks these attributes, establishing effective processes will be more difficult, and the processes you do adopt can be easily undermined by your management or other stakeholders. Adopting well-defined processes will be worthwhile, but gaining adequate support and commitment for them will require you to exert a good deal of the sort of influence discussed in Chapter 3.

While it is more common for organizations to lack a project management culture, there are organizations that overdo it. A periodic review of recent project problems at the organization level can identify and deal with the root causes of problems that arise from either too little process or excessive project overhead. When elaborate, formal, PMBOK-inspired project management is appropriate, project leaders have a solid basis for project control. If your organization finds that more informal, agile, or adaptive methods provide a better foundation, they can also work. It really doesn't matter a great deal what specific processes you adopt as long as they make good business sense, have ongoing support, and are really used. As long as the methods adopted in an organization are well understood and consistently applied, any organizational approach to managing projects can be used to improve project control.

Life Cycles and Methodologies

Life cycles (or stage gates, phase reviews, or other sequential project timing structures) and methodologies are related in that they impose discipline on projects. Life cycles primarily serve to coordinate related projects, whereas methodologies strive to ensure consistency in how project work is done. Mandatory process aspects of either (or both) can significantly enhance your project control.

Life Cycles

Nearly all projects have at least an informal life cycle to provide consistency for major project milestones. Life cycles are generally made up of sequential phases (initiating, planning, executing/controlling, and closing are process groups that effectively form a life cycle of this type) or are comprised of spirals (with iterative cycles of work). The details of an adopted life cycle are always customized to meet specific business, project, or customer needs, so there are many possible variations, even within a single organization. Requirements for thoroughness, documentation, specific deliverables, and communication are embedded in the checklists and standards associated with life-cycle milestones. Larger projects usually have more and longer phases; smaller projects tend to combine checkpoints and have fewer phases.

Formal life cycles are generally established to assist upper-level and program managers in coordinating related projects, determining progress at defined checkpoints, and facilitating visibility and communications. As desirable as these objectives may be, it's easy to overdo phase-exit and milestone requirements, and this is the process area where excessive overhead and structure are most common. Because life cycles are not primarily defined for the benefit of project leaders, they may impose overhead on the project team that impedes progress and diverts resources from other project work. For this reason, as a project leader you need to understand the requirements for the chosen life cycle and seek ways to customize it to improve your project's chances of success. For each requirement in the life cycle, ask both "Why is it necessary?" (so you can minimize the potential impact by low-value overhead) and "How can I use or modify this requirement to enhance my control over the work?"

Your requests and recommendations that relate directly to life-cycle requirements will have much more force than they would have otherwise. It's much more difficult for team members to ignore something that will be reviewed by managers and others, and you may also have opportunities to align project deliverables, documentation, and plans with defined checkpoints that fall earlier than might be typical. This can help you to minimize control problems (or at least to reveal them early enough in the project to better deal with them).

Life-cycle requirements are also a powerful tool for managing potential conflicts among different functional groups that may have contradictory interests. Team members in a project may come from a bewildering array of functions, such as engineering, finance, manufacturing, quality, sales, support, documentation, training, facilities, system management, and testing. If all commit to the requirements of a project life cycle, there will be fewer conflicts and you will have less difficulty managing the timing of project work. Activities in the project plan that arise from a life cycle are easier to control because they have corporate culture, not just your authority, behind them.

While specific life cycles vary a great deal, they do offer several universal opportunities for a project leader to eke out more control. One weak area in many projects relates to definitively closing the scoping process. Most life cycles have an initial phase that's usually called something like "Requirements definition," "Scoping," or "Initial investigation." A typical requirement for exit is a document that describes what the project will produce. The more precise you can make the requirements in this document, the easier it will be to develop an effective plan that you can use to control the project. Precision also will help in determining the consequences of proposed changes, and managing specification changes is essential to project control. Nailing down scope for a project is never easy, but you will be much more successful in achieving an early scope freeze with the help of mandatory life-cycle requirements.

One common issue with initial scoping involves listing "musts" and "wants" to describe what the project will produce. "Musts" are fine as long as they are well justified. "Wants" are a problem because they make planning the project much more difficult and they fail to set boundaries around what you and the project team are expected to produce. A standard that does not permit "wants" in the scoping document required for phase exit will force earlier decisions and make the project, and potential future changes, easier to control. Even better is to mandate explicit definition of the boundaries for the project through "Is" and "Is not" lists that make clear exactly what will be produced and what will not be included. An "Is not" list for a project is not a random list of silly things that would be illogical to include. It is a list of valid and, in some cases, very beneficial requirements that you and your sponsors have *explicitly chosen not to include* in the present project. The items listed will probably all be considered in the scoping for some future project, and perhaps most of them will ultimately be delivered—just not on this particular project. Failing to make an "Is not" list part of the project scoping makes it very likely that different people, looking at the project from their own perspective, will make wildly varying assumptions about what is in scope, because the limits are not clearly defined.

Another place where explicit life-cycle requirements are useful for improving project control is in ensuring that all testing, validation, and sign-off criteria are completely specified as part of the same phase of work that contains "design" (or whatever the "thinking" effort on your project is named that leads into the work of creating the deliverable). Ultimately, the success of your project depends on acceptance of what you produce. It's extremely dangerous to leave how successful completion will be evaluated undetermined until late in the project. As a requirement for entering the "doing" phase of the life cycle, mandate a thorough plan for testing all deliverables, including measurable criteria, owners and test participants, and any hardware or equipment that will be needed. It is much easier to pass a test when you know what the questions are going to be in advance. Project control on as fundamental an issue as final acceptance should never be left to the last minute.

There are many other possibilities embedded in the exit criteria of a life cycle to enhance your control over a project. The best way to start looking for them is to identify problems and difficulties with past projects that relate to the sequence or timing of key deliverables, information, and decisions. Since past problems tend to recur on future projects if you change nothing, identify ways to better or more clearly define interim project deliverables, or to move them into an earlier part of the project timeline. With compelling data, customizing the exit criteria for your life cycle, or even making permanent changes to the process used throughout your organization, should not be difficult. Some customizations will be more controversial than others, and for these you may need to be somewhat stealthy in slipping the changes you need into the process. When you are confident that the changes you are making will help the project, do what you have to do to adopt them. It's for a good cause.

Methodologies

Methodologies are similar in many ways to life cycles, and they often include life-cycle requirements. In addition to specific requirements associated with project milestones, a methodology also provides explicit guidelines on how to do the work. The process definitions generally include templates, checklists, forms, and other materials that project leaders are either required or strongly encouraged to use. Methodologies, like life cycles, are specific to a single type of project, so the level of detail can be very high. Product development methodologies often include specific advice on which tools and systems to use and how to use them. Information technology methodologies include standards for version controls, documentation, and other aspects of system development. Software methodologies often have defined variations that are specific to implementations of a single vendor's system. Methodologies that employ spiral or cyclic life cycles, such as extreme programming (XP) for agile software development, mandate processes for estimating, working in teams of two, and maximum timing between interim deliverables.

Methodologies are rarely adopted at the project level; they are defined by an organization for use on all projects, and there is generally not a lot of choice on whether to use them. Because they are mandatory and carry the authority of the management level where they are adopted, methodologies are also an important source of project control for you as a project leader. When considering the effect of an aspect of a methodology, always think of how that aspect could be used as effective leverage on project contributors to gain commitments that might otherwise be problematic. If the methodology requires specific documentation to be written in a certain format during development, reflect this in your planning and use the methodology requirement to ensure that it is done. If there are checklists and questionnaires in the methodology that can be used to highlight project issues, take advantage of them to gain visibility and assist you in resolving the issues. Common methodologies can also facilitate your management of dependencies on other departments, suppliers, and related projects.

Structural requirements such as life cycles and methodologies cut both ways—while they can provide a solid set of well-established boundaries that you can use to keep the project moving forward, they can also consume your effort and project resources doing things that may not help the project much. As with any process, you need to determine the net benefits of any methodology and work to avoid or minimize any parts of the methodology that will not help your project.

Project Definition

Clear, unambiguous, high-level project documentation is essential for project control. Whether or not some specific document and format is defined formally for your organization or is mandated as part of an adopted methodology, your ability to control a project depends on creating a thorough description, because it sets the stage for all subsequent work. Regardless of how and why you develop it, work to establish a written definition of your project that is readily available to the project stakeholders and team.

Project definitions take many forms and go by many different names: project charter, proposal, project datasheet, plan of record, project specification, statement of work, even simply a project definition document. Although the name "project charter" will be used in this chapter, the principles outlined apply to any project definition document whatever it may be called.

Project charters begin with top-down information from the project sponsor and other stakeholders on the results they desire. Collect and document the information you have, and if it is incomplete or not sufficiently clear, interview your sponsor (and others, if necessary) to discover the exact business need, problem statement, or other rationale for the project. Work to uncover any known constraints, and ask questions to understand any significant assumptions the sponsor and initial stakeholders have about the project regarding timing, staffing, and other project parameters.

Begin to assemble the project charter in an appropriate format. Use your organization's requirements for project documentation if these exist, but whether using a set format or one you have devised, be as thorough and clear as possible in the following areas:

- Project objective statement (providing in a short paragraph a high-level description of the project deliverable, the project deadline, and anticipated cost or staffing)
- Project priorities (rank ordering among scope, schedule, and resources)
- Project benefits (including a business case or return on investment analysis)
- Available information on user or customer needs
- A scope definition listing all anticipated project deliverables
- Goals for cost and timing
- Significant constraints and assumptions
- Descriptions of dependencies on other related projects
- High-level risks, new technologies required, and significant issues

Strive to include as much specific information as you can, and as you proceed, validate the content of your charter with the project sponsor and stakeholders.

A project charter is a living document that may grow and evolve throughout the project, but maintaining an unambiguous, easily accessed description of the project that is approved by your sponsor and others with influence is a very powerful tool that you can use to keep the project under control. Throughout the project, it will be easier to say no to proposed changes that conflict with the charter. Constraints that are documented in the charter, such as interim milestones or required standards, are a much more effective rationale to support your requests for commitment than simply claiming, "Because I said so." A well-written charter forms the basis for detailed scoping, planning, tracking, and periodic project reviews. Chapter 5 discusses development and initial use of the project charter and other documentation in more detail.

Contract and Procurement Management

However much influence and authority you have within your own organization, you will have less control over project contributors who work for other companies. While it is not always feasible, one tactic for improving your project control is to outsource as little work as possible.

If you must depend on the services of people outside your organization, you will face control challenges. One way to mitigate this situation is to scrupulously adhere to the standards and requirements your organization has for outsourced services. These processes will provide you with firm boundaries and guidance that are particularly effective in initiating and executing contract project work (as well as keeping you in the good graces of your management). Before considering the use of contractors or outside consultants on a project, review your organization's overall procurement process. Identify people you can go to for help (for example, in your procurement, legal, human resources, or other departments) who have experience with setting up the service contracts you will need. If any part of the required process is unclear to you, have one of the people who has expertise explain it to you, or get the person's commitment to assist you. Identify all the individuals who will need to be involved, other resources you will need, and all the forms, approvals, and communication required. Following tried-and-true processes will enhance your project control; failing to do so can result in chaos and potentially get you and your organization in trouble.

Establishing a successful outsourcing relationship takes time and effort, so determine when you need to start working on it so you will have all the details in place and contracts signed in time to meet your project's deadlines. Taking shortcuts and rushing into a contractual relationship will almost always leave you with far less control than you might otherwise be able to establish.

Control begins with detailed specification of all the deliverables that you intend to outsource. Document detailed feature specifications, measurable performance and acceptance criteria, any other relevant requirements, and the necessary timing. Ensure that the definition data is included in the contract, with all responsibilities clearly defined. Discuss these requirements with all the suppliers you may be considering throughout the process so your expectations are clear, and make a particular effort to ensure the final contract terms are well understood by the supplier who is ultimately selected.

Establish clear-cut language in the contract for managing changes, so all parties know what the process and consequences of any modifications will be. You can also improve your overall control of outsourced work by including contract language that includes specific incentives for early or exceptional performance and penalties for nonperformance. "If . . . then" clauses in the contract will provide you with more options for control than the basic "Do this and we will pay; fail and we won't" language that is the starting point in standard contracts.

As you proceed with the process, present periodic updates on your progress to your project sponsor and to any others who will need to approve or sign the contract. Identify any outstanding issues and correct problems as you work so that before signing you will have both a contract that includes all that it requires and the quick approval needed to get started.

Chapter 6 provides additional specifics on negotiating and planning for improving control of outsourced work, and Chapter 8 discusses ideas for maintaining control over contract work.

Project Planning, Execution, and Tracking

As a project leader, you can establish a solid basis for control by making a strong case for planning, tracking, and execution processes; getting buy-in for them from the project team; and using them throughout your projects.

Involving all the team members in planning and tracking activities builds buy-in and motivation. Wise project leaders encourage broad participation and include contributions from everybody in the resulting outputs from these processes. When people invest effort and see their influence on the project as it comes into focus, the project quickly shifts from "their project" to "our project." Controlling a project that people care about is a great deal easier, and more likely to be successful, than trying to manage one where the team is indifferent. Using project management processes collaboratively also encourages team member cooperation, which also makes your job of keeping things under control easier.

Chapter 6 includes details on using project planning processes to improve project control. Chapters 7 and 8 go into the specifics for maintaining control through execution and tracking processes. Even for the project leader who has little or no formal authority, using project management processes systematically is a very effective way to keep things moving forward.

Project infrastructure decisions in all of these areas are summarized later in this chapter. These decisions are a useful way to gain broad acceptance of specific project management practices, particularly when the decisions are made through team consensus.

Change Management

One of the most problematic aspects of technical projects is a lack of control over specification changes. Solving this problem involves two things: freezing project scope when setting the project baseline, and adopting an effective process for managing changes throughout the remainder of the project.

A Robust Process

Project leaders who have little formal authority are particularly dependent on a well-defined, documented process for managing scope changes; without one, "scope creep" and other general scope meanderings can easily render a project unmanageable. How formal the control process needs to be varies quite a bit, but even on trivial projects, a written process will help you avoid chasing a moving target. A project where the deliverable constantly changes begins, and remains, out of control.

Change management processes that contribute to your ability as leader to keep things under control have several things in common:

- Specific requirements for submitting change requests to ensure that all proposed changes (regardless of the source) provide consistent, sufficient information on each change
- A bias against accepting changes, to minimize unnecessary change
- Standards for timely response on change requests, and clear, public visibility for all decisions
- A review process for changes that includes the costs and consequences of accepting a change, in addition to any potential benefits
- Unambiguous authority for the owner of the process to make final decisions, including decisions to reject changes

If you, as the project leader, are the owner of the process, then you do in fact have a good deal of formal authority over your project. A lack of ability to manage scope change is often what separates successful projects from those that crash and burn. Even if you do not have ultimate responsibility for making decisions concerning proposed changes, there's still hope. You can still write or at least influence the process that will be used and facilitate the process to ensure that it meets the criteria you require to control project scope. You can also work to establish a strong relationship with the people who do own the process so that your inputs and opinions are used in making the final decisions.

A typical change management process flowchart appears in Figure 2-1. Simply having a process that is accepted by your team, sponsor, and project stakeholders is a powerful tool for overall project control. It puts people on notice that changes will be carefully examined before being accepted and establishes the hurdle of adequate documentation for changes being proposed.

A project leader can exert additional control at several key points in the change control process—namely, when ensuring that the submission is credible, and when considering all options for disposition of changes.

Project leaders are among the first people to see proposed changes, and they have responsibility, or at least shared responsibility, for the "Proposal complete" decision point. When reviewing a change, look for a clear, compelling description of the business case for the change. If the reason for a change (the "why?") is inadequately documented, send it back to the submitter with a request for a quantitative assessment of the benefits that the change represents. Be skeptical of change requests that specify narrowly defined technical solutions, because the submitters may not be in a position to judge the best technical changes for a specific problem situation. If the requested change includes too much focus on a solution and too little on the actual problem, return it

FIGURE 2-1. A TYPICAL CHANGE MANAGEMENT PROCESS.

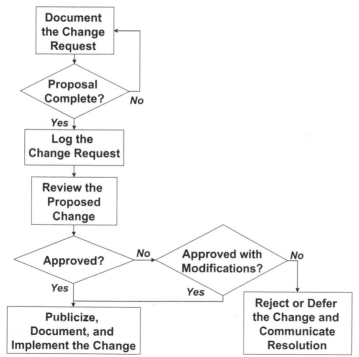

with a request to emphasize the business situation that inspired the requested change. Finally, ensure that the consequences of not adopting the change are credible and sufficiently detailed for analysis, and that any estimates on expected impact to project timing, cost, effort, or other factors are realistic. If you disagree with any of the information provided, send the change request back to the submitter with suggested changes or specific guidance where additional or better information is needed. Give particular attention to any change that you would characterize as an "enhancement," as these types of changes tend to be described with exaggerated benefits and grossly underestimated consequences. The first line of defense against unnecessary change is keeping people honest.

Accept/Reject Decisions

Another point in the process where a project leader may exercise control is the accept/reject decision. Again, the main principle involves maintaining credibility. Whether they are ultimately responsible for each decision or are a primary contributor of data, project leaders have two opportunities to guide the process. The first is to check the analysis information for each change to verify that it is realistic. Seek credible answers for all the following questions:

- Is the business benefit for the change well documented and believable?
- Does the proposed change represent the best available response?
- Do you have good reasons to believe that the change is feasible?
- Is the change likely to obtain the desired result?
- Will this change affect the project baseline? Are all estimates associated with the change credible? What milestones will change?
- How much additional effort will the new or changed project activities require? Are there people willing and able to staff the work?
- Who will bear any additional expense for equipment, material, training, rework, scrap, and contractual changes?
- What are any potential unintended consequences of the change?
- Will this change affect other projects?
- Does your sponsor support the change?

Use the answers to these questions to review each change and ensure that everyone involved in deciding how to proceed considers both the reasonably expected benefits and the costs and other consequences associated with the change. Keep in mind the information that people provide to support proposed changes can be highly uncertain; always probe for what the estimates are based on and ask for worst and best cases or ranges for all estimates, particularly estimates of projected benefits.

The second opportunity to provide guidance for the decision process is by keeping all four potential responses visible: approval, approval with modification, deferral, and rejection. "Reject" should always be the default decision, applied to all change requests for which the analysis fails to provide a compelling, credible business case. Even for beneficial changes, you can test the proposal to assess whether all of the proposed change is needed right now, and then counter-propose accepting only the part of a change that is urgent. Acceptance with modification can effectively minimize the impact on the project while still including key portions of the requested change. For desirable changes, determine the effect of delaying them to a later project. If the cost of accepting the change in the current project is larger than the estimated cost of delay, "not yet" may be your best decision. Work to approve changes sparingly and only when they are solidly supported by a strong business case.

Risk Management

Risk management is considered to be an important part of project planning, and much of the work required to do it well occurs during the initial analysis, scheduling, estimating, and other activities of planning. However, keeping a focus on risk throughout your project will reinforce the overall goals and keep your team's attention on the upcoming work. You can better control your project when you have a clearer notion of what lies ahead.

Some regard risk management in projects as a discretionary activity, but a project leader who has limited authority should not. The processes of risk management will, in fact, enable you to do more thorough planning, highlight potential troubles and build consensus on how to deal with them, and remove (or at least mitigate) serious project problems.

To maximize the effectiveness of your risk management efforts, make risk identification a parallel activity throughout project planning. Look for incomplete understanding of project activities as you develop the project work breakdown structure. Probe for risks when assigning activity ownership and developing estimates. Identify risks associated with dependencies both within and outside of your project. When resources are scarce or inadequate for project tasks, or when you are dependent on a single individual for project work, note the risks. Analyze assumptions and constraints to find exposures, and encourage all who are involved in planning to consider worst cases and potential difficulties throughout the development of the plan. Risk analysis, both qualitative and quantitative, will assist you in displaying the consequences of project risks and will make your requests for modifications to the initial plans to reduce or avoid risks far more persuasive. Specifics on integrating risk processes into project planning are detailed in Chapter 6. The more robust you can make your plan, the more likely it will be that you will be able to navigate through your project successfully.

Risk management also provides a lever for control throughout the project by allowing for the monitoring of risk trigger events, implementation of risk responses and contingency plans, and periodic reexamination of the project risk list. Enhancing your control through diligent focus on risk management throughout project execution is described in Chapter 8, on project tracking and monitoring.

Quality Management

Quality management provides another set of processes that provide project structure and "put teeth" into requests from a project leader that might otherwise be ignored. Standards for quality that relate to projects are of two kinds: global standards that are adopted within industries (and in some cases may be mandatory), and quality standards that are unique to a specific organization or even to a single project.

Adopted Standards

If your organization has adopted or is subject to standards for quality, review what they require of you and your project team. Specific examples of such standards include organizational compliance with ISO 9000 standards, Six Sigma, and commitment to maintaining a maturity level within the Capability Maturity Model defined by the Software Engineering Institute. Use your review to identify and integrate the checklists, quality processes, and other required elements into your project planning. The specific documented steps, reports, and evaluations that your project must comply with provide much more powerful motivation for team members to do things in a certain way than your simple requests to do so. Because processes related to quality management can be overdone, thus adding inappropriate and expensive overhead to projects, prudent project leaders identify and emphasize processes and standards that enhance their control over the work and minimize overkill processes that can slow the project.

Determine who in your organization has ultimate responsibility for quality management, then ensure that this individual or group understands and approves of your approach. If quality specialists will have specific responsibilities and deliverables for your project, get their commitment in advance, and don't hesitate to enlist their help when issues related to quality threaten the progress of your project. Similar to adopted project methodologies, quality standards give a project leader using them similar authority to the managers who define and monitor compliance with them.

Specific Quality Planning

Since quality standards, whether based on defined standards or general principles such as Total Quality Management or Six Sigma, are oriented toward consistently delivering what a customer requires, quality management is closely related to scope management. Another opportunity that quality management processes offer the project leader for better control is to align project requirements with the "voice of the customer." Strong emphasis will always be added to what you say when it is apparent that it aligns directly with a stated need of a customer or user. Market research, benchmarking, and customer interviews are useful in assessing and documenting user needs and defining the value of your project requirements. Understand what matters to your ultimate customers, and use what you learn to lead your project. Whatever you say or do will be more effective when you act with your customer standing behind you.

Incorporate quality-related activities into your project, such as process audits, tests, reviews, inspections, and approvals. For each process that you adopt, work to understand how the result is important to your customer. In particular, attempt to document the final approval criteria for your project early, and review acceptance tests and evaluations that will be required for scope verification with stakeholders and customers as soon as practical after the project begins.

Issue Management

With projects, issues will inevitably arise. At the start of your project, define a process to manage project issues relating to resources, timing, priority, and other matters. Get buy-in from your team for a disciplined process that recognizes, tracks, and resolves issues promptly. Establish an issue-tracking process that uses an easily accessed log of current issues and includes information on each current issue, such as a description of the issue; an identifier or code associated with the issue (to facilitate communications); the date opened; an assigned owner; the current status; and the due date for closure.

The process for dealing with open issues is generally very simple. It includes a description of the process for listing new items, a periodic review of open items (generally with some reporting), and a means for dealing with items that are overdue. The power of an issue-tracking process for a project leader who does not have much authority largely comes from the status and due-date information. Once the owner has accepted the item and committed to a date for resolution, you are free to report on any variance, and may in fact be obligated to do so. People don't like to see their name with a large red stoplight indicator next to it, whether the owner of an issue is a team member, someone from another project or organization, or even your manager. The public nature of an issues list provides the individual who maintains it a good deal of influence and control.

For overdue issues that cannot be resolved by an owner within the team, the process should also define a time limit for escalation to someone with more authority who can resolve the issue. Again, escalation should always be reserved as a last option. Using escalation too frequently to deal with issues (or with interpersonal conflicts) can produce unintended consequences and new problems.

Decision Making

Projects require many decisions, and making them quickly and well is essential to project control. A well-established process for group decision making is useful even when the project leader has a good deal of authority, because decisions made with shared input result in more team buy-in and can be expected to deliver better results.

Decisions are rarely easy in projects, and the spectrum of opinions on a diverse project team generally makes them even more contentious and difficult. A documented process for dealing with questions and options that the project contributors have agreed to use will streamline the process and deliver decisions that everyone will accept. Work with your team early in the project to develop a process for decisions or to adopt, perhaps with modifications, an existing process. A good decision process provides powerful support for control of your project. This process should include the following steps:

❑   Develop a clear, unambiguous statement of the question that must be answered.

❑   Obtain team support by involving all project team members who need to be involved with the decision or who will be affected by the decision; get their commitment to participate in the decision process.

❑   Review the statement among your project team and edit it as needed so that everyone interprets it the same way.

❑   Brainstorm and discuss potential criteria to use in making the decision (such as cost, time, usefulness, completeness, feasibility, or other considerations). Select criteria that relate to your defined goal, are measurable, and can be evaluated objectively by the project contributors who will assess them to make the decision.

❑   Work with the team to establish priorities for the criteria by giving each one a relative weight (where the weights of all criteria could sum to 100 percent).

❑   Set a time limit for the decision, and restrict the amount of time that you will spend in investigation, analysis, discussion, and making a final decision.

❏ Brainstorm and generate as many ideas and options for the decision as possible in the time you have allocated. Seek to develop multiple ideas that could be acceptable to the whole team.

❏ Use group voting techniques, if necessary, to filter the list down to no more than about six options before considering each one in detail. Analyze the options using objective assessments of how they conform to the decision criteria you have established.

❏ Quantify any objections that come up in discussion to the ideas, adding additional criteria for the decision if necessary.

❏ Sequence the options using the assessments and weighted criteria.

❏ Consider the consequences of adopting the top alternative. If there are no objections, come to closure and implement the decision. If there are significant risks or other valid concerns about the top-ranked option, reconsider the criteria or weights used for the decision. Discuss the situation and make adjustments quickly so you can use objective analysis to reach group consensus.

❏ Document the decision and communicate the results to others on the team and to appropriate stakeholders.

❏ Implement the decision and track the results. Be prepared to revisit and adjust the decision if you fail to achieve the desired results or if there are significant unintended consequences.

Information Management

Archiving project data serves as another foundation for project control. Information that is stored in your project management information system (PMIS), or whatever you may choose to call it, provides a solid foundation for project reference and communication. The project leader's "power of the pen" over the wide variety of formal project documents is a significant source of control. How and where the documents are stored can be equally influential.

Public storage of project documents is an essential aspect of control—you can support your requests and guide decisions throughout your project using project documents and reports that were previously archived. Your documents and plans form the foundation for your project, and the project contributors and stakeholders who helped to create them and gave their approval (or at least did not object at the time) will be obligated to cooperate with you in delivering on what they say. The longer that documents have been available publicly, the more force and influence they will have.

Project information is an essential project resource, so consider carefully where you put it. Some projects use websites, networked servers, or knowledge management systems to store key project data. For some projects, groupware applications are used to both maintain the project document archive and provide e-mail and other services. Online electronic storage allows easy access to a single master copy of each project document that everyone associated with the project can read at any time. Updates are instantaneous, so there is minimal chance that team members will have out-of-date information. If you do implement an online PMIS, verify that all software tools, Web browsers, and other applications that team members will use are up-to-date and compatible. Also, establish access to allow many to read, but few to write to shared documents, to avoid the "too many cooks" problem. Set up the archive to retain earlier versions of project documents for reference, and strictly limit the number of people who can delete information.

For small, colocated project teams, the PMIS might be a filing cabinet or even a notebook stored in a common area. Whatever method you select for storing project data, ensure that all project team members have adequate access at all times to at least hardcopy versions of project information. Provide current project documents in an easy-to-find place and clearly mark or remove all out-of-date information so it will not be used for project work.

In the PMIS, set up a logical structure to store project definition documents (such as the project charter and requirements definition), project planning documents (work breakdowns, Gantt charts, risk registers), and project execution documents (including status reports, issue logs, and other communications). For PMIS implementations that are not online (or for emergency backup), establish a method for distributing document copies to all the places where the project contributors are located. Implement a process to keep all sites synchronized and using only the most current project documents.

The processes concerning project documentation are not the most exciting part of a project, but if you invest in setting up a useful, easy-to-access repository for the information that people need to have, it will pay benefits throughout your project. A well-established, orderly project management information system adds immeasurably to the influence of any project leader, especially when you can reinforce your requests and actions using documents that have been available to the whole project team for weeks or even months.

▪ Project Infrastructure

All projects have an infrastructure. Most have an infrastructure that is a combination of organizational standards and generally accepted defaults. Other projects have an infrastructure created by adding to or changing some key decisions that the project leader believes could materially help the current project. Establishing processes for your project (the topic of the previous section of this chapter) sets a firm foundation for project control. Determining exactly how you will apply these processes requires a framework of decisions for project planning, execution, and tracking. Documenting your decisions clarifies how you will operate and provides you with enhanced support for overall project control.

Making infrastructure decisions requires only a few hours for smaller projects, but you may need to make a considerably larger investment for a major program. As with most project management matters, it depends on project scale. The best time to consider infrastructure decisions is at the start of a project. Once a project is fully underway no one will have much time or inclination to think about infrastructure questions.

One way to begin establishing an infrastructure for your project is to list key questions that you would like to work with your project team to answer. Your list can be one of your own making, one from an earlier project, a template used by your organization, or it may be based on a generic template, such as the one that you will find in Appendix A. However you proceed, include questions that relate to problem areas from earlier projects, things that could become control problems for you, and issues that may lead to trouble on your current project. A few examples are:

- Planning questions (related to project initiation, plan development, outsourced work, deliverables, and planning participants and tools)
- Execution questions (related to project status and metrics, the PMIS, meetings and informal communications, team concerns, life cycles, methodologies, and quality assurance)
- Control questions (related to project reporting, scope and specification control, individual performance problems, project reviews, project cancellation, and project closure)

You will find detailed, specific project infrastructure decision questions for each of these topics in Appendix A.

Fine-Tuning Your Infrastructure

It's worth repeating that you must develop the list of questions and decisions you would like to address in advance with your team during project initiation, when people are not overwhelmed with project deadlines. Otherwise, trying to change the way you are doing things midproject will be difficult—like trying to change the tire on a vehicle that is hurtling down a freeway.

Distribute the list of questions and issues to your team and ask each person to begin thinking about options for how the project should operate. If the team is very senior and has been involved with many projects, the list of questions alone will likely be enough to generate ideas. For a less experienced team, some thoughts that you have on alternatives worth considering might be useful for getting the discussion going.

To make decisions, set up a meeting (or teleconference) to gather the team's thoughts and discuss the alternatives. Set a time limit of no more than about ten minutes for each issue, and be scrupulous on timekeeping. For issues where there is little or no disagreement, document the consensus and move on to other issues. For questions where there is contention, you have several options:

- Extend the discussion slightly to seek closure.
- Delegate the issue to the people who are most vocal in their objections and have them bring a proposal to a future meeting.
- Make the decision yourself, explaining your justification.

For each question that you complete, document your decision and your key assumptions. Communicate your decisions to stakeholders and others involved in your project, and summarize the infrastructure decisions in your PMIS. Adopt the decisions to manage your project, and adjust your project processes as needed to conform to what you have decided.

Throughout your project, particularly following major changes and during project reviews, review your infrastructure decisions and consider any needed adjustments.

▪ The Project Office

One last process-oriented source of control is the project office. Some organizations invest in them and others do not, but if you are in an organization that has established a project office (or a program management office, center of excellence, support team, or similar group), it can also bolster your project control. Although there may be differing organizational roles, the three most common functions of a project office are auditing, enabling, and executing. Combinations of these functions are not unusual, but the precise nature of a project office depends on the organizational needs.

Auditing. Some project offices are primarily "process police," responsible for audits of methodologies and compliance with quality or other standards. Working closely with this type of project office potentially yields similar benefits to the adoption of process standards that were discussed earlier in the chapter. This type of project office tends to believe that "if some is good, more is better," so use your judgment in determining how much "help" is appropriate before the overhead starts to make things worse.

Enabling. A second type of project office works to improve the maturity and effectiveness of project leaders in the organization. Using a team of internal consultants, the project office provides training, assistance in setting up organizational processes, and help in tailoring life cycles. This "enabler" type of office gets involved in situations where the challenges exceed the capabilities of a particular team. This type of project office also is useful in boosting your credibility and authority as a project leader, because everyone always listens more carefully to apparently knowledgeable strangers. (One definition of an expert is someone who does not know any more than anyone else, but is from more than 50 miles away.) Many enabling project office organizations have staff available to help with initiating, planning, and closing projects.

Executing. Other project office implementations are even more actively engaged; they are responsible for facilitating and doing the project work. This type of project office has a staff of planners, administrators, and supervisors who coordinate and guide the execution of project work. For large programs, they ensure consistent planning among all the component projects. Again, the presence of outsiders who support (or even mandate) activities and processes that you need to keep your project under control can significantly enhance your apparent authority.

Some potential areas where project office help can be effective include:

- Facilitating project start-up workshops
- Support for project planning efforts and help with complex software tools
- Communications and meeting planning
- Enforcement of planning standards and auditing for completeness
- Establishment of templates and checklists for common project types
- Set-up of a central PMIS repository for sharing information among projects
- Organization-wide standards and reporting for change control
- Assistance with project escalations and recommendations for resolution
- Collection and analysis of project metrics organization-wide
- Assistance with set-up and execution of processes for conflict resolution, decision making, quality management, and other project processes
- Assistance with project reviews and follow-up
- Facilitation of post-project retrospective analyses and organization-wide storage of results
- Management of organizational change

While getting staff members from a project office involved with your project can considerably enhance the amount and effectiveness of your project, too much involvement results in it no longer being your project. Sharing leadership responsibility with someone from a project office can end up being difficult, like sharing a banana with a gorilla.

KEY IDEAS FOR PROJECT PROCESSES

- Get team buy-in for structured project management processes and clearly document how you will use them.
- Review past projects for problems related to structure and work with your team to make project infrastructure decisions to resolve them.
- Take advantage of organizational expertise and project office capabilities, but resist surrendering control over your own project.

CHAPTER 3

Control Through Influence

IT IS OFTEN SAID that management is assigned, but leadership must be earned. One aspect of earning the role of leader is building influence both within and outside of your project team. Your working style matters a great deal, and your influence with others depends on what you have to offer them in exchange for what you need and what you do to enhance your influence and maintain relationships with your team, your sponsor, and your project stakeholders.

▪ Appropriate Leadership Styles

The introduction that most people have to project work, especially in a business context, is as a contributor. Project contributors draw on a lot of background and experience that relates to the assignments for which they are responsible. Generally speaking, if contributors are good at what they do, sooner or later they find themselves leading a project, not just contributing to it. The transition may be gradual and involve taking a lead role in a portion of a project that depends on several people, or it may be abrupt—resulting in yet another "accidental project manager." However it occurs, a pair of challenges comes with the territory. The transition from primarily contributing to a project to leading one involves a different set of skills and responsibilities, and new leaders usually have very little or no formal authority. Becoming a successful project leader means that instead of spending most of your time with "things" and "stuff," you will now spend most of your time dealing with people and communications. To do this well, and to be successful leading a project when you have little power to coerce commitments out of people, you must establish and maintain influence over the team, stakeholders, and sponsors. This chapter outlines ideas that successful project leaders use to get their projects going and sustain progress, without having to resort to command-and-control tactics.

One of the most obvious differences between the typical day of a project contributor and the day of a project leader is how time is spent. For project team members, most time is spent doing technical tasks. The guideline that's frequently used for purposes of project estimating is that about two-thirds of the hours in a typical workday, or roughly five to six hours, are spent doing technical work. In many cases, this is approximately accurate, with the remaining one-third of the team member's time consumed by meetings, e-mail, telephone calls, biological imperatives, and miscellaneous other activities unrelated to the project. For a project leader, the overwhelming majority of time is consumed by meetings and communications. A study of several dozen project managers at Hewlett-Packard in the 1990s found that less than 5 percent of a leader's time was dedicated to technical work, while 85 percent was allocated to people management and project coordination. This pattern recurs in projects of all types and in all companies; project leaders inevitably become generalists, and as time goes on they assume less and less personal responsibility for technical project work.

This transition can be extremely difficult, because the image most people have of themselves is tied up in what they do. When I was asked to be a "group supervisor" and lead a team of twelve systems programmers at DuPont (which, despite the implication of the title, is not a management position), I found the transition literally painful. I delegated work to members of the team that I knew I could do faster and better. To an engineer who's always seeking the best result, this is about even on the aggravation spectrum with being forced to watch someone incorrectly fold a map. I knew, however, that leading a team that size while continuing to own significant technical responsibility would require me to do two full-time jobs: all day dealing with the team, communicating, and leading meetings, and all night catching up with technical task commitments. Many new project leaders learn this the hard way, at the expense of their personal life and also, frequently, the project. Some new project leaders never do make a successful transition because they can't let go of technical responsibilities, and eventually they resume their role as a project contributor (or worse).

If this were not enough for the new project leader to deal with, how your time is broken up also changes. Project contributors, like all knowledge workers, are more productive when they can concentrate and focus over longer periods of time. Interruptions are unwelcome and disruptive, so project contributors strive to protect their time blocks and minimize outside influences. The world of a project leader does not permit this; project leaders need to multitask, to work efficiently despite frequent interruptions. A technical contributor can say, "Leave me alone, I'm busy," but the leader who retains this attitude will encourage escalating project problems and increased probability of project failure.

Exactly how you spend your time as a project leader depends on the team, the project type, and a number of other factors. What tends not to vary is that effective team leaders spend about 10 percent of their time per team member throughout the project. This time will be spread among team meetings, one-on-one discussions, e-mail, collecting and sending status reports, telephone calls, problem solving, and other interactions. For a leader with a small team of three or four, there is certainly capacity to be a "player/coach" who carries a part of the technical load. However, for a leader with eight to twelve team members (or more) there is very little capacity to take on technical work. Even though little of this team-management work done by the project leader typically appears on the project work breakdown structure or schedule, it is "real project work." A project leader who invests too little time in leading, managing, and communicating with the team will slow progress and lose control.

Putting sufficient time into project leadership is essential for project control, but it also must be spent doing the right things. Project leaders need to be very good at communicating, which is discussed in detail later in this chapter. Depending on the project, effective leadership may also require effort in a number of other areas that were not part of the role of project contributor, such as:

- Staffing and hiring for the project
- Communicating a project vision and representing the project as a whole
- Managing the relationships with customers, stakeholders, and sponsors
- Serving as liaison to external suppliers, contributors, and leaders of related projects
- Facilitating the project planning process
- Mastering project scheduling and other needed software applications
- Being responsible for project budgets, contracts, and other financial matters
- Managing project changes
- Escalating problems and issues when necessary

None of this is easy, and few project contributors have much relevant experience with any of it before becoming a project leader. Moving into the role gradually may help, and having access to formal training and mentoring available in the organization will also make a difference.

You can improve your project control by building appropriate project leadership skills in areas such as:

- Finding and using an appropriate operating style
- Facilitating productive communications
- Motivating the team

Operating Style

Project leaders need to determine what operating style or styles will work best for their project teams. The best style to use depends on a lot of things—the specific needs of the team, team location (or locations), and the type of project. A leader may need to adopt a variety of styles to work effectively during different parts of a project or with separated parts of a project team.

The leadership style that you adopt will determine how members of the team perceive you. In most instances, perception matters more than actual authority; what team members think of you will affect how they respond to you much more directly than your title or your place on an organization chart.

Power in organizations is of several kinds:

- Power of position
- Power to coerce
- Power to reward
- Power of expertise
- Power of personality

The most visible power in most organizations is the power managers have because they are "the boss." Formal authority grants the first two types of power, the power of position and the power to coerce. Leading using these two types of power is not possible for many project leaders because they don't have much formal authority, and over some members of the project team they may have none at all. This is not necessarily as bad as project leaders, especially new ones, assume. Even managers with a great deal of formal authority are wise to use their position and the power to threaten and punish people sparingly, and only as a last resort. Overuse of this sort of power by "pulling rank" leads to resentment, demotivation, malicious compliance, and ultimately, turnover.

More effective are the other types of power. The power to reward is not the exclusive province of higher-level managers; anyone in the organization can nominate others for rewards, praise other people, and do other things that will be appreciated. While the upper managers in an organization may be able to grant bigger rewards, a project leader who remains alert for opportunities can thank and reward people frequently and thoughtfully, often with rewards that are appreciated more.

A primary and very effective source of project leader power derives from expertise. Power from your technical expertise is effective with your sponsors, managers, and stakeholders—they did, after all, put you in charge of the project. Your technical expertise may not be a great source of power on your team, because many, if not most, of your team members are probably a good deal more expert in their areas than you are. Even within the team, though, you might have an edge if you are the only generalist among a group of specialists in rather narrow fields. Your expertise in project management is also a source of power, both within your team and with those who surround your project. Finally, the expertise that you and you alone possess concerns your project. You are the world's foremost authority on your project, and it can be very useful to diplomatically remind people of this fact at strategic times during your project.

The final source of power derives from your personal relationships with others. Investing in team building, informal communication, and establishing a basis for mutual trust also provides the project leader a good deal of power, which is particularly important in times of stress and trouble. You don't need to be the most gregarious, happy, outgoing person on the planet to maintain friendly, respectful relationships with the members of your team.

How you operate, day to day, during your project is another important aspect of leadership style. Figure 3-1 shows a continuum of operating styles, with command and control on the left side and unanimous team consensus on the right. The ideal spot to be in this range of options is, of course, always situational. Regardless of the project type, in a crisis or emergency where quick action must be taken, the leader may have to act quickly, without consulting the team. Similarly, faced with excessive complexity, even a five-star general or CEO who has enormous authority will solicit input before proceeding and may even decide to delegate the ultimate decision making to individuals with high levels of specialized expertise.

In your project, particularly if you have little formal authority, you may normally only have options on the right side of this operating continuum. While this may appear to be a limitation on your project control, it may not turn out to be. Using position or coercive power too often, with no input from the team, can quickly result in rebellion and loss of control. On the other hand, your team will remain more motivated when they have a say in what they are doing. When the ultimate decisions and plans that the team has contributed to are consistent with what the project requires, operating with team consensus improves your control. Since, as project leader, you will generally facilitate the meetings and discussions, you will have ample opportunity to influence the ultimate decisions to ensure that they will serve the needs of the project.

FIGURE 3-1. OPERATING STYLES.

How Is Project Direction Determined?

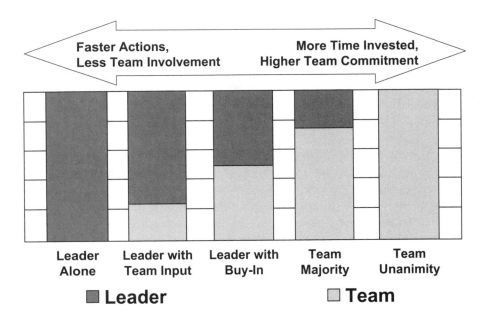

In selecting how to operate day to day, you need to consider a number of factors. If the team has mostly inexperienced team members who are new to the project work, your style will shift to the left and be somewhat more autocratic. With a team of experienced contributors who know what they need to do, you will probably be best served with a style that involves more team consensus. Collaborative planning and decision making leads to team member ownership and buy-in, which results in higher motivation, which in turn will more than compensate for the time and effort required to arrive at agreement.

When action must be taken quickly, shifting to the left is always an option, but be aware of the dangers if you do it too often. Good project leaders usually operate somewhere in the middle of the range, balancing the need for team discussion and buy-in with timing and other project requirements.

Communication

Good communication is the foundation of effective project management, and it is also your most powerful leadership tool.

What most people know about any project is shaped fundamentally by the project leader. Most status information collected is seen first by you, the project leader. You are responsible for summarizing, filtering, and reporting information to everyone who is involved with your project: to stakeholders and sponsors, to members of your team, and to leaders of related projects. Providing clear, factual information that conveys the current status of your project is essential, and doing this well can be a source of substantial influence. If things are going well, people are impressed with your work and your team. If things are not going well, factual data (just enough, never more than people need to hear) will show what you are doing to recover and provide appropriate visibility when you need to enlist help. To a great extent, what you say and how you say it determines how you are perceived as a leader, particularly by your managers and peers.

Communication methods also matter. Project communications take many forms, and project leaders must use all methods available to them. Effective project leaders tend to "overcommunicate" (running just short of being annoying) because it is always worse for people connected to your project to lack data that they require than it will be for them to receive extra copies of information that they do need to see. In fact, effective project leaders employ some important types of seemingly redundant communication practices—for example, following up complicated written communications with a telephone call (to clear up any potential confusion) and documenting the content of a phone call or discussion in a follow-up e-mail (to verify what was discussed and provide a permanent record). Thorough communication throughout a project is one of the most effective control tools available to the project leader.

Leadership also involves communication outside your project team. Regardless of your authority or formal position, as the project leader you are responsible for providing periodic project updates and presentations. Your communications to customers, stakeholders, and leaders of related projects will provide them with a window into your work and allow you to emphasize aspects of the project that you particularly need them to be aware of. Making visible the accomplishments that matter to these people will raise your profile with them and increase your influence. When you need involvement from stakeholders or leaders of other projects to resolve a problem situation, highlighting the issue will accelerate their assistance. When things are going well, reporting good progress will minimize any potential interference or unwanted "help" that might otherwise be inflicted on your project. What you say and how you say it has a very powerful effect on your overall project community.

Communications with people you report to, such as sponsors and managers, are equally important. Your reporting permits you to build a great deal of influence with those who have direct authority over your work. In addition, communication with sponsors and managers can allow you to turn the tables on these people when necessary. One key lever of control for the project leader is assignment of task ownership (the relationship between ownership and project control will be explored in more detail both later in this chapter and in Chapter 6). As project leader, you have an obligation to report on the progress of each identified activity in your project, naming the individual who is assigned responsibility for it. Savvy project leaders, especially those who have minimal authority, formally assign activities in their project to their managers and sponsors, such as approvals, decisions, and other responsibilities that the project leader may not be empowered to complete. Reporting that project progress is stalled, and including a big, red stoplight indicator next to a manager's name as the reason, provides a powerful incentive to meet the commitment. (Actually, savvy and *diplomatic* project leaders get the same result by warning their managers and sponsors in advance what the contents of their next status report will be if there is no action.)

Motivation

Project leaders who lack authority assume that they have little to offer that will have much effect on team members. In reality, there is much that a team leader can do that will make a lot of difference. In research into motivation of employees, most studies build on the work of Frederick Herzberg, who distinguishes between motivating factors and hygiene factors. Motivating factors include things that a manager or the workplace can provide that increase motivation and satisfaction with the work. These factors tend to be intrinsic to the work and are things over which project leaders have a great deal of control and influence. Hygiene factors, by comparison, have little effect on motivation when they are increased, but serve as powerful demotivators when they are inadequate. Hygiene factors are mainly outside the immediate job or project and usually only controlled by upper-level managers who have significant authority.

Motivating Factors

Herzberg cites six motivating factors: achievement, recognition, the work itself, responsibility, advancement, and growth. All project leaders, even project leaders with little formal authority, have control (or at least significant influence) over each of these factors.

The project leader is responsible for aligning the work with team members who will make commitments to get it done; as such, the project leader has a lot of influence over "achievement" and will delegate "responsibility" for all defined project activities. An effective project leader is always on the lookout for opportunities to align skill building for team members with the needs of the project, so "growth" is another factor over which an alert leader can exercise substantial control. These factors are all integral to effective project planning, and each is explored in detail in Chapter 6.

"Recognition" also seems well covered. As project leader, you write status reports and other communications where you can name names and highlight accomplishments. You can say "thank you" to anyone on the team whenever it seems appropriate. (On technical projects, no one does this enough.) You can celebrate accomplishments at the end of project phases, during project reviews, or, frankly, anytime that you choose to. It is also likely that you have access to established programs in your organization for reward and recognition, so you can give public awards to, or at least nominate, individuals or groups of individuals from your project team. Recognition is one of the most overlooked techniques that a project leader can use to maintain control and increase motivation. Specific ideas for rewards and recognition throughout your project are outlined in Chapter 8.

"The work itself" deserves particular attention because the way team members view a project, at least initially, can be heavily influenced by the project leader. The "vision thing" can be tricky, but if you are able to communicate the value of the project to your contributors in terms that are meaningful to each of them, it will make an enormous difference in motivation. All modern projects tend to have aggressive deadlines and tight resources. Projects don't succeed because they are trivial or easy—they succeed because the people working on them care about getting them done. To team members who see the project as a top personal priority, the project leader's principal activities are providing adequate guidance and then staying out of the way. Setting a vision for the project, perhaps with variations for different parts of the team, is a key element of control essential to project initiation, which is explored in more detail in Chapter 5.

Only "advancement" on Herzberg's list is really outside what a team leader can directly control, but even for this factor your reports on individual performance will exert a good deal of influence.

Hygiene Factors

Hygiene factors matter to workers only when they are unsatisfactory. Herzberg's hygiene factors include company policy and administration, supervision, relationship with supervisor, working conditions, and salary. Unless people are unhappy or frustrated with these factors, they are not much noticed. When workers view these aspects of their jobs as poor, compared with other comparable job opportunities, they will vote with their feet and leave.

Project leaders generally cannot control these factors, but they contribute little to increased motivation anyway. Two of the factors on Herzberg's hygiene factors list, "supervision" and "relationship with supervisor," are your responsibility (or at least partly yours). For this reason, maintaining relationships and trust with your team members is a high priority for an effective project leader.

▪ Getting Through Giving

Your sparkling personality and enormous talent as a project manager notwith-standing, you will never be able to get credible commitments for everything your project requires simply by asking. The fundamental basis for getting what you need will rely, as it always has, on exchange—giving something in return for something you have requested. Project leaders with little authority don't think they have much to offer, so they tend to believe that this won't be a very useful strategy for securing the necessary commitments for their projects. But as with the motivating factors discussed in the previous section, this is really not the case; project leaders have a great deal to work with in the realm of exchange.

Bartering is far older than humans. Exchange of things for things, or services for services, serves as the basis for reciprocal relationships throughout all of biology. Giving and getting is such a fundamental part of how we live and conduct our lives that we sometimes don't even consciously recognize it. Even in situations where it is possible to secure a commitment through coercion or exercise of power, some form of exchange is nearly always preferable. With exchange, no one feels taken advantage of, and equitable exchange serves as the foundation for trust and future interaction.

Given that exchange is a useful way to get what you need for your project, how do you do it? One way to start building an effective strategy for yourself is to identify people in your organization who are very good at getting others to cooperate. Think about how you were convinced to lead your current project. What were you offered? Why was the approach that was used to get your commitment effective? People who sponsor projects and are effective mid-level (and higher) managers seem to have a process for negotiation and gaining commitments embedded in their DNA.

You will generally notice a few things that are common to successful influencers. They approach others one-on-one, as equals, leveling any differ-ences in organizational power and authority, at least for the duration of the current discussion. You need to do the same. This isn't difficult when you are dealing with people who are in fact peers or who have less organizational power than you, but it can be a challenge when the situation is the other way around. To level a discussion with your sponsor or manager, or anyone who has more position power than you have, you may need to rely on your expertise or reputa-tion, or the value and importance of your project.

Successful influencers also identify common ground and shared interests quickly. While the two parties may begin with differing objectives and priorities, skillful questioning helps influencers to align what they need to do with some-thing that is of value to the other party. This sounds very difficult and even unlikely, but with justified projects in the context of a single organization, there is nearly always some common ground to work from.

Good influencers are also generally well liked. They are friendly and help-ful, and they have little difficulty initiating conversations about commitments, in part because they tend to be fearless, and in part because many people seem to owe them return favors. Experienced project leaders share these traits, at least the part about being owed return favors; they cooperate with requests whenever possible, especially small ones, because they know how valuable it is likely to be in the future when they need a favor in return.

What the people who have a lot of success at influencing seem to have that most of the rest of us do not, though, is knowledge of how to "close the deal." Anyone can learn how to do it. Even people for whom it does not come naturally can get a lot better at it with a little practice. The consequences of not understanding how to effectively come to an agreement will hurt you and your project more than you might think.

People who have little practice in influencing generally make their re-quests of others without much preamble. They assume that the other person will see things the same way they do and will quickly agree. In reality, other people see things from their own perspective, which might be wildly different. The response to these abrupt requests is generally a refusal. The requester, seeing this as illogical and inappropriate, repeats the request, a little louder. The other person refuses again, also a little more forcefully. After a few addi-tional rounds, things can escalate to substantial unpleasantness with no pros-pect for *ever* gaining the commitment required. In addition to failing to agree on the current request, such an exchange can also poison future dealings be-tween the two people involved.

Such disasters are far from inevitable. Project leaders can learn to listen better. They can discuss situations to learn more about the people they need to deal with and gain the commitments needed for their projects by offering some-thing appropriate to the other party to seal the bargain.

A Process for Influencing

Getting through giving requires negotiation, and it is most successful when all parties involved are better off after an agreement than they were before. You generally know what you want from others to make your project successful, but you may not know in advance what they want (or if offered, would like) from you. For minor requests, a generic offering might be sufficient, such as, "Would you mind spending a few minutes reviewing my project plan to see if I have missed anything? I would be grateful, and if you would like one you are wel-come to one of our project T-shirts." Unfortunately, not every commitment comes quite so easily, so a process for approaching more complicated situa-tions can help a great deal.

An overall process includes ten steps:

- Document your objective.
- Identify who could do the work.
- Evaluate your options and select the best person.
- Consider the other person's perspective.
- Possibilities for exchange.
- Meet with the other person.
- Verify your assumptions and determine what to exchange.
- Request a commitment.
- Document the agreement.
- Deliver on your offer and track the work to completion.

1. *Document your objective.* An overall process for negotiating begins with preparation. Clearly document what you need, in writing. Specific commitments you need to get for your project may be part of your overall project plan or details from other project documentation. In other cases it may be necessary to get out a blank piece of paper and specify the details from scratch.

2. *Identify who can do the work.* When you have a clear, written description of your needs, consider who could potentially fulfill them. If you have several options, list each alternative and capture the name of the person who you will need to approach, along with the individual's relationship (if any) to your project. List all possibilities; do not discount individuals who are not initially involved with your project. The more alternatives you can generate, the larger the probability that you will be able to secure an agreement with one of them.

3. *Evaluate your options and select the best person.* Your primary concern in reviewing alternatives, if you have more than one, is to identify who can best provide what your project needs to be successful. Assess your options using the best information you have available, and write down why you think that each the person you listed would be a good choice to contribute to your project. Document all relevant skills, experience, and other factors that you are aware of that would be useful for the specific objective at hand and to your project as a whole. For each person, also document any concerns, issues, or risks that you know about, so you can objectively consider both the advantages and disadvantages associated with each alternative. You are doing this for at least two reasons: to determine the people you should approach first, and to have a clear list of reasons why you are asking them to help. When you are able to convey to other people that you are aware of and respect their abilities and have confidence in them, it will get their attention. Flattery may not get you everything you seek, but it can move you a lot closer to agreement than you might expect.

In your analysis, also consider your relationship with the people you have listed. Identify everyone on your list with whom you already have an established relationship, whether it's someone you have worked with in the past, a friend, or anyone for whom you have recently done a favor. You will find it a good deal easier to influence and gain commitments from people when you already have established a relationship of trust with them. If you have no present relationship, or for some reason you have a poor relationship, reaching agreement will be more difficult.

4. *Consider the other person's perspective.* Continue your preparation by considering what you could do to improve (or establish) your relationship with all the people you plan to approach. Consider your project from their perspective and identify all existing connections that exist. Document why your project matters, or at least *should* matter, to each person on your list. For each situation, invest some time considering what you may have to offer that might potentially interest the person you are approaching. Based on what you know, brainstorm options that you might use to get their attention and obtain a credible commitment for your project. Think about what the other person does. What goals and challenges does this person face? What is important in this individual's working environment? What measures and evaluations are used? How will the other person benefit from your project when it is successful? What undesirable outcomes may the person experience if your project fails? What you ultimately agree to exchange may be quite different from what you initially come up with, but it pays to prepare in advance and to sequence the things you come up with, from the easiest to those that are more expensive or difficult.

5. *List possibilities for exchange.* With only a little thought, most project leaders can come up with a robust list of "exchange capital" that far exceeds what they might suspect. Your list of potential exchange ideas will strongly correlate to the motivating factors outlined by Herzberg, for obvious reasons—both are based upon things that people care about. To start your list of exchange ideas, consider some of these possibilities.

Overall Project Considerations

- *The Project Vision.* Provide a vivid description of how the world will be better, from the other person's perspective, when the project is completed.
- *The Project's Priority.* Provide documented evidence of the strategic importance and organizational commitment to the project.
- *Sponsorship.* Name-drop when your project is strongly supported by an important, respected individual.
- *Doing the "Right Thing."* Describe the aspects of your project that will appeal to the beliefs, ethics, and morals of others. If your project will resolve a situation that currently damages or could hurt the organization's reputation or standing, make this known to others.

- *Doing the "Best Thing."* If your project has goals that exceed what has been done before and will make a significant contribution, let people know. If your project will deliver exceptional quality, extraordinary reliability, or has other world-class characteristics, play them up.
- *Improving Customer or User Satisfaction.* Solving problems, addressing complaints, and improving customer loyalty can lead to appreciation and future work.
- *Secrets.* Knowledge is power, so if there are confidential or other aspects of your project that are not generally known, use them to appeal to contributors who would like to be in the inner circle.
- *Job Security.* Projects with committed resources, particularly lengthy ones, can be a safe refuge in turbulent economic times.

Project Work Considerations
- *Ownership.* Every activity in the project needs an owner, and delegation of responsibility by name is a powerful motivator.
- *New Skills.* Every project is unique, and there are always development opportunities to build new expertise.
- *New Technology.* Outline any specific areas that the project requires that are novel or extend beyond the foundations of past projects. Particularly for projects representing new platform development, architecture, or significant innovation, sell the excitement of being on the "bleeding edge."
- *New Resources and Equipment.* Emphasize any plans for upgrade and replacement of existing equipment to contributors who like "new toys."
- *Uniqueness.* Play up the elements of your project that differentiate it from other projects with people for whom the differentiators are important.
- *Challenge.* Outline the risks and potentially difficult aspects of your project to contributors who thrive on a challenge and are bored with the mundane.
- *Probable Success.* For risk-averse team members who gravitate toward the mundane, emphasize the parts of your project that are familiar territory and are likely to go well.
- *Self-Image.* The work we do represents a large part of how we see ourselves, so play up any status element inherent in your project's activities.
- *High-Quality Help.* If your project team or support network contains particularly able people who are well known for assisting others, use their presence to influence team members who want to learn from the experts.

Recognition Considerations

- *Visibility.* For projects that will get a lot of management attention, emphasize the opportunity to be noticed. For other projects, describe what you plan to do to ensure accomplishments are acknowledged. (For the risk averse, this two-edged sword may not have much value because with the potential for high-profile praise comes the chance of intense criticism.)
- *Reputation.* Describe relevant portions of the work that are seen as difficult and thus, when completed successfully, will result in kudos and respect. For work that is extremely difficult with high risk of failure, point out that others will be impressed simply by the attempt.
- *Gratitude.* While more of an ongoing tactic for enhancing control during the project, describing the gratitude that individuals on the project team can anticipate can be a powerful motivator.
- *Opportunity to Mentor.* Accomplished people generally like to hear how expert they are, and many will respond to sincere (and sometimes even not-so-sincere) flattery by sharing some of their knowledge with others.
- *"Stuff."* In some cases, inexpensive items such as T-shirts, mugs, buttons, hats, or other giveaways identified with your project may be useful in securing favors and commitments necessary for your project.

Interpersonal Team and Peer Considerations

- *Trust.* Project teams that succeed build trust for each other. Getting trust begins with offering trust, and even with people you don't know or don't know well, conducting discussions about commitments openly and honestly will get things started. For people you do know well, offer to maintain and enhance your existing relationship.
- *Contacts.* Emphasize the opportunity to get to know and work with specific team members, sponsors, managers, stakeholders, and others associated with your project, especially if any of these people are of particular interest.
- *Fast Turnaround.* Commit to quick responses to requests, problem escalations, decisions, and other project responsibilities you carry, especially if you are dealing with individuals for whom responsiveness has been a problem with other project leaders.
- *Empathy.* You and your project team are all in this together. For people who value teamwork, describe how you will work closely as a team, back each other up, and provide mutual support. Stress that acceptance and inclusion for all is automatic and sustained on your team for everyone who participates.
- *Loyalty.* Project leaders protect their teams. While criticism of individu-

als needs to be heard, an effective project leader commits to never taking action or joining in criticism before investigating and hearing out the situation from all sides. Even if fault is found, good project leaders commit to handling things within the team and minimizing external consequences.

- *Listening.* Commit to being available to everyone on the team to talk—about anything and nearly anytime. Display active listening in all discussions, and strive to talk less than your share of the time.
- *Fun.* Develop a reputation as a project leader who works hard, gets a lot done, and has a good time doing it. Use humor in meetings and in communications. Celebrate milestones and accomplishments with the team, doing things that the team as a group wants to do. Commit to doing as much as possible to establish and maintain a sane, comfortable, productive environment for the project team.

Interpersonal Considerations for Your Manager and Others in Authority

- *Competence.* Emphasize your capabilities and reputation for delivering on what you promise, and not causing frequent problems that have to be managed or escalated for attention. Work to deserve the confidence your managers had in you when you were asked to lead your project.
- *Confidentiality.* Develop a reputation as someone who can be trusted to properly manage sensitive information.
- *Feedback.* Offer to provide open, honest, constructive criticism on documents and presentations where you may be more knowledgeable than your managers. Give your feedback quickly and directly to them. Be a sounding board that your managers can rely on for credible, useful comments.
- *Backup.* Provide coverage for your managers in their absence, and keep things under control when they are away.
- *Proactivity.* Anticipate potential problems and propose responses to organizational problems to your managers before the situations become visible and serious.

You can find additional exchange "currencies," with a discussion of their use in a general context, in *Influence without Authority* by Allan Cohen and David Bradford. And you can undoubtedly add a number of additional ideas from your personal experience just by thinking about things that you have offered to others and things that have been offered to you.

The nature of projects varies enormously, so you need to think in terms of your own situation and list specific ideas that are realistic for your project. Only portions of what you have to offer will have appeal to each of the individuals from whom you'll be seeking cooperation. Select the ideas that are most appropriate in each case, and consider for each potential idea both the value you suspect that it will have for the other person and its cost or personal consequences to you.

When you have a clear idea of what you want, a target individual to approach, and some tactical ideas on how to proceed, you are almost ready to go into action. A role-play rehearsal with a trusted colleague is a good idea when you think there is a high risk that you will not be successful. Risky situations might involve approaching someone who has more authority than you in your organization, someone you do not know very well, or someone you have had problems with in the past. Practice will help you gain confidence in what you need to say in these difficult cases, and make you more comfortable dealing with potential objections or disagreements. Whether you need to formally practice or not, review your preparations thoroughly before scheduling a discussion with the person you plan to influence.

6. *Meet with the other person.* Schedule adequate time to discuss your project requirements with the other person, face-to-face if possible. Building trust and getting a reliable agreement by telephone is possible, but much more difficult. If you cannot get together to meet, provide any materials that you plan to discuss in advance of the meeting and ensure that the other person has reviewed them.

From your perspective, this meeting has one major objective—gaining the person's commitment to contribute to your project—and several preliminary smaller objectives. Your first preliminary objective is to verify that you already have a good working relationship with the other person or, in cases where you do not, to begin establishing one.

7. *Verify your assumptions and decide what to exchange.* Your next goals are to learn enough about what the other person is currently doing to validate any assumptions you made in preparing, and to ensure that the other person understands your project and what you need, at least in general terms. For people you know well and who are very likely to agree with most of your reasonable requests, these preliminary goals are easily met. For bigger requests, or when dealing with people you do not know well, you are wise to combine these objectives with relationship building—in other words, invest time building a foundation for your request. In general, the most powerful tool you have is the open question. Asking about another person's current activities in a friendly and interested way does several things for you. Showing interest in another person is the start of a small exchange, and the other person will probably reciprocate by showing increased interest in you. It also allows people to talk about a favorite subject ("But enough about you; let's talk about *me*") that they know a lot about and are nearly always comfortable discussing. It will also, through subtle follow-up questions, let you test if the assumptions you have

made are valid about how this person sees your project, you, and the overall relationship. In cases where the responses you get are consistent with your preparations, reaching agreement should not be difficult. When you learn things about the other person that invalidate what you expected, you need to begin considering new options for exchange.

8. *Request a commitment.* After establishing the groundwork through your preliminary objectives, you are ready to move on to the main event—getting a commitment. In some cases, formal exchange may not even be necessary. If, through your discussions, it seems that people are enthusiastic about your project, you may have provided sufficient incentive to them already and you might only need to simply ask, "How would you see yourself best contributing this project?" If the response is an offer to provide what you are seeking, accept it with thanks. Any commitment that the individuals you are approaching come up with on their own will be taken much more seriously than one that is requested, so if you can obtain an offer of what you need without asking for it, you will be much better off.

When a situation requires a formal exchange and you think you have something to offer that will probably get you what you need, offer it, request the commitment, and shut up. Wait for a response from the other person, patiently. Let the other person speak next. If the other person accepts, you are ready to move on to the hard part—getting your project completed.

If the other person says no, ask why. Simply offering more in exchange might be effective, but depending on why the other person said no, it may not make much difference. If you are dealing with a person who does not know you, or for some reason does not trust you, it may be necessary to retreat somewhat, revising your request to include only a small portion of what you initially requested. Starting small is an effective way to establish and build a trusting relationship, and once people start working on something it is easier to get future commitments to continue.

If the problem relates to the project or your approach to the work, try to find out how the other person might approach it. This technique may reveal options acceptable to the other person that could effectively move your project forward. The ideas that emerge from this sort of discussion may even be better than what you had in mind—remember, you are requesting a commitment from someone who you believe is expert and may well know a lot more about an issue than you do. In cases where the other person fails to come up with any other alternatives, the attempt may well result in a realization that the offer you made is acceptable. When the other person concludes that what initially seemed a poor idea might be the best approach, it can be extremely persuasive.

Often people say no because they are too busy, lack confidence or knowledge, or otherwise think that they will not be able to do the work. In these cases, any specific help or guidance that you can offer may tip the balance and help you secure a commitment. Continuing the discussion in an objective, friendly way will frequently result in at least a partial commitment to what you seek.

All of the ideas for exchange (in step 5) focused on positive factors for the other person, and it is always preferable to set up agreements where both parties have something after the agreement that they see as desirable and valuable. But when positive exchanges are ineffective, it may be necessary to explore the dark side. Negative factors may have a role in difficult situations, but even here it is best to focus on the avoidance of painful circumstances rather than threats and punishments. You may be able to overcome resistance by outlining the consequences that will result from your project not succeeding. The impact of your failed project may be on the person directly, or it may be to other employees or a department the person cares about, or to the organization as a whole. Projects that do not complete successfully may affect the environment of people we work with in many ways, and large failed projects threaten the overall health and stability of entire companies. Helping people avoid situations that they dislike can be very persuasive.

There may be cases where, after much questioning and discussion, you will be forced to admit defeat and recognize that you will probably never get a commitment. In these cases, you will need to go back to the drawing board and look for an alternative that will serve your project. If there are no acceptable alternatives, in extreme cases you can consider escalating the situation to someone who has sufficient authority to coerce a commitment from the other person for your project. But while coercion by others may work in the short term for your current project, this sort of "scorched earth" tactic should always be a last resort. Establishing teamwork and trust with someone who had to be dragged kicking and screaming into your project is almost impossible. Cooperation will be grudging, and the risks of malicious compliance—giving you something that meets the letter of a request but misses the spirit and intent entirely—will require you to do a great deal of surveillance and inspection. However the short-term situation works out, the real cost is in the long term. It is a small world, and we all tend to work with the same folks over and over. Instead of creating a trusted colleague who will make future projects easier and more fun, escalation and coercion may create an enemy who will likely find ways to make your future projects more difficult. It is often better to walk away from a situation where agreements prove elusive. You can either devise another approach to your project that does not rely on this specific commitment, or you can seek agreement with another person who will agree to the commitment, willingly.

9. *Document the agreement.* In most cases where you prepare well, have a reasonable request to assist with a meaningful project, and are persistent, you

will be able to secure an agreement. When you have an agreement that you and the other person are both satisfied with, thank the other person, then document the agreement *in writing*. Some agreements will be formal contracts, or terms added to contracts that are already in force, so this requirement is necessary anyway. Other agreements are less formal, but it is still a good idea to capture them in written form. You are creating a formal version of the agreement for several reasons. In written form, you and the other party can check the agreement to ensure that it clearly states what you both had in mind and correct any misunderstandings right at the start. Whether it is signed or not, it will serve as a permanent record of the commitments that you and the other person have made, which might be very useful later in the project if there are problems. Finally, written agreements carry a lot more weight than verbal ones. Once something is written, it is taken far more seriously, which is why self-help programs of all types have participants write a list of specific changes that they intend to follow through on, and why we write down our New Year's resolutions. Writing down our intentions in these cases still results in a meager success rate, but goals that are only spoken (or worse yet, only thought) have a success rate that is essentially zero. Writing down specific commitments, supported by meaningful exchanges, powerfully enhances your ability to control work on your project.

10. *Deliver on your offer and track the work to completion.* An agreement without follow-through is generally worthless. If either party fails to live up to the commitments made, it will undermine the ongoing relationships with others with whom you will probably work and depend upon in future projects. Follow though to ensure that others will hold up their agreements with you. Deliver on what you offered, and respect both the letter and the spirit of your part of the agreement. Providing more than you promised is often prudent, both to show your good faith and to set up future exchanges. If you committed to providing help or information once a week, do it at least that often. If you committed to specific resources, quick turnarounds on decisions, or other actions, deliver on them. Strive to deliver what people really need from you on your project, not just what you promised. Thank people sincerely when they deliver on their commitments, and provide positive feedback on a regular basis to project contributors.

Project leaders who are generous with favors build up a reserve of goodwill and can maintain control in times of stress by calling in favors that they are owed. Reciprocity represents the most powerful generic contingency tool available to any project leader.

▪ Enhancing Influence

In addition to reciprocity, there are a number of other ways for you to build influence. Some methods are useful for increasing your influence within your team, while other methods are more appropriate for increasing your influence with other project leaders, stakeholders, and managers. Some people are naturally good at influencing others, and these people will find everything in this section obvious and trivial because they do these things all the time. Other people are very analytical and will find some of these ideas alien, and perhaps vaguely dishonest. Effective project leaders are often in a group about midway between these extremes—adept at some influencing techniques and unaware of, or at least unpracticed at, others. For most of us, consciously thinking about how better to influence others we work with once in a while is a good practice to get into, because few of us are as influential as we would like to be.

Building Influence Within Your Team

At the beginning of a project that you have been asked to lead, the project is your responsibility. At the start, though, it may be far from guaranteed that the project team will look to you as a leader, cooperate with you and the other contributors, and do their part to ensure success. Even if you are the manager of every member of the project staff, you will still be wise to earn their recognition as leader of the team.

You can probably think of many additional ways to go about this, but the following techniques should serve as a good starting point:

• *Lead by example.* On a project, you have activities and responsibilities along with everyone else on the team. It is good practice to ensure that you are doing as much or more for your project as anyone else, and that you are not asking others to do things that you are not willing to do (or at least *try* to do) yourself. Leading by example includes pitching in when someone or some part of the team needs help, putting in as many off-hours as others on the team, and providing personal support and encouragement when contributors put in extra effort. One large, very important product development project at Hewlett-Packard in the early 1990s was able to maintain its schedule despite a large number of unforeseen difficulties. The project required a substantial amount of late-evening work by most of the development team and could have completely broken the team's morale. To counter this, all the managers involved supported the extraordinary effort with a nightly competition to see who could find and deliver the best food for those working late. It turned out that very few restaurants refused takeout orders, so everyone ate well, no one got tired of pizza, and motivation was never a problem.

• *Use random positive reinforcement.* When a leader provides the same recognition or thanks again and again, and does it at every possible opportunity, it soon loses its effect. To be effective, expressions of gratitude must be (or at least seem) sincere. What works most effectively is random *positive* reinforcement—praise and thanks to team members in varied forms and at times that are not automatically anticipated by the recipient. Many are puzzled that "salary" is on Frederick Herzberg's list of hygiene factors; after all, who would come to work day after day unless they were paid? Why is a paycheck not motivating? Once in a while, it is—when it goes up. The rest of the time it fades to the background, and if we think of it at all, it is generally to wonder why we are so underpaid. Nonmonetary rewards that are granted occasionally tend to get the best results in most cases. Rewards that do not involve money (like greater recognition) may be granted publicly, whereas monetary rewards (like your salary) are typically private. To enhance your influence, be generous with praise, but pick meaningful opportunities and don't overdo it.

• *Strive to remove barriers.* Project leaders also increase their influence by being proactive. Throughout the project, be vigilant for potential problems. Ask team members, particularly team members who are having trouble with their commitments, what you might be able to do to make their work easier or to avoid future trouble. While you cannot always remove all barriers or anticipate every future problem, your influence will expand whenever you succeed in eliminating obstacles to progress, and even when you are unsuccessful, your influence will improve if you have made an honest attempt.

• *Always provide reasons.* Certain words have a lot more power to influence than others. The word "because" appears to lead all lists. You will always gain more cooperation if you provide reasons with your requests, particularly when the reason directly relates to something that the other person cares about. Interestingly, though, in a study cited by Robert Cialdini in *Influence: Science and Practice,* people trying to cut into long lines at a photocopier who said, "Excuse me, I have five pages. May I use the machine next because I have to make some copies?" were as successful as those who made a similar request but provided an actual reason for needing to break into the queue ("I'm in the middle of an important meeting and need to distribute these copies"). When you ask anything of anybody, always formulate your request with a "because" statement, followed by a reason, and whenever possible find a reason that the other person will respond to favorably.

• *Coach, mentor, and assist.* The principle of reciprocity, of course, also works in situations when the giving and getting are not simultaneous. Effective project leaders are as generous with their time as they can afford to be, and they frequently find opportunities to coach, mentor, and assist people on their teams as well as others. This begins with establishing an environment where people will feel free to discuss any matter or topic without fear of criticism. Encourage project team members to let you know when they are inexperienced or lack skills needed for their assigned activities, then provide guidance and help when you are able, and find help for them when you are not. Be willing to teach and share your expertise with others. This is actually easier to do with people that you are not directly managing, since they may be reluctant to reveal their shortcomings or ask "dumb questions" of their own manager. Ensure that people are confident in your discretion and that there will be no repercussions or consequences when they reveal shortcomings to you. Assisting and mentoring others builds your influence in the short run and increases your stock of goodwill and favors owed to you over the long term.

• *Practice credibility and integrity.* Influence also relies on how people perceive you. Your credibility with others depends on them believing that you mean what you say. Being straightforward and conveying information as accurately and truthfully as you are able is important, but you will enhance your influence even more by showing integrity—delivering on what you say that you will do. A reputation for credibility and integrity, particularly inside your project team, will significantly increase your influence.

• *Be inclusive.* Humans divide those they deal with into "us" and "them." We usually listen to and like "us," and we tend to ignore and mistrust "them." Effective project leaders are quick to include new contributors into the team, making them comfortable and helping them to feel like they are part of the team. Being inclusive requires you to let go of your own tendency to mistrust others and take the first step. When you offer trust and respect, your actions will frequently be reciprocated and accelerate the acceptance of new team members, and the trust you gain with others is essential to building your influence. When new contributors resist becoming part of the team, sometimes trying harder and being persistent helps. With extreme cases, where the person continues to operate independently of the team, you may need to rely on other influence methods (or even find alternative contributors who will become effective team members).

• *Use referent power (but sparingly).* Our influence also depends on "who we know." Referent power—power that you have because managers or others with influence support you—is also a source of influence. It can help you to win arguments and persuade people to do things, but using it too frequently and overtly can backfire. Referent power is most effective when used subtly, ensuring that people know you have it and that you know that they know you have it, but never actually referring to it directly. Mentioning the results of your meetings with your sponsors and others in authority and conveying any appreciation that they have expressed to the project team are effective methods for keeping your team aware of the support you have. Only as a last resort should you attempt to influence others by threatening to involve others higher up in the organization. While it may work in the near term, doing this too frequently will damage your relationship with the person you were attempting to influence, perhaps permanently.

• *Effectively build consensus.* Another effective way to improve your influence is to systematically build consensus around any ideas that you wish your team to accept. Instead of simply inflicting your desires on your team, do some planning in advance and use discussion to build support for your recommendation. Prepare by considering reasons why your idea would be attractive to each of your team members. Look at your recommendation from the team's perspective and outline any reasons why anyone on the team might object to it. Develop responses for potential objections before you convene a team meeting. Begin your team meeting by discussing the overall situation that requires action and the consequences if you do nothing. Present a summary of your proposed response, emphasizing its main benefits and showing how your idea directly addresses the need. Invite objections and criticism, and answer questions that arise. Respond to any objections using the information you have prepared. Encourage modifications for improvement and adopt any beneficial suggestions. Ask for alternatives and discuss any suggestions among the team. Summarize the merits of your proposal, as well as any alternative ideas discussed, and seek consensus from the group for a single idea. If your preparation was thorough and your proposal has merit, the group will choose your idea. If your idea with modifications or some alternative has more support, it is nearly always better for the project anyway. Preparation and systematic analysis that gives your idea a head start, though, adds a great deal to your influence.

   • *Always get it in writing.* Following discussions of almost any kind where you have requested something of another person, it is a good idea to follow up in writing, to reinforce the commitment and to get it in a tangible form. If it is difficult to get the other person to document what was discussed, you do it. Personally written commitments are the most powerful, but an e-mail from you summarizing the request and reinforcing any timing or other factors with a statement such as "Please let me know if this is not what you agreed to" will be nearly as effective. A tangible, backup document increases the likelihood that the other people will follow through and influences their behavior.

   • *Dress for success.* While it is yet another thing in life that is not fair, studies repeatedly show that for most people, influence depends on visual cues. A popular book of the 1970s was *Dress for Success,* which made the point that you should dress for the job you want to have, not necessarily the one you currently have. The way people respond to you changes depending on what you wear and how you look, so give some thought to how you wish others to see you before you come to work, meetings, and other face-to-face encounters. Dressing neatly and similarly to those in your organization who have the amount of formal authority that you would like to have will help close the gap between their influence and yours substantially. If you are male, it might mean wearing a suit or at least a tie if you work in the northeastern United States, or wearing a clean T-shirt with no holes in it if you live in Silicon Valley. When you look the part, sometimes people fail to notice that you may have little actual power.

• *Be positive.* Finally, be positive. People who are cheerful and use humor to good effect are much more influential than grumpy, doleful, depressing people. Even on the telephone, people actually can tell when you are smiling, and it makes a big difference in how other people hear what you are saying. Even when delivering bad news, focus on what has been accomplished and what you are doing (and will do) to resolve any problems. In the film *Harvey,* Jimmy Stewart's character, Elwood P. Dowd, says, "Years ago my mother used to say to me . . . 'In this world, you must be oh so smart or oh so pleasant.' Well, for years I was smart. I recommend pleasant. And you may quote me." Pleasant worked for Jimmy Stewart, and it works pretty well for everyone else too, especially project leaders who have limited authority. You catch more flies with honey than vinegar, and you can influence people more effectively with it, too.

Building Influence with your Manager, Project Sponsor, and Stakeholders

To be successful, you need to influence upward, as well as within your team. Many of the ideas in the previous section apply to building influence with the people that you report to, particularly leading by example, providing reasons with requests, being helpful, practicing credibility and integrity, effectively building consensus, and being positive. In addition, you can improve your influence with your management by asking revealing questions and collaborating with your peers—there is strength in numbers.

Asking Revealing Questions

Project leaders rarely are able to control things by saying no or simply telling people what to do. However, by virtue of their role, leaders may ask questions, which can be equally effective. Asking revealing and even potentially embarrassing questions—questions that shine a bright light on aspects of your project that otherwise would remain murky and fuzzy—allows you to apply logic and reason to situations that might otherwise be settled using emotion, politics, or a coin flip. Project leaders bring a unique perspective to many discussions, merging a technical, analytical viewpoint with pragmatic business considerations. With sponsors and stakeholders, an affinity for numbers is useful when the rationale for some proposed change or other project request is not based on very thorough analysis. The right question, *diplomatically* posed at the right time, can help you to avoid a great deal of aggravation on your projects. Specific questions relating to project initiation are discussed in Chapter 5, and examples useful for scope management and specification changes are explored in Chapter 8.

As project leader, you need to remain skeptical throughout the project, checking all the information that you hear and working to understand where the information is coming from. Some questions that can help are:

- What problem are we trying to solve? (This one shortens a lot of meetings.)
- How sure are we of the information? How can we verify it?
- What is the source of the information?
- Can we quantify what we are hearing? What are the financial, timing, and other measurable aspects?
- Are there uncertainties or data ranges associated with the information?
- What might we have overlooked?
- Has this situation occurred before? How did we deal with it (or similar situations) in the past?
- Is this approach the only option? What other alternatives should we consider?
- What is the overall business case for what is being proposed?
- What are the risks associated with the proposal?
- Is the proposal consistent with our overall priorities?
- What are this proposal's benefits? How can we verify their value?
- What is the maximum tolerable project impact for this proposal?
- Are there possible unintended consequences of the proposal that could affect others?
- How will we evaluate success? Who will be responsible for verifying successful closure?

A healthy skepticism and an ability to shine a bright light into the often murky corners of technical projects forces people to consider things that they might prefer to overlook. Asking revealing questions within your team will keep people honest. Strategically worded questions posed to your sponsor and stakeholders can substantially increase the influence and control you have on your project.

Collaborating with Peers—Strength in Numbers

Another source of influence, particularly with upper-level managers, sponsors, and others responsible for the organizational infrastructure, comes through collaboration with your peers. Recommendations that come from a task force or a council of project leaders carry a good deal more weight than those that originate from a single person. You can work with others who face similar challenges to gain support for your project processes (as outlined in Chapter 2) or to change them and improve how they work. Doing this from the ground up is not easy and may take some persistence, but it is possible. There is strength in numbers. When speaking in unison, backed up with data from recent project experience, working within a group of like-minded project leaders can amplify your influence enormously.

Building influence with managers is largely about relationships, so working throughout your project to keep your sponsor and stakeholders involved and supportive will be a good investment of your time. Providing them with frequent evidence of your progress and ensuring that they remain confident in your ability to lead the project to successful completion will help you maintain the influence with them that you require.

In the early 1990s, I had the opportunity to participate for several years in a Hewlett-Packard internal task force on project management comprised of grizzled practitioners from all of HP's product groups and corporate functions. This Project Management Council met quarterly, and as a member I interacted often with Lew Platt, the CEO, and other members of the HP executive committee. As individuals, none of us had a great deal of influence, even within our own organizations. As a council, though, our work over several years made much progress in establishing better, more consistent practices for project management companywide, with sustaining impact even today.

▪ Maintaining Relationships

Most of your work in establishing good relationships using ideas in this chapter will be during project initiation and project planning (discussed in Chapters 5 and 6). Maintaining influence and control throughout the project depends on your ability to maintain solid relationships with all the members of your team throughout project execution. Effective communications, both formal and informal, are vital, but there is much more you can and should do to maintain good relationships over the course of your project.

One key to maintaining relationships is taking advantage of the things that you have in common with the people on your team. The most obvious thing you have in common is the project itself. Even though the specific reasons for why the project matters for each person may differ, keeping the common goal of project success front and center can be a powerful unifying force.

Especially when you are working to establish a relationship with someone new, find out if you have any colleagues or friends in common. Building your relationship through mutual acquaintances, particularly people for whom you both have respect, can result in very durable relationships.

Common experiences and educational backgrounds are another good foundation for building trust and respect. Similar past projects will give you things to discuss and exchange information about, as will your academic studies, professional affiliations, and even training classes that you both have attended.

Another effective way to connect with people, especially on a personal level, is to find common interests, hobbies, and travels. What people do with their own time is always of interest to them, and when you share interests in a type of music, sport, cinema, books, or other pastimes, you will always have something to talk about. Similarly, a shared interest in a hobby such as bird watching, home repair, photography, vintage cars, skiing, playing a musical instrument, hang gliding, gardening, cooking, sailing, or any of thousands of other activities can create an enduring bond. Even visits to the same destinations on vacation will provide opportunities for interesting conversations. Uncovering things that you have in common with members of your team increases your ability to influence them (and their ability to influence you as well) and will support ongoing teamwork and effective communication.

You will find a number of additional ideas and suggestions for maintaining relationships in the final section of Chapter 7 on project execution.

KEY IDEAS FOR INFLUENCE

- Adopt a leadership style that will work with your team members and work to deliver on what people care about the most.
- Build your awareness and skill for influencing others.
- Learn what people you need commitments from want that you can provide, and use exchanges to negotiate credible agreements.
- Work to increase your influence through your actions and demeanor.
- Build and maintain relationships of trust and respect with each of your team members.
- Provide snacks.

CHAPTER 4

Control Through Project Metrics

ALL PROJECTS MOVE FORWARD little by little, especially long, complex ones. Lacking metrics to demonstrate progress, the timely discovery of inadequate progress may be impossible. Even worse, without adequate data your project could be headed in the wrong direction without your knowledge.

The most commonly used measures for most projects are aimed at progress reporting. Status metrics also contribute to project control by helping you identify issues and uncover potential future problems. Project control requires timely information about resource and funding consumption, progress relative to milestones and other dates, and performance against scoping commitments. Metrics can also be used to better understand your project, to adjust the project's objectives, to improve your processes and working methods, and to motivate team members. Measures based on analysis and planning are useful for understanding the project, particularly early on the work. Project assessment metrics that use numerical data can show what you are getting yourself into. Typical measures for sizing a project, and for allowing comparison with other project opportunities and the validation of relative priorities, include:

- Resource allocations and cost estimates
- Project deliverable benefits and value assessments
- Complexity
- Forecasted volume of output

- Measures of risk and uncertainty
- Project duration

Measurement is also central to decision making. From the perspective of project control, one of the most important uses for plan-based measurements is influencing decisions concerning scoping and overall objectives. Project leaders who lack much authority frequently find themselves taking on fundamentally infeasible projects, and throughout their project additional changes are imposed that make project success more and more unlikely. Metrics related to project size provide your first line of defense against this, providing compelling data you can use to frame successful counterproposals to change unrealistic project objectives. You can use the same measurements to demonstrate the consequences of proposed project changes, allowing you to avoid unnecessary changes throughout your project.

Metrics show the effectiveness of project processes, both at review points during the project and at project completion. The measures that trigger action to review process effectiveness also guide process improvement efforts and assist you in improving your working methods in the future and on following projects.

For a project leader with little real authority over team members, measurement is also an essential tactic for motivating project contributors. Used well, such metrics are a force for good that will significantly increase your ability to keep things under control and moving ahead. Used less well, measurement aimed at motivation can backfire on you and make a shaky situation a good deal worse. For this reason, you need to carefully select and manage the measurements you adopt on your projects.

▪ Desired Behaviors

Fulfilling our objectives requires action. In a simple case you don't need any measures. When the objectives are simple and the necessary behaviors are obvious and easily accomplished, things generally play out as we hope, as illustrated in Figure 4-1.

We easily complete simple goals that consume little time or effort without any special tactics to link the objectives and the necessary actions. We are able to act quickly and succeed without too much forethought or intervention most of the time.

Unfortunately, we rarely work in such a trivial environment, so we must introduce measures into our projects to align appropriate behaviors with desired objectives. Projects are complex, so measures that relate both to your overall objectives and the behaviors you desire will help you ensure that people on your team are doing what they need to do to support the project goals. For

FIGURE 4-1. LINKING GOALS AND BEHAVIORS.

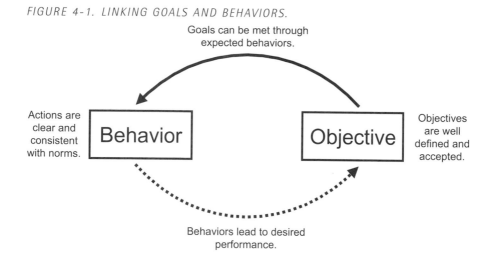

better or for worse, measurement *always* affects behavior. If you select metrics with care, they will provide you with a powerful tool for guiding your team that requires very little actual managerial authority.

Aligning behaviors and objectives requires you to think through the relationships indicated in Figure 4-2. It is far from simple to determine behaviors that will support your project objectives and define appropriate linking measures, but it is worthwhile.

While specific project objectives are highly variable (projects are, after all, by definition unique), some *broad objectives* that are universal can significantly contribute to your project control. These objectives should be:

- Predictable project performance versus plans
- Clearly defined, managed project scope
- Efficient and effective use of resources
- Infrequent conflicts and disagreement
- Appropriately managed risks

Behaviors that contribute to these objectives could include:

- Preference for careful planning, execution, and communication over project heroism and reactive firefighting
- Tolerating innovation and change only within appropriate, well-understood business and customer requirements
- Contributors enthusiastically moving from completed projects to follow-on projects, with rare cases of burnout

- Cooperation, with team members supporting one another and work and rewards balanced within the team
- Minimizing overall uncertainty through analysis and planning, but with people willingly to accept appropriate risks (being too cautious can be risky also)

FIGURE 4-2. GOALS AND BEHAVIORS ALIGNED THROUGH METRICS.

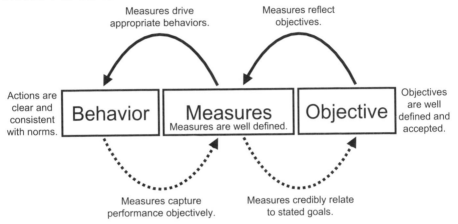

Methods for selecting measures that encourage these desired behaviors and support the objectives are discussed later in this chapter, but a few examples follow. The first of the broad objectives, performing to plan, is the genesis of many common project metrics, such as:

- Variance between actual timing versus baseline schedule
- Variance between actual costs versus baseline budgets
- Task closure rate (or earned value measurements)
- The number of "stoplight" red or yellow indicators on published status reports

For the objective of managed project scope, some selected measures may include:

- Assessment measures related to deliverable definition (through assessment surveys and other means of detecting gaps and weaknesses)
- The volume of changes submitted during the project, particularly changes late in the project
- The percentage of changes accepted and implemented during the project
- Measured results from tests of project outputs

Resource usage and staffing are also measured on many projects using metrics such as:

- Cumulative overtime
- Incidents of idle time
- Comparative staffing compared with norms from earlier, similar projects
- Staff retention and turnover statistics

Metrics may also relate to encouraging cooperation and avoiding conflict. Examples would be:

- Frequency of unplanned meetings
- Number of escalations
- Quantity of team rewards and recognition

Measures related to risk must track the risk tolerance that is appropriate for each project, but they can involve:

- The number of risks identified and assessed
- The number of unanticipated problems by severity (compared with norms)
- The value of delivered project results versus expectations

Setting up a system of measures that both encourage desirable behaviors and support project goals can be difficult to do for a specific project and can vary from location to location or even from contributor to contributor. Measurement must always be sensitive to the context and consider the people involved. For example, you might consider inflicting identical measures on teams in India, England, and California. All three teams predominantly communicate in English and would presumably be able to interpret what is to be done consistently. In spite of this, the same metric will almost certainly drive different behaviors due to culture, background, and values. Even in the same geographical location, working across company boundaries or with people within your own organization soon after a merger, you may find complicating cultural implications due to differences in organizational culture. Metrics can be very powerful and useful, but unless you carefully chose and test them in your specific environment, they may have unintended consequences that cause great dysfunction and harm.

▪ Types and Uses of Project Metrics

Overall, the main reason for measurement in business organizations is to assist in achieving goals. In the context of this book, the principle business objective for measurement is good project management and control. There are three basic types of metrics, and each plays a different role in project management.

1. Predictive project metrics are based on definition and planning information and help set realistic expectations for the project.
2. Diagnostic metrics are based on current status and serve as indicators of progress and as timely triggers for risk response, problem solving, and decision making.
3. Retrospective metrics assess how well the work you have completed was done and provide insight into process issues and recurring problems.

Predictive Project Metrics

Predictive project metrics are primarily used in project initiation and project planning. They serve to help you understand the project and function as a distant early-warning system for unrealistic constraints and potential project problems. These metrics use forecast information derived from analysis and planning and are based primarily on speculative rather than empirical data. Because of this, predictive metrics are the least precise of the three metric types. Predictive project measures support project management by:

- Determining the scale of your project
- Justifying the need for revisions to the project objective
- Quantifying schedule and budget reserve requirements
- Validating cost and timing assumptions for project prioritization and value assessment

Some predictive metrics related to the overall project are explored in more detail in Chapter 5, on project initiation, but most predictive project metrics related to timing, resources, and setting a realistic project baseline are covered in Chapter 6, on project planning.

Diagnostic Project Metrics

Based on project status information, diagnostic project metrics help you assess the current state of your project. It's said that a frog dropped into boiling water will hop out promptly, but a frog set in cool water that is gradually heated will sit there until he becomes consommé. Project leaders too often find themselves in hot water for similar reasons: An initially reasonable-sounding project gradually becomes impossible. This happens because of the accumulation of many small problems and incremental changes in scope, resources, and timing. If you lack an adequate set of status measures, the transition to a failed project can occur long before you realize it. Diagnostic project metrics are designed to provide real-time information about your project, and they serve as your thermometer for assessing just how hot the water is getting. Control-related uses of these metrics include:

- Identifying resource consumption and timing problems and trends
- Showing the consequences of scope changes
- Making process and staff performance issues visible
- Managing potential future problems and project risks
- Monitoring the need to revalidate the project objective for (or shut down) the project

Status collection and defining diagnostic metrics are main topics of Chapter 7, on project execution. Using diagnostic metrics is discussed in Chapter 8, on tracking and monitoring.

Retrospective Project Metrics

Retrospective metrics determine how well a process worked when it is finished. These metrics are a project's rearview mirror. Project process metrics can be assessed at the conclusion of any completed process-oriented activity throughout a project, such as during a project review (as discussed in Chapter 8). Backward-looking project-level metrics assess the overall effectiveness and efficiency of overall project processes when a project has finished (or has been canceled). Use retrospective project metrics to:

- Improve or replace existing processes
- Evaluate long-term trends
- Validate and improve the accuracy of predictive metrics
- Quantify systemic project and organizational issues, risks, and problems

Metrics related to process improvement and overall project assessment are explored in Chapter 9, on project closure.

▪ Measurement Definition and Baselines

Projects are complicated, and selecting the right measures for your project may be challenging. One or two metrics will probably not be enough, but committing to collection of metrics for everything that could be measured is also problematic; the overhead would be huge and important information will be impossible to find in all the data volume. Selecting metrics for a project is about balance and utility.

The basic process steps for establishing a system of metrics are documented in Figure 4-3.

FIGURE 4-3. PROCESS FOR DEFINING METRICS.

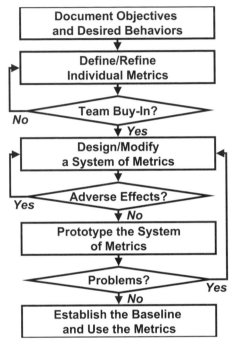

Determining Objectives and Desired Behaviors

Determining objectives was discussed earlier in this chapter, and for some project measures this is not very complicated. We collect estimates for each activity in a project, and each estimate (whether of effort or duration) is a predictive metric based on an analysis of the work required. We collect estimates to support the overall goal of a coherent, realistic plan, and we expect that the processes we use for estimating will be supported by appropriate behaviors. If we think about the behaviors that this metric will lead to, things begin to get a little more complicated. If inaccurate estimates are not tolerated and lead to criticism or punishment, the behaviors this metric inspires will lead to padding and systemic overestimating, which is in contradiction of the objective: realistic plans. If we do not provide adequate time to systematically analyze the work and all estimates are "rough order of magnitude" or, even worse, derived from arbitrary deadline constraints, we not only fail to meet our planning objective, we also display that we do not care very much how well, or even if, this project is completed. Behaviors in this case will be very undesirable for nearly all contributors.

Defining the desired behaviors and objectives *before* considering the question of what to measure will lead to more consistent, appropriate results. The objective of realistic plans and the desired behavior of thorough, systematic analysis may not seem very complicated, but they are in fact easily (and often) undermined as a result of too little forethought. Even in this simple case, you may need to consider several types metrics and implement a system of measures with care and attention to how the information is collected and used.

Designing Individual Metrics

You can design individual metrics using several different approaches. Some approaches begin with objectives. Others begin with behaviors. Wherever you begin and whatever process you use initially, the final steps of the process require you to evaluate your measures for appropriateness, consistency, and potential dysfunction.

Methods for defining metrics include goal question metric, balanced scorecard, process measurement, and behavioral methods.

Goal Question Metric Approach

In the early 1990s, Victor Basili of the University of Maryland and several colleagues working with NASA developed the goal question metric (GQM) method for defining metrics. Since then, this means of definition has been widely applied, particularly for software projects, in commercial and other environments.

GQM is a systematic process based on a three-tiered hierarchy. The first tier is at the top of the hierarchy and defines the desired outputs and results. The second tier is in the middle and is composed of questions through which you can determine whether you have achieved these objectives. The third and lowest level of the hierarchy contains measures that can be used in answering the questions. Figure 4-4 shows a schematic example of a GQM hierarchy.

As an example, if one of the goals for your project was to "improve the accuracy of project duration estimates," one question might relate to the overall current accuracy and another might be about change in accuracy over time. To quantify these questions, primitive metrics such as estimated and actual duration for activities would be needed, along with composite metrics to determine ratios and differences. Of course, you can improve estimating accuracy simply by padding all your estimates, completing the work faster than that, and then waiting until the expected time to deliver your results. To guard against this, a

FIGURE 4-4. A GOAL QUESTION METRIC (GQM) HIERARCHY.

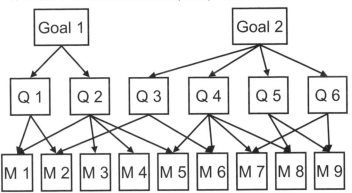

second goal could be to not increase the overall average durations of completed work. Questions related to this goal could be about current actual durations and changes in activity duration over time. Some of the same metrics are needed to answer these two questions, but some measures will be used uniquely by one question.

Will these two questions alone, with their metrics, actually achieve our intended overall objective of better, more realistic plans? Probably not, because we have not considered the possibility of contributors defining shorter, simpler activities going forward or other ways that these objectives might be undermined by unexpected team behavior. GQM is a good way to start the process of metric definition, but we still must validate the measurements and check that they are consistent with what we are trying to use them to achieve.

Balanced Scorecard Approach

Robert Kaplan devised the balanced scorecard method for defining metrics in the mid-1990s, in large part to deal with the potential for abuse and other problems that arise when measures are applied selectively. When too few measures or the wrong measures are deployed, it is possible—and in many cases likely—that the measures will look just fine even when the behaviors are undesirable and none of the objectives are being met. Kaplan devised a four-quadrant view that provides tension between the measures and helps to ensure that the metrics are less likely to result in dysfunctional behavior. The balanced scorecard method is principally aimed at the business or business-unit level, but it can be applied to projects and programs with a little creativity.

Kaplan's quadrants are "customer," "finance," "internal process," and "learning and growth." The context for these four categories is the overall strategy and vision for the organization, so the primary questions relate to how both external and internal constituencies perceive the organization, as determined using objective measures. The same type of model can be applied to projects and programs, yielding a similar system of metrics that can provide good results and minimize the possibility of overemphasis of a single dimension or dysfunctional behavior. An example of the balanced scorecard approach applied to a project is shown in Figure 4-5.

In the center of the figure is the reason the project exists, the specific technical goals and why they matter. While the project objective is common to all perspectives, vision tends to be in the eye of the beholder and can vary considerably from quadrant to quadrant.

Ultimately, the end user (or customer) perspective for a project is primarily about scoping. If you can get the feature set just right, other considerations of timing and cost are much less important, particularly in the long run. Sponsors and most stakeholders tend to be more focused on timing and cost, as these dimensions of a project affect what else the organization can take on, and time is money. These two perspectives are external to the project and need to be balanced against internal considerations, including your need for control and survival.

The internal process view revisits themes that have figured prominently in earlier chapters. Process is one of your most important control tools, and fine-tuning the process dimension relates to execution efficiency and elements of timing and resource consumption. Teamwork and development are also central to the project and pull in the human motivation factors as well as support the team's capacity to deliver on the more challenging aspects of project scope.

FIGURE 4-5. A BALANCED SCORECARD CONTEXT FOR PROJECT METRICS.

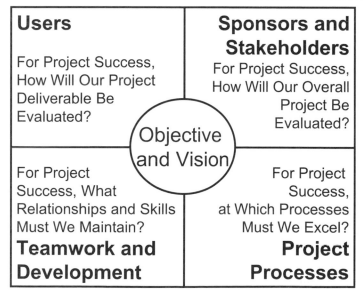

Your version of a balanced scorecard for developing a set of metrics may be different from this example, but the basic idea of looking at all significant aspects of the project and setting up metrics in tension that force objective evaluation of trade-offs is a useful approach.

Process Measurement

Another approach for defining metrics rests on the ideas in Chapter 2. When you have defined a set of processes well, you have established rules and standards for performance. You can then establish expectations for performance from these rules and define metrics that will show you how well the process is working. Some metrics relate to the outputs of the process, such as accuracy, quantity of omissions or defects, and degree of acceptance. Other metrics relate to the execution of the process, such as throughput, timeliness, or effort consumed.

As an example, a key process for overall project control is scope change management. Metrics of both of these types are useful in dealing with proposed specification changes. Examples of output-related measures include:

- The number of changes accepted as a percentage of those proposed
- The number of changes accepted into scope that are later modified, require significant clarification, or are subsequently dropped
- The number of initial decisions that result in escalation for reconsideration

The effectiveness of the process may also be measured by:

- How long it takes to accept submitted change proposals for review
- How much time the review process and initial decision requires
- How much effort is used dealing with submitted changes

Defining measures as part of an overall process is a good way to provide visibility for the process and make its use more universal. Carefully selected measures will let you see when a process needs revision, when it lacks appropriate priority, or when people need training or assistance. Before finalizing measures as part of a process, carefully consider whether there could be any adverse behavioral consequences; undue emphasis on efficiency measures such as cycle time and effort consumption often lead to shortcuts, and inadequate analysis undermines the intended purpose of the process.

Behavioral Methods

Finally, of course, you can simply start where this chapter did—with behavior. Metrics tied to rewards are nearly always defined starting with a behavior that is viewed as desirable and associating monetary payment, recognition, or some potential for reward with specific behavior. In projects, the most universal measure, performance to schedule, is defined to encourage the project team members to do what the project plan calls for and complete it by the appointed time. While not all slips on the project schedule are created equal, attention to this metric does reinforce the importance of completing work on time and contributes to cooperation in keeping the overall project on track.

Because you are starting from the perspective of desired behavior, you may have some confidence that the measure will help you achieve the behaviors you are seeking. It is particularly important with this approach that you validate the connection to the larger objectives in addition to driving behavior. If the "right" behaviors do not consistently deliver the results you need, metrics defined this way will not contribute much to your ability to control your project.

Documenting the Metrics

After deciding what to measure, you need to clearly define each metric and then discuss it with all the people who will affect it or be affected by it. This step will further refine your understanding for each prospective metric. In addition to defining how and when information is to be collected, you will need to describe how you plan to use the data. For each prospective metric, consider:

- The name and a description of the metric
- The principal objective for this metric
- The method or process used to collect the data
- The person or persons who will collect the data
- If appropriate, the person who will verify or audit the data
- The frequency for data collection (frequent enough to support your objectives, but not so often that it represents excessive overhead or generates "noise")
- For metrics that are not simple counts or ratios, specific units of measure (such as days, euros, effort-months) for reporting the data
- Where the data will be stored and how it will be managed
- How the information collected will be reported and used
- Any barriers or potential data collection problems

As you are documenting each metric, consider the following factors:

- Is the metric unnecessarily complicated? Could you get essentially the same information more easily?
- Is the metric easy to collect? Could you learn what you need to know with less overhead?

- What will it cost to collect the data? Does your expected value for the information justify the investment?
- Is the information to be measured as timely as possible? Could we define an earlier or more leading indicator?
- Could personal information collected hurt someone? Is any part of the information proprietary or secret? How will you manage confidentiality and privacy issues?
- Is the metric objective? Will two different people measuring the same thing obtain the same result?
- Is the description of the metric and the process for collecting it clearly understandable by all the people who are involved?
- If there are people on the team who speak different languages, have you verified that all translations are consistent? Have you checked for possible cultural misinterpretations?

While this probably sounds like a great deal of effort, most of these considerations are a natural outcome of the defining process, so most of the work is already done. An example project metric is documented in Table 4-1.

Obtaining Support for Data Collection and Use

No metric will be of much use if the people who are collecting the data and are affected by it do not support it. There are many ways that measurements systems can be subverted. Ideas for minimizing "gaming" of metrics and other potential barriers are explored later in this chapter, but it is better by far to

TABLE 4-1. METRIC DEFINITION.

Activity Closure Index	
Objective:	Provide project progress information
Normal range:	0.95 to 1.1 (higher is better)
Tension:	Output quality, deliverable cost
Calculation:	(Number of activities closed) / (Total activities) / (Percent of timeline consumed)
Data:	Activities completed, current date
Reported by:	Activity owners
Frequency:	Weekly
Tools used:	Project scheduling tool database
Potential barrier:	Performing easy, short activities first; declaring activities complete when work remains or output is unsatisfactory

establish metrics with broad support to start with so that such problems are uncommon.

People are rarely neutral on measurement; they either think that it's a great idea or the worst thing that they have ever heard of. In general, people tend to support measurement when they think they will excel, or when they think that measurement will contribute to significantly better results. Very good students look forward to report cards, and Olympic athletes have no problem with timekeepers and other scorers because they are generally pleased and validated by the measurements. We also value measurements that allow us to make better decisions or obtain consistently better results; buyer's guides are popular with shoppers because they are full of facts and figures, and cooks rely heavily for good results on their oven's mechanism for temperature monitoring and control.

People dislike measurements when they suspect that it will show what they are doing in a bad light, particularly when there are potential adverse personal consequences. One of the most common factors in failed measurement systems is using the results to punish, criticize, or increase hardship on the people who are responsible for collecting the needed data. The reliability of the collected data will be suspect, at best, if project metrics are used to select projects to cancel, or if activity performance information regularly serves as the basis for personnel cutbacks. Shooting the messengers bearing bad news is a formula for project chaos and ultimate failure.

For projects, the most controversial metrics tend to be diagnostic, because they are collected most frequently, are generally visible, and require the broadest input and participation. Predictive and retrospective metrics are often primarily your responsibility and are based on information that you collect, manage, and interpret, so there is generally less need to build support for them.

The first step in obtaining team buy-in for project status metrics is personal involvement. Team members' compliance and cooperation with any ongoing measurement effort tends to be proportionate to how much they participated in establishing it (or trust those who did set it up). As part of project initiation or planning, solicit input from your team on what status information each person thinks would be useful for the project. Before actual data collection begins, measurement usually will seem like a great idea to most people, especially those who have had recent unpleasant project experiences. You can build substantial opportunities to explore (and influence) measurement options in project start-up and other planning meetings. You will find many examples of diagnostic project measures in Chapter 7, with tips for reporting and other uses for them in Chapter 8. These examples—and other metrics that you and your team agree would provide useful, ongoing information for your project—are all possibilities for consensus choices.

Another aspect of buy-in is the projected use of the data. When people see that the main intended use will be to improve response to problems and to support important processes, you can get their commitment and willing cooperation. If they suspect that other uses are intended, or even likely, you will encounter substantial resistance.

People support status metrics that have obvious use in better execution or process improvement. Some examples are measurements that can be used to avoid frivolous or unnecessary project change and status information useful for identification of project problems early enough to trigger effective responses or reallocation of resources.

Measurements that support recognition systems are easy to gain support for, and since recognition is one of the duties that you own as project leader, you can ensure that this happens. In particular, if you are able to establish with your team that you will reward accurate and timely reporting of bad results, setting up an effective system of status measures is easy to sell.

The hardest part of getting buy-in for ongoing measurement is the potential for abuse, especially for information that will be publicly reported. In general, the more you are able to keep visibility of your project measures internal to your team, the easier it will be to gain cooperation, especially if you have established a relationship of trust and respect within the team. One possibility for minimizing public embarrassment (or worse) in broadcast reporting is to show your project measurements only in aggregate. This will depersonalize the measurement process, at least for individual members of your team. (Of course, your project measurements will still reflect on you, but that's one of the reasons that project leaders have such thick skin).

Another idea for handling publicly available project information is to work with your sponsors and stakeholders to get their commitment that measurement results will only be used constructively, avoiding punitive uses of the data. For example, when progress measures are lagging on your project, you have advance commitment from your sponsor to review your staffing levels and investigate how you might use outside or additional help to catch up. Adverse measures can also be set up as semiautomatic triggers (though some review is always prudent) that make budget or other reserves available to the project.

However you go about it, for each metric that you intend to adopt, discuss it with the team members who are involved. For each candidate metric, work to get consensus from all members of the project team on the definition, the planned collection and use of the data, and the meaning of the results. One of the most effective ways to counter "gaming" of the metrics is to seek each person's agreement not to do it. Work to ensure that each person affected by the measures willingly commits in advance to collecting or supplying accurate data.

Developing a System of Measures and Evaluating Potential Adverse Consequences

While a single metric may encourage desired behavior and link to an important objective, for something as complicated as a project, you will generally need a collection of measures. In addition, it is generally the case that individual metrics by themselves can put so much emphasis on one thing that it gets too much attention (the "if some is good, more must be better" effect). Metrics assessing execution speed alone may encourage incomplete analysis or shoddy results. Too much emphasis on precision and accuracy can lead to unacceptably slow throughput and delay. The solution is to use opposing metrics together to create tension, where improvement in one measure diminishes the other one. Opposing metrics in this way forces trade-offs and will result in behavior that is more appropriate than you can expect using either measurement by itself.

A system of measures should be kept lean; you can always measure many more things than will be justified, so your goal should be a small set of meaningful metrics. Each metric you select should pass a number of tests, in the context of the overall set of measures you are adopting. These tests include sole focus, reward and evaluation system consistency, and environment consistency.

Sole Focus

The sole focus test asks what would happen if this were the only measure you used or if the measure were emphasized substantially more than other metrics. What potentially problematic behaviors might result? Would there be any unintended consequences to others outside of your project? If so, consider modifying the metric or looking for a better alternative. If there are no particularly good alternatives, seek one or more additional metrics that will provide tension to offset the undesirable effects of the metric. When adopting a metric that can lead to adverse outcomes, clearly communicate the purpose and your concern about potential abuse, and plan to monitor your project diligently to detect any problems promptly so you can manage them.

Reward and Evaluation System Consistency

Each metric must also be consistent with your organization's reward and evaluation systems. There are always metrics that are used to determine individual performance in any organization. These measures, however informally they may be defined, trump all others. They determine how people are paid, how secure their jobs are, and many other fundamental aspects of the employee-employer relationship. Consider carefully how people and teams are evaluated, rewarded, and recognized in your organization from the perspective of each metric you are considering. Your metric will be a problem if it could encourage individual behavior that would be viewed negatively in the organization, or even if it would potentially interfere with actions that are more valued. While you could work to modify the rewards and evaluation systems, this is generally a long-term proposition and you may have little realistic ability to influence it, in any case. You might be able to contrast other consequences with project recognition based on the metric for which you are responsible, but if there are significant impediments, the organizational imperatives will always prevail. If you face serious issues with a given metric, you can look for an alternative project measure that might be better aligned with established practices, or simply chose not to use the measure.

Environment Consistency

Similarly, you also need to consider the work environment for each of your team members. Metrics expected to encourage behaviors will never work when they are inconsistent with a team member's culture, traditions, or established practices. When working across international boundaries or with people from other companies, this may result in significant issues that you may not be aware of at the start of your project. When discussing potential measures with unfamiliar contributors, probe hard for potential problems and surface issues as effectively as you can. For example, you would measure differently based upon geography. Inflicting common measures across parts of your team in Japan, Germany, and Canada is perilous. Working with newly hired people in your own company or with external contractors who are working on your project may raise similar issues. When faced with this kind of challenge, you have several options. You might be able to gain overall buy-in for your metric using your influence and working hard with all the individuals to get them to accept required changes. This solution, though, takes time and may not be practical, so you might need to consider an entirely different candidate metric if you can define one that avoids cultural deployment problems. You may also need to consider different measures for each disparate part of your team that you hope will yield consistent desired results. This is very difficult and requires a great deal of knowledge about all the others, so it may not be effective, either. Using your prospective metric only with part of the team is another option, but then you'll need to devise some analogous method for monitoring work where you are not applying the metric. If expected challenges prove too substantial, the best course will probably be to simply abandon the metric.

When you have looked at each metric individually in the context of the others, examine the whole set, asking the following questions:

- Does the set of measurements reflect the aspects of your project that are most important?
- Is it missing anything that you need to include to understand and control your project?
- Is the set of measures as simple as you can make it? Have you eliminated all redundancy?
- Is there a smaller or more easily collected combination of metrics that could provide a comparable result?
- Are your metrics defined to provide you with the timeliest, most leading indicators?
- Is it possible for the measurement goals to be achieved with no impact on the desired objectives?
- Can the measurement goals be achieved without any beneficial behavior change?
- Will your use of this information make a meaningful difference, or are you collecting data just because it's there?
- Have you dropped all measures that cost more to collect than they are worth?

Work to define a set of metrics that represents the minimal set of information that you need to understand and control your project. Seek a set of measures that will aid you in controlling your project through tension between the measures you select. As with balanced scorecard approach, establish a set of measures that will encourage appropriate overall team behavior through trade-offs in the measures.

In general, if you are unsure whether a metric will be useful but think that it probably will be, retain it in your initial list. It is much easier to drop a piece of status from your collection process later, if you find that you no longer need it, than it is to add new overhead during a busy, stressful project.

Testing the Metrics and Resolving Problems

After you think that you have a good, useful set of measures for your project, it is good practice to test at least any of them that are new to ensure that the descriptions are clear and they will work for you. Testing metrics requires you to set up a context and collect status on each. And you'll need to watch for some potential problems, including:

- Pockets of resistance to measurement and reporting
- Reported data that's inconsistent with expectations
- Greater-than-anticipated effort required to collect and provide the data

Find potential problems with your metrics and resolve them by adjusting the individual metric definitions, modifying the overall set of metrics, or having a through discussion with team members to deal with understanding or compliance issues.

Setting a Baseline for the Measures and Establishing a Normal Range

Before starting to use a set of diagnostic metrics to control your project, validate the baseline for the measures. Until you have a validated normal range, you will be unable to interpret your metrics or use them to make good project decisions. Without an established measurement baseline, you also cannot assess the effects of any process modifications or other changes that you make.

For well-established metrics, baselines may already be documented. For new measures, or for defined metrics used in a new context, you will need to establish an initial data range. While you can always start your project using an educated guess for a new metric, you will need to confirm it using data from the first few cycles of status collection.

For predictive metrics, verify baselines and assumptions using corresponding retrospective metrics from earlier projects (for example, you can check your estimates against actual durations and costs from similar work done before). For retrospective metrics, you can also use the data from earlier, completed projects to set your baselines.

Using the Metrics

Once you have defined and set up a set of measures, using them is fairly straightforward, though it does require a good deal of effort and discipline.

Using predictive metrics to plan for and negotiate realistic project objectives will enhance your control over a project; this topic is explored in Chapter 6. Selecting specific diagnostic measures and evaluating the data to assess the status of your project is discussed in Chapter 7 on project execution. Chapter 8 includes pointers on measurement reporting, other uses for your metrics, and data archiving. Capturing lessons learned and improving processes using retrospective metrics is explored in Chapter 9 on project closure.

▪ Potential Problems and Measurement Barriers

No set of metrics can ever be bullet-proof. It is possible, some say inevitable, that any metric will be undermined. Defining metrics clearly to minimize differing interpretations and loopholes is one of your first lines of defense. You also need to understand the main reasons that metrics are "gamed" so that you can be vigilant and eliminate the causes for measurement dysfunction and failure.

The most common causes of gaming, more or less in order of importance, are as follows:

- Metrics are used primarily as "report cards" or for punishment.
- Metrics require public reporting of private or personally embarrassing information.
- Honest reporting of bad results is discouraged.
- Reporting good outcomes, even when untrue, is encouraged.
- Metrics are not aligned with rewards and recognition systems.
- There are no significant consequences of failure to report data or reporting of inaccurate information.
- Metrics are poorly defined or imprecise.
- Metrics are not motivating.
- Metrics have inappropriate emphasis and lack tension.

Dealing with some of these factors is part of the overall definition process, as discussed earlier in this chapter. Managing other factors requires surveillance, discipline, and a good deal of influence all through the project, particularly if your project is undertaken in an organizational context where some of these problems are common and tolerated. The topic of verifying status information throughout your project and confronting gaming behavior within your team is a major part of Chapter 7, on project execution.

The best overall technique for minimizing the barriers and potential problems associated with project metrics is simple, however. It's this: *Ask people not to game the measurements and get their commitment to send you the data you need.* Your part of this bargain is also not complicated, though it is very difficult at times. You need to treat all the people on your team fairly, thank them for the information they supply (even when it is not what you were hoping to hear), and do everything in your power to prevent others from misusing the data you collect.

KEY IDEAS FOR PROJECT METRICS

- Outline desired behaviors that you need on your team to maintain project control.
- Identify metrics that align with project objectives and desired behaviors.
- Select a small set of key measures and obtain team support for them.
- Test the metrics and establish a measurement baseline.
- Use the metrics to monitor and control your project.

CHAPTER 5

Beginning Control with Project Initiation

TROUBLED PROJECTS FREQUENTLY HAVE tentative beginnings. Control begins as soon as the project does, ideally with both the leader and the project team fully engaged and ready to "hit the ground running." To do this, you will need the support of your sponsor, solid documentation, and a project start-up workshop.

▪ Sponsorship

Your project sponsor has considerable organizational authority, at least enough to initiate your project. This person's authority can be useful to you, regardless of how much or little formal authority you may have. Sponsors are most enthusiastic and engaged at the start of a project, so take full advantage of your sponsor's interest to get things off to a great start. By retaining management's attention and focus throughout your project, you can use your sponsor's authority to substantially enhance your project control.

One of the first things you can do to ensure ongoing support and attention from your sponsor and other influential stakeholders is to set expectations right away and get specific commitments. Do it while they are still enthusiastic about your project and the value of your project is fresh in their mind. In the context of this discussion, a project sponsor is the person who provides strategic direction, formal support, and sets the organizational priority for your project. Your sponsor also approves funding and staffing for the project, and will generally be the person who makes project decisions that are beyond your authority. If any of these functions are shared among several people, or other stakeholders have influence in these matters, work to gain their support and commitments, too.

In a perfect world, all sponsors would stay interested and involved until the end of every project they initiate; unfortunately, people with enough organizational authority and power to get projects and programs going have many other matters competing for their attention. Shortly after you assume responsibility for your project, use your influencing skills to extract some commitments from your sponsor (and other key stakeholders) in exchange for your agreeing to lead the project. In particular, request commitments for:

- Managing the project environment
- Active involvement in project start-up
- Support for robust project management processes
- Initial validation and baseline setting (and revalidation as required throughout the project)
- Protection for the project (retaining resources, removal of barriers, prompt response to escalations, and minimization of project change)
- Organizational learning

Meaningful participation in each of these areas by higher-level managers who take interest in your project will make controlling your project a good deal easier. You should, however, strive to avoid getting your sponsor too involved with the day-to-day execution of your project. You want your sponsor's support, not detailed involvement—it's your project, after all.

Managing the Project Environment

Your ability to control your project relies on a stable environment and advance warning of any upcoming surprises. Your sponsor probably has more knowledge of what is going on in the organization than you do, so get a commitment from your sponsor to inform you of any changes that will impact your project proactively. Periodically remind your sponsor of this commitment, or use your interactions with your sponsor throughout the project to ask about upcoming organizational or other changes.

Your sponsor also needs to be the project's agent inside your organization, to serve as a liaison with even higher-level management and be a spokesperson for the project during project portfolio analysis and overall prioritization. Ask your sponsor to describe to you why, from his perspective, the project is being undertaken, and capture the rationale using your sponsor's words. Offer to help your sponsor to build a strong business case for the project and align the project goals with strategic business objectives. Identify significant project risks and plan to work with your sponsor to minimize and then manage them. If your sponsor understands your project well it will receive more attention, and your sponsor can be a more effective advocate for you. Work to get a meaningful commitment from your sponsor to monitor and manage your project's ecosystem.

In addition to specific involvement in each of these areas, request a regular time to periodically review your project with your sponsor, about an hour at least once a month. Use this time to share accomplishments, discuss issues, and have a one-on-one opportunity to explore general matters concerning your project. Use this time to keep your sponsor aware that you are still there.

Active Involvement in Project Start-Up

Some of your power to control and manage your project comes vicariously from others who do possess organizational power. Your sponsor can confer status on you by formally appointing you as manager (or at least leader) of the project; you can even offer to write the memo for your sponsor to sign or send that announces the start of the project and your responsibilities.

You may also need formal involvement from your sponsor to secure commitments for staffing, funding, or other resources, particularly resources from outside organizations. If your project will require funding for travel, training, or to cover other direct expenses, get commitments for these as well. Identify any new equipment or upgrades to existing hardware or software that you will need, and begin working with your sponsor to obtain the necessary approvals. Use discussions with your sponsor to identify all the project stakeholders who can affect your project or depend upon its successful completion.

Next you may need to get commitment from your sponsor to support an appropriate project start-up workshop. If your project start-up will require funding for travel and other costs, begin building the case to justify it in your initial sponsor discussions. Sponsor involvement in your project start-up will help convey the importance of your project. Request that your sponsor participate, either by attending the beginning or the close of your project start-up workshop. Specific suggestions for conducting a project start-up workshop are explored later in this chapter.

Support for Robust Project Management Processes

As discussed in Chapter 2, project management processes are an essential part of project control. If your sponsor formally supports the processes that you intend to adopt, you will have better cooperation and less resistance from your team members. You do not necessarily need detailed, item-by-item mandates for every process step from your sponsor for this to be helpful, and you probably won't have the time or access to arrange this anyway. High-level support from your sponsor for your overall project processes, particularly for fact-based, bottom-up planning, will assist you in getting the cooperation and collaboration you need from your team for better control.

A commitment from your sponsor to review key project planning deliverables is another way to facilitate process adoption. An announcement that your sponsor will examine the Is/Is NOT criteria for major deliverables or the high-level project work breakdown structure will help you communicate that the processes you plan to use in developing these outputs are mandatory, not discretionary.

If you anticipate friction in gaining support from your sponsor for key project processes, then try to help your sponsor understand why the processes are important and relate them to your project success. Focus particularly on getting support from your sponsor for a reality-based overall planning process for your project. Sponsors who view planning and other project management processes as frivolous overhead significantly undermine your ability to control and finish your project. If you are unable to obtain wholehearted, enthusiastic support for the processes you need, try to get a concession from your sponsor to support your approach "as an experiment," just this once, to test the value of project management processes. For some organizations, gaining meaningful support from project sponsors for project processes may be a longer-term goal, but ultimately the work will pay off and it will result in more successful, better controlled projects.

Initial Validation, Baseline Setting, and Revalidation as Required

Two keys to overall project control are robust sponsor validation of the project objectives *prior to* planning and a meaningful commitment for project baseline validation *following* project planning. The initial validation of objectives is to ensure alignment of sponsor and stakeholder goals with the understanding that you and your team carry into the planning process. Validation by the sponsor of the project baseline, using bottom-up, fact-based planning deliverables, may require modifying the initial project goals to ensure that you are committing to a realistic, credible project objective. Project baselines that are supported only by hopes, wishes, and prayers cannot serve as a foundation for a controllable project.

Set a firm expectation with your sponsor that the initial objectives and expectations for the project are targets, not commitments, until you, working with your team, have had an opportunity to analyze the work and figure out what you need to do. Even if you are unable to get a commitment from your

sponsor in advance to consider potential project adjustments based on the results of your planning, when your planning shows that the initial project goals
are not achievable you will still have an opportunity to propose alternatives for
your sponsor's consideration when you set the project baseline. Without an
advance commitment you are likely to encounter a good deal more resistance,
but you can use your planning data to successfully negotiate project changes.
(For more discussion on negotiating a credible project baseline, see Chapter 6
on project planning.)

Initial baseline validation is necessary for project control, but it may not
be sufficient. Most projects encounter change. For large changes, your committed project baseline may no longer describe what you must do to complete the
project. Unexpected problems may also trigger replanning and lead to modified
objectives. Periodic project reviews for projects that run a year or longer may
also result in replanning and revalidation of the project baseline. In each of
these cases, you will need to meet with your sponsor and revalidate the new
project baseline. Set an expectation with your sponsor that major shifts will
require revalidation, and provide your sponsor with as much advance notification as possible whenever it appears to be necessary. Also, incorporate process
steps for revalidating the project baseline into your change control and project
review processes to be used when appropriate.

Protection for the Project

Project control relies on ongoing attention and support from the project sponsor. One of the most important ongoing responsibilities for the sponsor is retaining staffing and budget for the project. In modern organizations there are
always more great ideas for projects than there are people to adequately staff
them, and there are chronic pressures to reduce costs. Frequently, the most
imminent threat to your project will be directly from your project sponsor.
That's because the person who started your project will undoubtedly be
tempted to start more new projects that will need to execute in parallel with
your work. New projects need people and money, and since both are always in
short supply, the most likely solution will be to reduce what is allocated to your
project. Requesting a formal commitment from your sponsor to protect your
resources can help. Periodically reminding your sponsor of this commitment is
prudent, as is having a list of consequences ready at all times to use against
threats to pull away people, funding, or other resources from your project.

Dealing with major obstructions and barriers is also a sponsor responsibility. When you lack the authority or organizational power to resolve issues that
impede your project, you can turn to your sponsor to deal with the situation.
Some situations that may require sponsor assistance include:

- Arbitration and resolution on deliverables needed from other projects
- Escalations involving individual performance of cross-functional team members and other cross-organizational issues
- Decision making in project matters that are beyond your authority
- Settling differences of opinion that are blocking project progress
- Resolution of problems with outside contractors, suppliers, and partners

Set up a process with your sponsor for escalation (but only plan to use it after exhausting all of your other options). Get a formal commitment from your sponsor for prompt response to escalations, a workday or two at most. In addition, authority for decisions should always be delegated to another manager (or to you) whenever your sponsor is unavailable because of business travel, vacation, or other absence.

Also work with your sponsor to get a commitment to reject discretionary project changes. Your sponsor will be able to say "no" to a wider range of proposed changes than you can, so obtaining your sponsor's assistance in helping you to avoid unnecessary changes will improve your overall ability to keep things on track. This request also will help you to close down one of the most common (and hard to manage) sources of unessential change—your sponsor.

Ongoing protection of your project also requires ongoing visibility, so set up regular meetings to discuss the project status with your sponsor and provide frequent, high-level project summaries that are brief, easy to read, and succinct. (And did I mention short?)

Organizational Learning

A final area where sponsors can enhance your overall control is in providing support for process improvement, infrastructure modifications, and knowledge sharing. Commitments for setting up databases and other network repositories for organizational project data often exceed the capabilities of project leaders, so establishing facilities and better environments that support well-run, controllable projects requires sponsorship at a higher level.

If your review of the infrastructure checklist in Appendix A, observations made during your project start-up workshop, or other initial analysis raises an issue that could be resolved through higher-level intervention, work with your sponsor to deal with it.

Another situation where sponsor action can be effective is in implementing recommendations made during post-project retrospective analyses. If earlier projects that you or your peers have completed have resulted in specific recommended changes related to control problems, raise them with your sponsor and either get approval to make the changes or request permission to work differently. Also seek support from your sponsor to implement at least one recommended change that emerges from the post-project retrospective that you will do following your current project.

If you believe that better facilities or other major changes would afford improved control for projects throughout your organization over the long run, work through your sponsor to propose these ideas. If you are not initially successful, don't give up. Continue to collect information on the issues and plan to propose the changes again later on. Continue to work for changes that will improve project control over time until they are accepted.

▪ Project Vision

There is a great deal of confusion, or at least lack of consistency, around a number of closely related project ideas. *Purpose, mission, objective, vision, goal*, and many other terms are used somewhat interchangeably to describe what a project is initiated to accomplish. It's useful to define these terms and make some distinctions.

Purpose is a durable part of the context for a project. Purpose is linked to organizational strategy and will be shared by several, perhaps many, projects and other undertakings of your entire organization. Purpose changes slowly over time and is consistent with long-term organizational planning. Because retaining sponsorship depends on contributing to the broader goals that higher-level managers care about, controllable projects are well aligned with overall organizational purpose.

Missions, objectives, goals, and other tactical concepts relate to separate projects. These concepts describe what the project will accomplish and must be clearly and consistently defined for a project to be controllable. A project objective is best described in terms that are the same (or at least equivalent) for everyone involved, regardless of perspective. Clearly defining your overall project objective and scope is a central part of project launch (as discussed later in this chapter). Ongoing control of your project depends on managing all changes to the project objectives; change management is explored in Chapter 8.

Where these other ideas are consistent for all team members, stakeholders, sponsors, and other project participants, *vision* for the project may or may not be. Project vision is about why the project matters, and while this might be the same for everyone, it may have aspects that are personal and unique for each individual. Creating a vision (or visions) that will motivate members of your team and others you depend upon is never mandatory, and for short, straightforward projects the effort may not be justified—a clear objective and adequate sponsorship could be sufficient. However, for longer, more complicated projects, investing some time in "the vision thing" can be what differentiates a successful project that everyone cares about from a chaotic disaster. An inspiring project vision will increase your influence, particularly during project initiation.

Projects these days are always difficult– they succeed because the project team cares about them and finds a way to get it done. An effective project vision that uses compelling, vivid language can help you build the commitment and perseverance you will need, and it will significantly assist you in controlling your project.

Value Analysis: Why Does This Project Matter?

One starting point for your project vision is your sponsor's reasons for undertaking the project. These will probably include at least some broad description of the project's value. If project benefits from your sponsor's perspective are not obvious, start probing with questions such as, "What is the most important aspect of this project to you? How will things be better (or easier, or faster, or less complicated) when we are finished?" The value of a project is usually a consequence of why the project is being considered. Projects are initiated to solve particular problems, to respond to requests from customers or users, to meet regulatory requirements or comply with industry standards, to conform with organizational strategies and initiatives, to save money or improve the performance of a business process, to bring a product or service to market that will generate profit by meeting a perceived need, to conduct research and exploit technical advances, or to pursue a business opportunity.

Work to understand your sponsor's expectations for the project. Write down what you learn using your sponsor's words, and use active listening to paraphrase and validate what you hear. Your sponsor's motivations are the foundation for your overall project definition, and understanding the genesis of your project will help you uncover assumptions and constraints that you will need to manage and control for your project.

One Size Does Not Fit All

In some cases, a project vision based simply on what your sponsor values will be sufficiently compelling to you, your team, and to others. But most of the time, what your sponsor values ("I will be able to run this organization with fewer people . . .") will not necessarily translate into a compelling project vision for everyone else. Sometimes, you can develop an overall vision statement on your own, based on what you know about your team. In other cases, you may want to schedule some time, possibly during your project start-up workshop, to discuss the project with all the project contributors and collect their input for a shared vision created by the entire team. Developing a vision on your own will probably be faster, but it entails the risk that you may miss something, coming up with a vision that is not motivating, or worse, is demotivating. Developing a vision as a team requires some time, and some team members may resent or try to obstruct this effort, but when done well it will enhance trust, build relationships, and improve cooperation. With very diverse teams, a single vision may not be feasible, so developing a separate understanding of what individuals or subteams care about most may be necessary.

However you proceed, your main goal is to make the ultimate success of the project align closely with the interests and concerns of your team members. Use the influencing skills from Chapter 3 to listen to your team members and identify aspects of the project that support or connect to what they really care about. Seek words that people will respond to with passion; get people excited. If your project team is incomplete or you expect significant staffing changes during your project, discuss and revalidate the vision with new contributors as they become part of your team.

Confirm that the vision is consistent with the values of your team and your organization as a whole. Craft project vision statements that are brief, compelling, and easy to remember. Verify that you have a vision that passes the "What's in it for me?" test with each project contributor. Does your proposed vision inspire pride and the confidence of your team? To motivate, a vision must be accepted as credible. Is your vision statement realistic, or at least plausible? The more you are able to involve your team in discussing the vision and using it to build emotional buy-in for your project, the more control and influence you will wield.

▪ Project Launch

With a sense of who wants the project and why, the project leader can begin defining a foundation for project control by documenting and defining the project. It would be useful if each new project emerged fully and clearly documented, and it is not unheard of for much of the information that you will need to be available in one form or another. Nonetheless, in the interest of control and communication, you should review and validate any data that is available and ensure that it is credible and appropriate through your own analysis. Careful review will also uncover any gaps so that you can work to fill them in. Some of the documentation that you will need to assemble for initial project communication will include a project charter, project priorities, return on investment analysis, initial scoping, and project staffing requirements.

Project Charter

Begin documenting your project by assembling available information. The process for project definition outlined in Chapter 2 is one of your most durable tactics for control because it provides written information that you can use throughout your project to keep things on track. The most common starting point for initial project documentation is the information provided by your sponsor or obtained through your interviews and discussion. Wherever you obtain your information, work closely with your sponsor to verify and gain support for your documents, to maximize their weight and increase their influence for controlling your project.

A project charter is one way to collect initial high-level project information. Because projects differ, even the name of this document varies, and in some environments a comparable document may be called a project proposal, definition document, project datasheet, system specification, plan of record, or a statement of work.

Regardless of the name, format, or primary author, what matters most for project control is that you capture initial project expectations in writing. Review the information as you collect it, then validate that what you have written is consistent with your sponsor's understanding. Typical contents for a project charter include the following:

- *The Project Objective Statement.* At a high level, develop a brief summary statement that summarizes the principal project deliverable and the sponsor's goals for project cost and timing. The project objective, validated by the project sponsor, serves as the foundation for all project definition and planning. Good project objectives avoid the use of acronyms, jargon, and technical language; include the desired deadline in a format that includes the day, month, and year; and summarize the budgeted investment either in terms of monetary cost or overall effort/staffing.
- *Project Priorities.* For the project, document the relative importance of the scope, schedule, and resources. (You will find more detail on setting and using project priorities later in this section.)
- *Project Benefits.* Summarize the value of this project from the perspective of the sponsor and those who are funding it. Combining the forecasted value of the project deliverables and expected project resource costs is the basis for return on investment (ROI) analysis, which is also explored later in this section.
- *User or Customer Needs.* To support the expected value of the project, describe who will benefit from the project and outline which of their specific needs will be met by the project.
- *Initial Scoping.* Draft a preliminary scope definition, listing all expected project deliverables. For each deliverable you define, include timing information if it is not consistent with the project deadline. Initial scoping is described in more detail later in this section.
- *Committed Staffing.* List all the core project team members who are

initially committed to the project team, including their contact information and their role on the project. Also list other contributors with relevant additional information, such as when they will be available, the percentage of their time committed to your project, and contact information for their managers. Initial project staffing analysis is also discussed later in the section.

• *Significant Constraints and Assumptions.* Based on discussions with your project sponsor and other stakeholders, document any project constraints that you are aware of, such as limitations on staffing, interim milestones that have established timing requirements, or other factors that will impact the project. Determine expectations for travel, equipment, training, and other potential expenses for your project. Document all the organizational requirements (including life cycles and methodologies), legal and regulatory constraints, and industry standards that will affect your project. Also document any assumptions that you uncover (or make), particularly those that are potentially controversial or seem unrealistic.

• *Dependencies on Other Projects.* Particularly for projects that are part of a larger program, identify each project that could affect, or be affected by, your project. For each, list the leader's name and describe how the project relates to your project. (Planning and managing the interfaces that interconnect projects is covered in Chapter 6 on project planning.)

• *High-level Risks and Identified Issues.* Document any known high-level risks and significant issues for your project, including any that relate to potential problems arising from project constraints and assumptions.

Project Priorities

Documented priorities for your project will help you assess trade-offs and develop alternatives during project planning, minimize controversy over decisions throughout the project, negotiate project changes, and support disciplined change control for your project. The initial priorities that are part of the project charter may or may not remain static throughout the project, but the initial priorities are one part of the project charter that can provide a lot of leverage for influencing your sponsor. Too frequently projects are undertaken with a belief on the sponsor's part that any combination of scoping, time, and cost for a project can be forced on a project leader and result in a commitment to a realistic project. Setting priorities allows you to set expectations for your sponsor; it's your chance to inform your sponsor that the initial objective may not necessarily translate into a credible project baseline.

Setting priorities is equivalent to the old project management adage: "Fast, cheap, good—pick two." For any given project, the triple constraint of time, cost, and scope can be manipulated through trade-offs to conform to a wide spectrum of possible projects. You do, however, need at least one degree of freedom available before you can start nailing down the other two parameters. Establishing and documenting priorities is an effective way to drive home to your sponsor and stakeholders that if the deadline is firm and resources are limited, they may need to give a little on the deliverable.

Your objective in rank ordering the parameters of the triple constraint is to determine which of the three is most critical to your sponsor and stakeholders. If you are unable to select one of the parameters using the information you have, discuss small two-way trade-offs with your sponsor to reveal preferences. Ask questions such as:

- Given the choice, would it be better to extend the project by several days or drop a feature expected in the deliverable?
- Would you prefer to add an additional staff member to this project or let the schedule slip slightly beyond the deadline?
- Would you consider a small increase to the project budget to protect the project scope?

It is much better to ask these questions early and set credible expectations for your project than to have to deal with them in crisis mode late in your project.

As you explore the consequences, pain, and difficulties associated with small project changes, you will begin to see the relative priorities emerge. If there is a lack of consensus between your sponsor(s) and stakeholders, initiate dialogue among them to determine which view prevails. (One colleague refers to this process as "getting all the liars in the same room.")

Document your project priorities using a three-by-three matrix. There are a number of formats possible, but the message is most visible if the priorities are listed in the rows top to bottom, with each parameter of the triple constraint in a separate column, as in Figure 5-1. Place one mark in each row, showing which parameter has the highest, middle, and lowest priority for your project.

There are six ways that this matrix may be drawn, and each has implications for control of your project. All three of the parameters are important to your project, and you will bear the consequences of failing to meet any of them. One purpose of establishing the priorities, in addition to helping you dissuade management from prematurely constraining your project, is to reveal the relative severity of the consequences of failing to deliver on each parameter. If timing is the highest priority for your project, missing your deadline may well be career-threatening. If the next priority is scope, failing to deliver part of the documented scope might be almost as dire. Failing to comply with even the lowest priority will usually result in unpleasant consequences, but most of the time these are limited to verbal abuse. Project leaders tend to develop relatively

FIGURE 5-1. THE PRIORITY MATRIX.

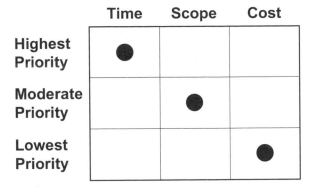

thick skins, so the prospect of being yelled at for going a bit over budget in order to deliver on time is likely an acceptable outcome.

Keeping the priorities visible is an essential control tool. In general, whenever you find your project in difficulty, your maximum flexibility and first options to explore will involve your lowest-priority project parameter. The two higher-priority parameters are more greatly constrained, so any proposed project changes that will adversely affect them should be easy to reject. Similarly, you can confidently make project decisions that protect the highest priorities and use the matrix to defend them.

Return on Investment Analysis

The use of predictive metrics was discussed in Chapter 4 on project metrics. In general, most predictive project metrics are plan based, and a number of them that are useful for project control are explored in the next chapter on project planning. The first predictive metric that you may encounter on many projects, however, involves a very early, high-level project return on investment (ROI) analysis that may have been completed even before you hear about your project.

Project ROI analysis requires two separate predictive metrics—monetary inflows and monetary outflows. All versions of ROI analysis contrast estimates of expected project benefits with preliminary cost estimates, jamming them together to derive a compound measurement showing project "goodness" that can be used to assess, compare, rank order, and select from a portfolio of potential projects. Both of these estimates tend to be highly speculative and inaccurate, especially if the project analysis is done without any input from the project team. There is generally a significant bias in benefit estimates on the high side, due to enthusiasm and optimism. There is also a persistent bias in project cost estimates on the low side, due again to optimism coupled with a lack of information. These biases tend to be most significant the earlier the estimates are done. Because these estimates are rarely realistic, the accuracy of ROI metrics can be highly variable. Because of their prominence in many organizations, however, you should be comfortable discussing ROI concepts. Influencing how the inputs are assembled and how ROI is used will also help you control your project.

Before getting too deep in the mechanics of ROI, a word about the incentives for gaming the metrics. Some incentives align with the biases that are inherent in the ROI process and result in ROI measurements that are less credible. If the benefits are estimated generously and the costs are low-balled for your project, it will be more likely that your project will be approved and funded in the first place. The higher the overall return is assessed to be, the more relative priority your project will have, and you will gain influence and organizational clout based on your role as project leader. On the other hand, though, if the costs are significantly underestimated, your budget will likely be too low and you will either have to negotiate for more funding or have great difficulty finishing the work. Also, if the assessment is based on estimates of value that are impossible to realize, there is always the risk (admittedly infinitesimal, in most organizations) that someone will later check and you will suffer the consequences of the shortfall.

In spite of all these pressures to the contrary, in the long run, the best course will be to strive for accuracy on both benefits and costs. For this to be equitable you will need to influence your managers and peers to also strive for credible estimates (which, of course, everyone *says* they want to use anyway). Since early estimates for ROI are based on sparse data, it is prudent to revisit ROI assessments for ongoing projects as better, more complete information becomes available. It is also always prudent to do a sanity check on ROI analysis using before-and-after results from recently completed projects to determine whether the information you are working with is in a realistic range.

In addition to monetary information, ROI depends on timing. There are a number of different ways to combine the financial estimates and timing data, each with good and bad points. These ROI measures are calculated differently, so although they all use essentially the same data, project comparisons using them can generate wildly varying results. Standard ROI calculation methods include simple payback, discounted payback, net present value, and internal rate of return.

• *Simple Payback.* This is the easiest method for assessing ROI. It uses a running sum of costs and benefits (or returns or revenue) starting at the beginning of the project. It extends as far into the future as required for the accumulated costs (all negative cash flows from all the time periods estimated) to be balanced out by accumulated benefits (all positive cash flows for the same periods). This method for ROI is measured in months or years and provides an indication of how quickly a project "pays for itself." Simple payback can be easily implemented in a spreadsheet application or even with pencil and paper.

• *Discounted Payback.* This ROI method is similar to simple payback, but it introduces the time value of money. Future costs and benefits are discounted using an interest rate, and they affect the measure less and less the further out in the future they are. For example, if the annual interest rate used for discounting is 7 percent, a benefit one year in the future of $107 would balance a current cost of $100. Discounted payback, net present value, and internal rate of return all use a discount rate in evaluating cash flows, diminishing future values back to an equivalent present value using the formula:

$$PV = FV/(1 + i)^n$$

where PV is the present value, FV is the future value, i is the periodic interest rate, and n is the number of periods.

The discount rate used to assess discounted payback and net present value is often equivalent to a published interest rate, such as the rate at which your organization borrows money from a bank or pays on bonds that it issues. The interest rate used for discounting is also sometimes set using your organization's goal for return on internal capital investments (which is what your project is, after all), which is generally a bit higher than the interest rate for borrowing.

Because project costs are up-front and project benefits generally do not begin until the project is completed a good deal later, the discounted payback period is always at least slightly longer than the simple payback period, and is also measured in months or years.

• *Net Present Value.* Probably the most common ROI calculation method, net present value (NPV) uses the same data as discounted payback analysis, but it also includes estimates following the project breakeven point. All expected future benefits over the life of the project deliverable are discounted back to the present, and from this all discounted project costs are deducted to give a single monetary measure. NPV can be assessed in dollars, euros, yen, or any currency you choose.

• *Internal Rate of Return.* The most complicated ROI metric, internal rate of return (IRR) is based on the same data as NPV, but it does not use an assumed discount rate to calculate the monetary value of the project. IRR forces the present value of each project to zero. IRR requires you to determine the interest rate needed to discount all the costs and benefits so that they exactly balance. For streams of cash flow that reverse multiple times, IRR assessment may not be unique; there can be more than one interest rate that will work. Because most projects are characterized by a stream of outlays followed by a stream of inflows, a unique IRR generally emerges. Before computers and financial calculators were widely available, IRR was not widely used because the iterative calculations used to determine the required interest rate were too tedious to make it worthwhile. Systems for assessing IRR are widely available today, but they still rely on guessing an interest rate and gradually iterating to converge on the IRR. IRR is reported as a simple percentage.

Getting a Return on ROI

Assessment of a project's ROI using any of these metrics requires two series of estimates: costs for the duration of the project and returns through some or all of the expected useful life of the deliverable. The analysis required to do this well involves a good deal of effort. Even doing it poorly (which is more common) can be a lot of work. In many situations, ROI analysis on projects will generate small overall benefits relative to its cost. If you have the option of avoiding extensive ROI analysis for your project, do so.

If you do not have a choice, the exercise will be most worthwhile if you can make the uncertainty in the input data visible and ensure that the resulting ROI (whichever versions you are using) is interpreted with this in mind. Early cost data, before any detailed planning is done, typically has error bars of at least plus or minus 50 percent—mostly plus. Early estimates of financial return are based on sales projections or other speculative forecasts, and these are notoriously inaccurate for projects. Both of these arrays of estimates become even more unreliable as the amount of research and innovation required for the project increases. Keeping this in mind, ROI analyses are most reasonably done using a number of scenarios that establish a range of possible results. One of your scenarios should be a "worst case," including the highest potential costs and the lowest estimated benefits. Presenting an ROI as a range clearly communicates the level of uncertainty in the input data and can significantly improve decisions made using it. A project with a net present value of "between $1.5 million and $5 million" reflects the actual precision of the ROI better than a deterministic-sounding NPV of "$4.57 million."

As projects progress, cost information improves because estimates for future project work are based on better planning data and the cost of completed work is known. Over time, you will also have greater certainty about the project completion date, and you can get additional feedback from users (or potential users) that will increase your confidence in the benefit estimates. Revisiting all initial ROI assessments when you set the project baseline will result in smaller ranges and a more realistic ROI for your project. On longer projects, subsequent periodic reassessment of ROI as part of a project review will result in further convergence. All of this will let you monitor trends and better manage project expectations.

ROI metrics are most accurate when the project is complete and you can do all the calculations using actual historical measurements. Validating ROI assessments retrospectively is one way to gauge the magnitude of your initial biases and improve your organization's processes for developing credible ROI information on new projects.

Each of the ROI calculation methods has both positive and negative aspects, summarized in Table 5-1.

Due to their differing assumptions, comparing or rank-ordering projects based on these metrics can vary widely. If your organization is using only one method for ROI and it does not show your project in the best light, propose adding another metric to the analysis to your sponsor. You might also consider additionally calculating the other metrics (the same basic data is used for all of them) to find one that you can use to better illustrate your project's value.

Overall, it is generally better to focus on the value of the project inherent in your vision instead of getting too wrapped up in financial ROI analysis. ROI information is never very motivating, and because it is difficult to ensure much accuracy, many people find it hard to take ROI analysis very seriously. Many projects have justifications that are at least partially noneconomic, or their expected benefits are hard to assess in monetary terms. Projects that develop new technologies or invest in process or platform changes may have little direct

TABLE 5-1. COMPARISONS OF ROI METRICS.

Metric	Positive Aspects	Negative Aspects
Simple Payback	• Easily calculated. • Retrospective auditing is straightforward and timely	• Benefits beyond payback are ignored. • Favors short projects.
Discounted Payback	• Simple to calculate, more realistic than simple payback. • Easily audited.	• Same as simple payback.
Net Present Value	• Relatively easy to calculate. • Compares projects with differing time scales.	• Favors large projects. • Requires more estimates, further in the future. • Verification is not timely.
Internal Rate of Return	• Compares projects with differing sizes.	• Requires specialized financial calculations. • Requires more estimates, further in the future. • Verification is not timely.

benefit, but they are expected to establish foundations that will generate value for an indeterminate number of future projects. Some projects are undertaken primarily to comply with legal or other mandatory requirements. If this type of "indirect" but nonetheless meaningful benefit is a significant factor for your project, work to ensure that it is not obscured by overemphasis on ROI analysis.

Initial Scoping

One of your most important objectives in initiating a project that you can control is to get an early, solid fix on what "done" looks like. Changes, particularly late project changes, are the enemy of control. On most projects, much of what looks like change to you and your project team is in reality overlooked scoping information that was available at the start of the project. To begin well, you need to ask a lot of questions, be persistent, verify what you learn, and visibly document project scope. For your initial scoping you need to define deliverables, verify requirements, test the limits, and validate initial scoping.

Defining Deliverables

If you do not yet have a list of major project deliverables listed in your project charter, you will need to summarize them before you can focus on what they include. Be as thorough as you can with your list. Brainstorm with your stakeholders, sponsor, and any team members already identified to pick up anything that your project will need to produce or do that you might have missed. Your major deliverables list will be the foundation for the project work breakdown structure, so whatever you fail to include can't be part of your plans. Whether you list something or not, if it is legitimately part of the reason you are taking on the project, you will need to deal with it. It is better to know early and plan for the work than to discover it late and react to a subsequent project crisis. In addition to any obvious products, subassemblies, processes, services, or other deliverables, consider such deliverables as:

- Documentation (published materials, online references, and other written matter)
- Training materials and other instructional requirements
- Certification, legal, environmental, and standards compliance
- External testing needs
- Marketing or promotional collateral
- Deliverables that will facilitate needed organizational changes
- Translation of written material into additional languages
- Mandatory deliverables required for your organization's life cycles or methodologies

- Logistical requirements for packaging, shipping, setup, installation, on-going support, or other post-release work

Develop a description for each listed deliverable aimed at minimizing the project's "fuzzy front end." For each item on your list, set completion criteria in measurable terms and outline how you plan to evaluate or test the deliverable on completion to ensure that it meets the criteria. For any deliverables that will require external sign-offs or other approvals, identify the individual who will be responsible. Document the prevailing expectations for timing and closure.

Refine your understanding of each deliverable using an Is/Is Not list. For each deliverable, create a list with two columns, one headed "Is" and the other headed "Is Not." Put all the mandatory requirements based on constraints or other imperatives into the "Is" column. If common practice for projects in your organization uses the idea of "musts" and "wants," all of the "must" requirements belong in the "Is" column. "Wants" are a significant enemy of project control, particularly for project leaders who lack much authority. As a starting point, list all of the "wants," along with any other features and aspects of the project deliverables that are desirable but not mandatory, in the "Is Not" column. The "Is Not" column is not for frivolous or silly requirements that no one would take seriously. It is for legitimate requirements that have value and are known to be important to at least some project stakeholders, but will not be part of the current project. These requirements must still be listed to set visible boundaries for the project, and to permit you to better manage expectations and proposed changes throughout your project.

Candidates for the "Is Not" list include:

- Specific things requested by users that seem inappropriately aggressive
- Lower-priority requirements that can be deferred to a subsequent project
- Items that have not been mentioned but that you anticipate might be later proposed as project changes
- Things that you or your team might wish to include that are not actually necessary, such as use of new technologies, processes, or equipment

Explicitly listing what you plan to exclude is a powerful use of communication. It will generate discussion, probably arguments. Some of the items you have provisionally excluded from your project will emerge as valid, high-priority requirements, and if you lose the arguments, they will move over to the "Is" list. Others will remain firmly out of scope and will provide you with a clear delineation between what is included and what is out-of-bounds, which will help you maintain control throughout your project.

Verifying Requirements

As part of your scoping, review the requirements until you know what you need to know to begin your project. For your defined deliverables, assess what you know about:

- Documented market analysis or verified user needs
- Regulatory, environmental, legal, and standards requirements
- Specific local requirements for deliverables in each place where they will be used
- Analysis of any other project options and competitive alternatives
- Core competencies and specific skills needed
- Availability of adequate project staffing
- Logistical requirements related to distribution, installation, delivery, and support
- Alignment of your project's objectives with overall organizational strategy
- Dependability and credibility of project finances
- High-level project risks
- Cross-functional dependencies and interfaces with other projects

Document what you know and do not know in each of these areas, and work with your sponsor and team to resolve gaps that you discover. For any of these factors where you lack information, take note of it and define activities that you will make part of your project work breakdown structure and overall plans. If there are any gaps that you will be unable to resolve, make note of them for later analysis as part of project risk management. What you do not know about your project can, and likely will, hurt you.

Testing the Limits

Initial scoping also involves reviewing and testing project constraints and assumptions. Not all of the initially identified constraints are necessarily hard-and-fast requirements; some of them may be sponsor preferences, desired goals, or otherwise not really essential to the success of your project. Testing project assumptions is also a good idea, because there will inevitably be cases where your project can be made more straightforward and controllable through relaxing some of the assumptions. Retaining a healthy skepticism and asking lots of questions is a very good way to use communication to enhance both your project understanding and control. In the following list you will find some questions that you can use to learn what your sponsor and other key project stakeholders know, and to find out what they feel most strongly about. Documenting what you learn and using it to refine the scoping for your project is a strong defense against the sort of fuzzy definition that leads to excessive change and poor project control.

- Is each requirement defined in terms that make the business problem or issue clear? (Restate any requirements that are simply summaries of a technical solution, with no indication of why.)
- Are all improvement requirements (such as performance, throughput, or efficiency) quantified? What is the present baseline, and why does the particular improvement goal matter?
- What are the ramifications of failing to fully meet a requirement? What portion of the expected value is lost if a project requirement is largely, but not entirely, achieved?
- What additional value, if any, could be realized by exceeding any of the project requirements?
- What is the basis for the expected benefits associated with each project deliverable? How were benefits estimated? How uncertain are the estimates (what are the lowest and highest credible values)?
- How certain are the project assumptions? What are they based upon? What are the consequences of small changes to any of them?
- If any project data seems unrealistic, where did it come from? Can you verify the information source?
- Are the requirements identified sufficient? Are there potential failure modes for the project related to possible other requirements? Are they safely excluded?

Validating Initial Scoping

Gather your data in a high-level scope document that includes the information on all project deliverables, such as:

- Specific functions included, with reasons
- What *is not* included in the deliverable
- User and interface needs
- Quantitative performance and reliability requirements
- Documentation, training, support, and any other post-delivery needs
- Acceptance tests information, including the person responsible for assessing and approving the results

Review the initial scoping with your project sponsor and with other stakeholders as appropriate. Explain your documentation to defend what it contains when issues arise. Make modifications as needed to reach consensus on the scoping for your project. Then finalize the document and communicate the detailed output objectives for your project. Make it clear to everyone that this is still a goal, not a commitment. Scoping commitment is done following project planning when the project baseline is established, so some change to the initial scoping may be expected.

Project Staffing

Following your analysis of preliminary scoping (or in parallel with it), confirm who will be on your project team. Particularly for project leaders who will not directly manage the contributors on the project team, early identification and commitments for staffing are essential to project control.

Collect information about anyone who's already assigned to your project, then begin developing a staff roster to summarize contact information and other data. Most initial project team members will probably be part of your core team and focused primarily on your project, but your roster may also include others who are as-yet unidentified. Extended team members will have other responsibilities in addition to your project, and these contributors often pose significant control problems for a project leader with limited authority.

Use your project objective and scoping information to assess whether your committed staffing seems adequate for the project. Compare the skills on your existing team with the core competencies required by your initial scoping. Do a rough estimate of the number of project contributors needed for the required project roles and skill areas. Assess the overall effort that your committed project staff can supply. Inquire about anticipated time-off and other commitments, and use realistic estimates. Be skeptical about the level of effort your extended team members will provide, and ask about the relative priority of your project compared with other responsibilities. Update your project roster with assigned roles that meet your staffing requirements, identifying the members of your initial team who have appropriate experience and talents to take on those responsibilities.

Use this high-level analysis to identify any skill gaps or resource shortfalls, then promptly begin to work with your sponsor to locate people to resolve project staffing issues. Be clear with your sponsor about the consequences of inadequate staffing. Options for resolving project staffing issues include:

- Arranging for more time from extended project team members
- Acquiring additional staff from within the organization
- Hiring new permanent staff for the project
- Contracting for outside help
- Training existing team members to develop unavailable skills
- Changing project scope or timing to be consistent with available staffing
- Planning for overtime work by project team members (even a small

dependence on this option is risky, and it will diminish your overall control)

Develop a plan to resolve the staffing issues as early in your project as possible. Be realistic about acquiring new or outside resources; getting approvals to hire or outsource can be time-consuming, and finding and adding the right people takes a lot of effort. Learning curve issues and reduced initial productivity are also factors that you will need to consider.

If there are staffing issues that you are unable to resolve with your sponsor, note them as risks and integrate them into your overall project risk planning.

Use your roster to visibly identify all formal staffing commitments to your project. Once a name is added and published, the membership is real, and you can begin to the build trust and good relationships with each person that you will need to control your project. As you add team members, start working to learn about their personal desires and goals. Use discussions with your team members to help you secure firm, unambiguous commitments to your project.

▪ Start-Up Workshops

There are many similar names for this event, such as project launch, kickoff, project planning workshop, and project initiation meeting. Whatever you choose to call it, a project start-up workshop serves to build teamwork and to establish a solid, shared understanding of what the project is about. Both the influence and control aspects of a well-run start-up workshop are substantial.

The workshop can be scheduled anytime after staffing is set and the project objectives have been stated. The most common times are during project initiation, when the focus is on initial planning and team building, and toward the end of planning, when the main objectives are a shared understanding of the project baseline and integrating any new staff members into the team who will contribute to project execution. With some projects, it's useful to conduct both types of project start-up workshops.

Justifying the Start-Up Workshop

Workshops are most valuable when you can involve everyone on your project team in a face-to-face meeting. The most effective ones are conducted in a location that minimizes distractions and interruptions, so sufficient time can be allocated to fully discuss project information and issues. Whatever the timing, you can use a project start-up workshop to:

- Build relationships and trust among team members
- Build common understanding of the project

- Establish shared processes and terminology
- Discuss and resolve conflicts and differences among project team members
- Clarify roles and responsibilities
- Collaborate on project planning
- Get strong team member buy-in and commitment to the project

For all their value, there is often resistance to holding a project start-up workshop. They take time, consume money and other resources, and can be difficult to coordinate and schedule. Face-to-face workshops require travel by nonlocal team members. These factors are real and must be dealt with if they become barriers to your conducting a start-up workshop.

Project contributors who claim to be too busy need to understand that the time invested is one of the best ways to deal with today's extreme time pressures. The common direction and coherent information developed in the workshop are essential for avoiding unnecessary or redundant effort and project rework. The productivity of a focused project start-up will also produce a lot of results in a very short time. Most people are surprised at how much work a group can accomplish during a start-up workshop.

For sponsors who need to approve the expense and travel, the same points can be made. Overall, projects that begin well and minimize execution problems reduce project budgets and finish more quickly. Build the business case for your workshop and get approval from your sponsor to conduct one that will be as effective as possible. The trade-off is simple: Pay a little now, or risk paying a lot later.

Traveling time, coordination, and scheduling issues are usually excuses raised by people who do not see much value in a project start-up workshop. People will make time and go anywhere to take part in activities that are important to them, so gaining a commitment to participate is largely about setting up a meaningful agenda and communicating the value of the workshop.

Sometimes you will need to compromise on how—but never whether—you conduct your project start-up workshop. If you can't arrange a face-to-face gathering, hold your workshop via videoconference or teleconference. The important thing is to do it, using the most effective means available. (Toward the end of this chapter, you will find more pointers on building control on global and distributed teams that can apply to technically assisted project start-up workshops.)

Creating the Agenda

Running an effective workshop requires a detailed agenda. The workshop length can vary from less than a day up to several days, depending on the size and complexity of the project. Even a short project that has many complicated interdependencies may warrant a two- or three-day workshop. A minimum of a half-day is beneficial even for small projects, and a series of multiday workshops may be prudent for large multiteam programs. In your agenda, also allocate time for breaks and meals, as required.

Although you will undoubtedly need to include additional items, a basic workshop agenda should always include these main elements:

- Welcome to participants
- Introductions of each team member
- Shared project vision
- Project charter, objective, and initial scoping
- Individual roles and responsibilities
- Collaborative planning
- Close and follow-up actions

The welcome and introductions are primarily about team and relationship building. The shared vision and project information items are both about information sharing, with vision aimed at building motivation and buy-in and the project summary intended to create a common understanding of the project. Additional agenda items that are often added include:

- Further analysis of deliverables and scoping
- Project infrastructure discussions
- Specific planning activities
- Team-building activities, meals, and other items that are not directly related to the project (particularly for longer workshops)

Selecting Participants and Confirming Attendance

In general, workshops are most effective with no more than about twenty people. All of the core project team will need to participate, along with key members of your extended team who will be responsible for major project deliverables or will make significant contributions to the project. Include people who will be involved in any part of the life cycle of your project. Once you determine a good time when everyone (including your sponsor) will be able to attend, distribute your proposed agenda to each invited participant, and get commitments from all team members to participate in your entire workshop.

For large programs with significantly more than twenty participants, hold a series of smaller project start-up workshops, with a summary session to integrate all of the information.

Handling Logistics

Prior to the workshop, distribute any pre-meeting materials to all participants far enough in advance so that everyone will have ample opportunity to review them.

Arrange for a room that is large enough for your meeting. When it's possible, use an off-site location. You can get more accomplished faster when you are away from your normal workplace with few interruptions, and avoiding normal interruptions will give you more control over the workshop. Just before the meeting, set up the room by arranging seating and tables for work. Especially if the participants have not met before, use a U-shaped arrangement so people face each other.

Many project leaders like to facilitate their own workshops, but if you are running your workshop, particularly if there are more than a dozen participants, it can interfere with your full participation because you may become more focused on the mechanics of the meeting and less on the project (or worse, you'll become so focused on project issues that the workshop spins out of control). Arranging for another person to facilitate your workshop will allow you to contribute and participate in discussions more fully. Some options for obtaining a facilitator from outside your team are hiring an outside professional or requesting help from a specialist within your organization, if available—for example, from a project management office or other team of internal consultants. Outside consultants are very experienced at getting results quickly and efficiently, but cost may be an issue. If there are no suitable specialists inside your organization, another approach is to ask a peer project leader to participate in your meeting, in exchange for your returning the favor later. If you do use an outsider to help run your workshop, involve your facilitator in planning for the workshop and get feedback on your agenda.

Be well prepared for your project start-up workshop. The way the workshop runs will set expectations for your whole project. Have all the documents you will need, including copies of the project charter, scoping and user needs information, project planning data, and any other project information. Have ready all the office supplies you might need for the workshop, including pencils, pens, notepads, masking tape, easels, flipchart paper, and lots of yellow sticky notes.

Opening the Workshop

Start on time. When possible, get your sponsor to begin the workshop and welcome participants. Convince your sponsor to also attend the introduction and vision portions of your agenda, to get to know the team and to reinforce both the importance of the project and support for you as project leader. Alternatively, involve your sponsor in the close of your workshop, where you can summarize your results and request reinforcement in the form of the sponsor's support and view of your project.

Following a general welcome, review your agenda and ensure that all the participants understand what you plan to accomplish. Make adjustments to the agenda if necessary and post it where it will be visible and easy to use to keep your workshop on track.

After finalizing the agenda, let your team start to get to know each other through introductions. In addition to names and factual information, such as what they do and where they work, have people describe why they were selected to be part of the team and the contribution they think they will make to the project. Invest the time to let people see how they and the others will fit together as a team. If most of the people don't know each other at all, have each person share some additional piece of personal information—about favorite foods, hobbies, recent films, or almost anything that will start to let people see each other as fellow human beings, not strangers. The idea is to start to build personal connections and show what the team does have in common.

Reviewing Project Information

Before getting into the "nuts and bolts" of the project, and preferably while your sponsor is still there, spend some time at the start of the workshop on the project vision, which is the common, shared view of why this project matters. A credible, shared project vision will draw the team together and is a very powerful tool for any project leader who lacks authority.

After that, it's time to shift focus to project facts and figures, drilling into the project objective, charter, scoping, major deliverables, and initial planning information. For these sections of the workshop, delegate the role of scribe to one of the participants so that key ideas, issues, assumptions, decisions, and actions are captured accurately during the meeting. Capture workshop information on a flipchart, whiteboard, or a laptop computer hooked to a data projector so that the notes will be visible to everyone in the room as they are written. Track the information that is captured for accuracy, and fix anything that is not correct or complete during the meeting. During lengthy meetings, shift the recording responsibilities around so that it falls equally on each team member (or at least those who can write legibly) so that your team members can participate as fully as possible.

Reviewing documents, brainstorming, proposing changes and improvements, and other activities will help project team members contribute to the overall documents and plans. This process, as well as subsequent collaborative planning, converts the initial situation where everyone perceives the project as "yours" into the more desirable state where it is "ours." As people invest time and effort into the overall direction of the project and become more involved, their ownership and buy-in increase. Projects are successful because the people who work on them care. Collaboration and open discussion lead to caring.

Another important goal for this portion of the project start-up workshop is a deep understanding of the objectives and priorities of the project. Team members who understand what is most important for the project can make fast decisions on their own that support the overall project. A discussion of the Is/Is NOT criteria for the project deliverables will both allow the team to refine and improve what it says and let you communicate the specific goals and boundaries for the project. Maintaining control over your project requires you to manage changes, and one of the most common sources of unnecessary change is scope creep within your team. Contributors who have a clear understanding of what is out-of-bounds for the project are much less likely to add "cool extra features" or strike out on inappropriate development tangents.

Whether you or someone else is facilitating, monitor participation throughout the workshop to ensure that each participant is contributing about equally. If the workshop is hijacked by a single person or a small clique of people who dominate all the discussion, the workshop result will be the opposite of your goal. Isolated, uninvolved participants will not care about your project and are not likely to make meaningful, reliable commitments.

Confirming Roles

Another key portion of the workshop agenda focuses on roles and responsibilities. Detailed planning (discussed in the next chapter) includes setting individual goals and assigning ownership for all defined project activities. During the project start-up workshop, you can get a head start by beginning to delegate and identify who will be responsible for project deliverables, processes, and other requirements.

One technique, which goes by the acronyms RACI or DACI, uses a two-dimensional matrix and codes for assigning individuals specific roles for project work or decisions. Responsibilities are listed in the first column of the matrix, one per row. You and the members of your project team are listed across the top, one per column. Codes defining each person's role are added to the cells where the activities and individuals intersect. RACI stands for:

Responsible: A responsible party makes a commitment to do the work.
Accountable: The accountable party has ultimate decision authority and bears any consequences related to the objectives. There can only be one A, and this role may be combined with R.
Consulted: Any stakeholder is consulted who could participate in planning and decision making.

Informed: Informed parties are regularly provided status on progress, deci-
             sions, and other information to coordinate related work and fa-
             cilitate collaboration.

One reason to use a RACI chart is to delegate ownership and make responsibilities visible, which is important for motivation. Meaningful involvement of any sort reinforces connections and teamwork, though, so this process
is even more useful for projects.

During your project start-up workshop, develop a RACI chart to record
roles for high-level project responsibilities such as quality management, risk
analysis, training, systems management, project metrics, vendor liaison, communications, testing, and sign-off. When you complete the matrix and document it for posterity, populate the cells with the complete terms, not just a
single letter, or at least incorporate a legend and definitions to minimize potential confusion by casual readers.

DOING THE PAPERWORK

The DACI model is similar, with the same roles defined, but the letters
standing for Driver, Approver, Contributor, and Informed. The DACI model
is used at Intuit Inc. and is effective there even for fairly small projects.
Scott Beth, a senior manager with Intuit, tells this story about starting a
project to converting Intuit's paper stock to recycled paper:

> "After initial discussions with the sourcing manager for office
> and paper supplies, I asked her, 'Who's the Driver for this proj-
> ect?' She said wasn't sure, and we realized there really was no
> owner for that area. I agreed to be the Approver and to be
> accountable for the decision to convert to recycled paper.
> After discussing this, I asked the sourcing manager to be the
> Driver, to own the responsibility for making this change. We
> set up milestones for reviewing progress. When we clarified
> the DACI for the project, we immediately started making
> progress and easily met all the timing and expense goals for
> converting to recycled paper. Defining roles and responsibili-
> ties, especially in writing, is a very effective way to secure the
> reliable commitments that you need to depend on to control
> any project."

Digging into the Project

If time allows in your agenda, start to develop some of the planning deliverables
discussed in the next chapter, such as the project work breakdown structure,

activity estimates, dependencies, and identified risks. Though you will not likely be able to complete all project planning in a typical start-up workshop, it is particularly beneficial for distributed teams who will be unable to meet face-to-face later in the project to start to build a solid foundation for subsequent planning while everyone is together.

Having Some Fun

Structure some workshop activities to have people work together in pairs or in small groups to facilitate team building. Even during shorter project start-up workshops, include at least one opportunity to engage in a suitable team-building activity. During longer workshops, activities such a low-impact sporting event (a program manager I worked with recently organized a boccie match—we were all quite pathetic), a meal at a restaurant, or some other outside event is a great opportunity for people to converse and get to know one another. Even during a half-day workshop, you can set up some game or activity that will get people moving and informally interacting with each other. Have some fun during the workshop. Rarely will people become best friends in a single workshop, but that isn't necessary. It will be enough if people start to know, trust, and respect each other (and you) so that they don't develop into adversaries.

Capturing Issues and Closing the Workshop

The final part of the agenda is to close the workshop. As the workshop progresses, capture all the action items requiring follow up on a posted piece of flipchart paper, whiteboard, or in some other visible place. At the end of the workshop, collect all the items requiring follow up and get owners to volunteer to manage each one and commit to an appropriate completion date. Collect final impressions and complete the workshop on time. Strive to end on a high note, and thank all the participants for their contributions.

Following Up After the Workshop

Document the results and distribute the information to your team. In general, it is better to do this quickly rather than spend a great deal of time making all the documents look perfect. Strive for accuracy, but get the workshop documents out to all participants and stakeholders as soon as possible. If you have captured most of the workshop information on a computer, much of it can be sent immediately following the workshop.

Update your project management information system, too, with all the project documentation that you have changed, and enter all the information you created during the workshop.

Set up time with your sponsor to discuss the results of your start-up workshop. If you generated any proposals to modify the project charter, initial scoping, or any other information you developed with your sponsor or stakeholders, schedule extra time to discuss and validate the changes.

Finally, follow up on any workshop items that you were unable to finish and track each captured action item to completion. The initial progress you made in the workshop should carry forward into your overall project planning process.

THE 90-DAY MIRACLE

Richard Simonds, an experienced project leader at Hewlett-Packard, shares the story of the role a project start-up workshop played in a particularly difficult project he faced:

> "I was asked by my general manager to prepare a training guide for field engineers who would sell and support one of the division's soon-to-be-released products. As usual, no one on the development team had given this any thought. The new and complex product was scheduled to go to market in just three months."

Richard agreed to take on this aggressive, time-constrained project, but only after gaining a strong, high-level support commitment from his general manager. His first action was to clearly define the scope and to gain commitments for the project from eight key team members (and from their managers). This team spanned eighteen time zones, from Europe to Asia, and none of the project team members was dedicated solely to this project; they all had to do it in on top of their regular, full-time responsibilities. He immediately arranged for a project start-up workshop and brought all eight team members to the division's headquarters. He distributed information about the project, the workshop agenda, and other project documents in advance so that the team would arrive well prepared.

> "Over the course of the three very long days we were together, we worked very hard to identify all the key elements of the project and agree on the specific assignments for each team member. We also decided how I would coordinate project activities and stay on top of progress for the eighty days we had left until the deadline. Despite the challenges of a globally dispersed team with competing commitments, the re-

lationships and solid project planning resulting from the project start-up workshop enabled us to bring the project in on time and *under* budget."

At the end of the project, the division general manager called it the ninety-day miracle. Richard's team had not only delivered the training guide as requested, they had also developed a training workshop to ensure that everything would be in place for the product release. The initially aggressive goal of a well-trained sales and support organization was easily met, and in the end the entire team was recognized for exemplary performance on this crash program. "The results would not have been realistic or even possible without the project start-up workshop," he concludes. "It reinforced the project's strong sponsorship, gained the commitment of the project team [and their managers], and gave me the personal leverage to be a bulldog in managing the established baseline schedule and project scope."

▪ Working with Cross-Functional, Distributed, and Global Team Members

Initiating a project with a team made up of people from different functions or from different locations entails additional challenges. Such teams are a main reason why project leaders lack authority over their team members, so managing these challenges is crucial for project success. This section contains general ideas to help you along, as well as specific advice for running a long-distance project start-up workshop.

Establishing Your Team

Most of the advice for managing a "matrix team" (where contributors report in effect to more than one manager) applies, whether the team is cross-functional, multidisciplinary, distributed, or global. Initiating an effective team in these environments requires you to develop as much influence within your team as possible (as outlined in Chapter 3). Building influence, particularly with distant team members, takes a good deal of extra effort, but it pays off—and can be the biggest difference between a well-controlled, successful project and a global, cross-functional disaster. Here are some specific ideas for increasing your influence at the start of a project:

- Identify and build on shared personal backgrounds, such as interests, hobbies, and experiences.

- Find specific, personal reasons why a successful project is important to each of your team members.
- Share pictures of distant team members, preferably pictures outside of the work environment to let people see what team members look like. (For digital pictures, reduce the file size before sending when necessary.)
- Put additional effort into informal communications. Be willing to make calls and hold meetings at times that are convenient for your team members.
- Communicate inclusively, minimizing jargon, acronyms, confusing technical language, local idioms, unusual figures of speech, and other sources of potential confusion for cross-functional teams.
- Be persistent in all communications, and always maintain a friendly tone.
- Experiment with a number of communication styles to determine what works best for individual team members.
- Reread all written communications, particularly to team members with a different native language, to ensure that what you are sending is as clear and unambiguous as possible. Avoid jargon, acronyms, and local idioms.
- Promptly follow up conversations with written summaries and meetings with minutes.
- Follow up on complicated written materials that you distribute with at least a telephone call to verify that they have been received, read, and are not confusing.
- Whenever it appears to be necessary to avoid confusion, provide translations of all project documentation into the native languages of your team members.
- Build on any past working relationships, especially previous work with your team members on successful projects.
- Discover and take advantage of personal relationships with mutually respected colleagues that you have in common with your contributors.
- Name your team, and create a shared identity.
- Reinforce team identity by using a dedicated project "war room" for a colocated team or a team website for a distributed team.
- Do whatever you can to bring people together for a face-to-face project start-up workshop. If distant team members are unable to travel to meet with you but you are able to travel to them, do it.
- Seek additional sponsorship for your project from the functions and locations of your team members. (Managing multiple sponsors can be tricky, but it may be necessary to influence some team members.)

- Praise each team member's specific talents and the pivotal contribution each person will make to your project.
- Personally thank team members frequently for their contributions, and copy their managers on all your communications expressing gratitude.
- Be unflaggingly loyal to your team members and avoid all public criticism. Keep negative feedback one-on-one or within your team, involving individuals' managers only as a last resort.
- Find and use all available programs for formal rewards and recognition for each of your team members.
- Get strong buy-in for collaborative planning and always be persistent in getting each person's input and feedback.

Conducting a Long-Distance Project Start-Up Workshop

If you are not able to arrange a face-to-face workshop for all the members of your team, use the best meeting technology available to you to accomplish most of the same goals. You can't use a teleconference to build the level of relationships and trust that you can establish in person, but you should be able to adequately achieve most of the goals related to project understanding.

Set up one or more short meetings with your team, each no longer than two or three hours. Longer technology-based meetings are not as productive, and shorter meetings will help you to minimize time-zone problems. Use the best technical tools for long-distance meetings that you have access to: videoconferencing, telephone conferencing, computer network presentation-sharing software, server-based file storage systems, and anything else you can think of. Before initial meetings, check that all the locations involved have access to compatible equipment and software. Also, resolve all access and security issues in advance, especially for participating contributors who are external to your organization.

Check that all of your team members have up-to-date versions of all the applications needed to open all documents that you attach to e-mails or save on network servers. Distribute all workshop materials well in advance of the meetings, and verify that each person has received them. Avoid the use of any networking or conferencing techniques that require a lot of bandwidth if part of your team has limited or low-speed network access.

Structure the agenda for a multipart workshop to take advantage of the time between meeting sessions for offline work. Plan for small colocated subteams or individuals to do follow-up work from earlier sessions or to prepare for the next session. Schedule the workshop segments no more than several days apart to maintain continuity. Personally contact all participants for your workshop to confirm their commitment to attend each scheduled portion of the workshop. Request that all of your team members focus full attention on the workshop during the sessions, and get acknowledgment from each of them that they will not answer e-mails, work on other tasks, or engage in recreational Web surfing during the meeting.

As preparation, assign pairs of team members who do not know each other to get in contact and do interviews so that they can introduce the other person at the start of the meeting. Challenge each person to discover at least one interesting fact about the other person to include in the introduction. If you do not have videoconferencing available, collect a photograph of each team member to distribute before the first session or present over the network during introductions.

Even if your project start-up workshop is not face-to-face, if there are opportunities to visit and work in person with distant team members in follow-up activities or planning, take full advantage of them.

KEY IDEAS FOR PROJECT INITIATION

- Secure commitments from your sponsor for ongoing support and begin to establish a good relationship.
- Develop a compelling project vision and fine-tune it as needed to inspire and motivate your team.
- Thoroughly understand your objectives and document your project charter.
- Conduct an effective project start-up workshop to get your project off to a healthy start.
- Put extra effort into building relationships and trust with your team members in distant locations.

CHAPTER 6

Building Control Through Project Planning

P ROJECT INITIATION FOCUSES on where your project is going. Creating the plan for your project forces you to figure out how you are going to get there, giving you a foundation for tracking. Project planning contributes more to your overall control than just a baseline for monitoring. Planning is a collaborative process that establishes buy-in and ownership of project work and motivates your whole project team. A credible plan shows that your project is, in fact, possible (though rarely easy). Lacking a plan, expectations for the project are based on hopes, dreams, and wishes—not good foundations for building confidence, or control. Your plan will also provide you with predictive metrics that will give you negotiating leverage with stakeholders and sponsors when your project faces unrealistic objectives.

▪ Plan Collaboratively

For project leaders who lack substantial authority, an important objective of collaborative planning is a common, shared, and coherent understanding of the work required to complete the project. This is useful on any project, but it is crucial for project leaders who do not directly manage their staff. Independent team members are much less likely to cooperate with your requests when they don't understand them or agree with them. Developing the plan as a team ensures that all the necessary commitments are based, at least in part, on choices and decisions that have been made by the contributors themselves.

Collaborative project planning builds on the project charter, initial scoping, and other documentation outlined in Chapter 5. Where initiation focuses primarily on what the project is expected to look like from the outside, planning is about seeing the project's structure and logic from the inside. The discussion here is not a complete reiteration of project planning processes. There are many other books and places to learn about basic planning (such as *The Project Management Tool Kit* mentioned in the Appendix B). As discussed in Chapter 2, planning is a critical process for project control, so clearly define the practices and methods you intend to use and get support for them up-front from both your sponsor and your team.

Certain planning concepts are particularly useful for increasing your influence and control. These include:

- Project infrastructure
- Breaking down the work with your team
- Individual goals
- Collaborative estimating
- Outsourced activities
- Interface management
- Constraints and plan optimization
- Risk identification and assessment
- Plan review

Much of this planning can be incorporated, at least for small projects, into your project start-up workshop agenda, as discussed in Chapter 5. Even for large projects, you can at least begin your collaborative planning during the workshop. If the project start-up workshop will be your only opportunity to work with your team face-to-face, build the strongest case possible to lengthen the workshop and incorporate most of your planning effort into the agenda. (In this case, where you invest multiple days primarily focused on project planning, it might more correctly be called a project planning workshop.)

GETTING EVERYONE HEADED IN THE SAME DIRECTION

To underscore the importance of collaborative planning on cross-functional teams, Al DeLucia, director of the Project Management Division for the U.S. Government General Services Administration (GSA) in Philadelphia, tells of a particularly challenging project he led. GSA's mission is to find and provide appropriate space for federal government "customer" agencies, and this project involved establishing a new headquarters for an agency that would consolidate many functions from leased space in a number of dispersed locations into one integrated facility. Al explains:

"A cross-functional project team was created using resources from GSA and representatives from the customer agency. I was assigned the official role leading the 'source selection' process of choosing a developer. Unofficially, however, I was assigned because much animosity had developed among team members early on. This animosity was the consequence of a long history of distrust between the customer agency and GSA over the previous leased space. The team had become polarized, stalling important decisions that needed to be made to move the project forward on schedule. The customer agency kept 'gold plating' their requirements because they didn't trust the judgment of the GSA people.

"My job was to break this deadlock. I had recently read Jon Katzenbach's *The Wisdom of Teams* and remembered his assertion that team development requires that members work on something 'real' together. So, as source selection official, I required the team to attend a five-day source selection training session at an off-site facility. The trainer was asked to use our project as the case study for the training, with the goal of producing the actual source selection plan."

The first day of the training, hostility was very much in evidence. Team members were reticent and conversations were strained. Day by day, however, as the training progressed and the team worked side by side on the plan, tensions drained and people relaxed and they began working together more and more constructively. Team spirit was bolstered even more by going out for drinks and dinner each evening. "By the end of the week," he says, "we had a good plan that everyone had bought into, and a healthy, functioning team."

The spirit of the planning session was maintained by setting up a war room for the remainder of the project, outfitting vacant space nearby with necessary equipment and desks for each team member. "Although team members retained other workload, they were directed to work on this project in the war room and to keep all documents related to the project there," he explains. "In this way, security and confidentiality during the source selection process were maintained, but the clear overriding benefit was the relationships established by team members by the close proximity afforded by the war room." The team posted pictures and personal items around the space in addition to the project-related materials on the walls, and it became "their" room, where they ended up spending a good percentage of their time working, talking, and just hanging out, even after hours.

"In the end," Al reports, "the project proved very successful, and team members remain friends to this day—a result of having participated together on a high-performing team."

Project Infrastructure

As the story illustrates, the environment for a project is an important place to begin establishing control for your project. Start with a quick review of post-project lessons learned from recent projects and your own experiences to identify problems, issues, and barriers that you may face. With your team, consider these factors and review a list of project decisions, such as the one in Appendix A. Work to pick out a short list of decisions from the list or develop your own questions that relate to recent problems or to any new aspects of your current project that you are concerned about.

Collect options and ideas from each contributor for the questions you need to answer, and discuss how you all think it would be best to run the project. Work for consensus and document the decisions as you make them. If your team is unable to reach agreement on a single approach in a reasonable time, either propose what you prefer as a way to operate, at least provisionally, or skip the decision, or, as a last resort, escalate crucial decisions for resolution.

Consensus decisions on infrastructure questions are a powerful tool for project control because you can rely on your team's own determinations, instead of your personal authority, to back up your requests. Even when you are not successful in reaching consensus on an issue, the discussion will reveal things that you need to watch out for and individuals with whom you may have difficulty. Forewarned is forearmed.

Make your infrastructure decisions visible to your stakeholders and others involved in your project. Plan to review these decisions periodically, especially on longer projects, to keep them visible.

Breaking Down the Work with Your Team

The project work breakdown structure (WBS) is a complicated-sounding idea that is essentially the equivalent of a to-do list for your project. A WBS differs from a simple list in that it is displayed as a hierarchy in order to make the complexity of a typical project easier to understand and deal with. A project WBS is best developed by a team that includes a wide spectrum of perspectives—the more the better for surfacing bits of essential work that may not be obvious to all. You want to include people who are not yet involved in your project but will participate later, or at a minimum find people who can represent those viewpoints. When the size of the effort grows too large, both the process and the resulting WBS can become unwieldy. For that reason, this section will offer some specific ideas for developing a WBS with more than a dozen people involved or when the project work extends beyond about six months.

Your goal in developing a WBS is to understand your project as completely as possible, and early enough to use the information proactively to set up a coherent project that you can control. Every project has only two choices for defining the work: You can do it at the start, or you can do it incrementally, day by day, throughout your project. Either way, you will have to define the work. With the incremental approach you have no hope of control and a high likelihood of doing things out of order, incorrectly, and more than once. Control of your project demands that you get the WBS right (or at least close to right) as soon as is practical.

The top level of a project WBS is a single item, which is the entire project. The next level contains subdivisions of the project that can be aggregated to describe the project's work. Each subsequent level follows the same rules, with the elements of the lower hierarchy levels representing smaller and smaller pieces of the project that can be more clearly defined and better understood. The lowest levels of the overall breakdown comprise a list of project tasks that aggregate to the overall project's effort and are easy to describe. A project plan built using these lowest-level fragments (usually called tasks, activities, or work packages, though the terminology varies widely) will be as inclusive and thorough as you can make it.

The first-level breakdowns for projects are often (the PMI PMBOK says always) based on major deliverables, and the elements come from the initial scoping work discussed in Chapter 5. Further breakdown can be based on components and subcomponents of these deliverables, populating the lower levels of the breakdown down to the granularity that you seek.

Since the main objective of a WBS is to identify the work, other starting points can also be used, such as components of your life cycle, the locations of your team members, functions or expertise of your contributors, or the iterative release cycles used for evolutionary or agile development. However you approach it and whatever you call it, the result of a thorough work decomposition becomes the foundation for project planning.

Some ideas for a developing a WBS collaboratively include working "up against the wall"; minimizing missing work; dealing with long, multiteam, and high innovation projects; and documenting your results.

Up Against the Wall

At the risk of sounding like a 1960s radical, to create the most thorough WBS for your project, get up against the wall. Get your team together, give each person several pads of yellow sticky notes, and find a big chunk of blank wall (or whiteboard, collection of easel-pad sheets, or any other large, flat vertical surface). Developing a WBS is a creative right-brain process. Posting it on a wall where everyone can see it, using pieces of paper that you can move around and easily replace, is a great way to quickly develop a sense of what you are going to need to do. Working with a computer tool initially is like working with blinders on; it's easy to miss things even if you use "right brain" computer tools that support mind-mapping or other graphical representations.

If you find it necessary to develop your WBS with a distributed team, consider initially breaking the project into a structure by individual site, so most of the decomposition can be done on a wall by members of your team who are colocated. Then use computer networking or videoconferencing to share results and stitch everything together. When you are unable to develop the WBS face-to-face, such long-distance methods are always far superior to doing it all by yourself.

Minimizing Missing Work

Begin by reviewing several existing WBSs for similar projects. Request that each member of your team with access to plans from earlier projects bring and use them for brainstorming. Include all activities listed in any of the earlier project plans that are relevant to your project. Include activities needed to comply with legal requirements, organizational standards, and applicable life cycles or methodologies. Include "overhead" activities such as vendor and subcontractor management, special reporting, and preparation for reviews, presentations, and other meetings. Review retrospectives from recent, similar projects to identify all the things that were left out, then scan what those projects would do differently and incorporate pertinent advice in your WBS.

For each item identified, ask: What must be done before this work can begin? Is all the prerequisite work defined? Similarly, ask: What work logically follows this piece of the project? List any tasks you discover that are connected to those already listed. For each piece of work, capture and document any assumptions.

Consider the project WBS provisional until you have done a thorough evaluation of the whole structure with your team and have had it reviewed by at least one experienced peer project leader.

Long Duration Projects

For most projects, the planning horizon, or the longest period that you can expect to plan with much precision, is six to nine months. The initial WBS for projects expected to take a year or longer will necessarily be incomplete. There are a number of methods for dealing with this situation, and all of them essentially convert a long project or program into a succession of shorter-duration pieces—essentially doing the initial breakdown for the project across a timeline.

One common approach is to use "rolling wave" planning to develop a detailed WBS and schedule for the upcoming three- to six-month phase of the project. Work further out is defined and planned in general terms, but not at the level required for tracking and control. Control is based on detailed planning for the next phase of work, which is a defined activity built into the WBS for the current phase. At the end of each phase or wave, you will need to make a decision to continue, to proceed with changes, or to cancel the project based on the newly developed detailed plans for the next wave and updated general forecasts for remaining future work.

A related idea, used for software development, is to structure the project around a series of short development and testing cycles. Each evolutionary cycle delivers incremental functionality to the target users; then, based on testing, the following cycles are scoped, executed, and completed one by one. The incremental scoping of such evolutionary development cycles that are part of agile methodologies, extreme programming, and related approaches may shorten the planning horizon, but they add quite a bit of uncertainty around the overall project budget and completion date.

Some long programs can be broken into a succession of shorter projects that deploy in discrete waves. Each wave is independently planned and controlled as a separate project within the overall program, using similar WBS and schedule information with minor modifications and shifted dates.

On longer projects, identify both what you know and what you still need to find out. Assess risk for work that lies beyond about a six-month planning horizon. Allow a margin for reserve in both budget and timing for distant work based on your assessment of what you do not know.

Multiteam Projects or Programs

Having too many people involved in a project creates challenges similar to long duration. The bigger your project staff becomes, the more complex your WBS will be. In addition, the process of developing a good WBS in a face-to-face meeting (or any other way) with more than about a dozen people can be chaotic, frustrating, and nonproductive. Where the initial decomposition for lengthy projects tends to be along the timeline, projects with large staffs are usually broken down at the first level by functional or geographical subsets of the overall project or program team. If any of these smaller teams is too unwieldy, further decomposition may be warranted. One of the differentiators between project and program management is this initial decomposition of programs with a large staff into parts. These parts can be led, planned, and managed as independent projects by individual project leaders, and coordinated by a program manager responsible for project interconnections and integration of the plans and deliverables. Whether you delegate leadership to others for parts of your project or not, planning in general—and WBS creation in particular—is best done by a small, focused team.

Organize the sessions for developing WBS information around the smaller teams, and either assign a leader for each of the teams to coordinate the effort or plan to participate in each one. If you plan to delegate the facilitation, define the roles and responsibilities of project leaders at each location. Provide for language translation assistance when needed to develop your WBS. To make ultimate plan integration easier, establish standards for naming and documenting items in the WBS. To ensure consistency, make sure to clearly define any project terminology that will be used. Wherever possible, use common methods, formats, and templates.

When stitching together independently created pieces of the overall WBS, clearly and fully document all interconnections between the defined work. Add any activities needed to create the inputs required by defined activities, and ensure that all activity deliverables are needed. Look for and eliminate any redundancy you find, and then consider the most logical placement in the WBS for the activities that remain. Check the overall WBS to test whether the hierarchy minimizes interconnections and interfaces with other branches. If there are excessive dependencies, explore other possible structures that could make coordination and control more straightforward.

If your geographically distributed team can't meet in person, schedule meetings to even out the inconvenience of time-zone problems. Rotate the times so that the same people don't have to get up in the middle of the night to attend every time. Consider using a series of "rolling meetings" that bring portions of the team together who share at least a few working hours, and have meetings that swing around the globe involving everyone in a pair of meetings—one with their team members to the west and one with team members to the east.

For multiteam projects, add activities to your WBS to support necessary communication, coordination, and issue resolution between the teams.

As with planning for lengthy projects, take advantage of all the help you can find from peers and others who have successfully completed similar projects.

High Innovation or Investigation Projects

Projects are unique. Each project is different, so some participants and even some project leaders give up on developing a WBS before they start. You'll hear them say, "What's the point? No one has ever done this before, so we can't possibly write down what work is necessary." The best response to this argument is that while projects are indeed unique, most of the work they involve is not. For the most part, any sequence of projects within an organization will contain almost precisely the same activities, differentiated by a small number of additions, deletions, and modifications.

Project management principles apply best to work that can be well understood and controlled, which are the activities that recur project after project. Projects exist across a large spectrum; they may contain a lot, some, or very little work that has been done before.

That said, even the most leading-edge, high-tech projects have at least some standard, well-defined work that can be used to begin populating a project WBS. Projects that are initiated to conduct a wide-ranging investigation are another example where the precise direction in which the work may go is not clear at the outset, but even here there are always some activities that are known and can be defined and planned. Separating the work for your project into "knowns" and "unknowns" is a useful way to begin developing a WBS for a project with a lot of initial uncertainty.

Capture all the activities you are able to define, and treat them the same way you would in any project. That is, delegate them to an owner, schedule them, and keep them in control using garden-variety project management tracking techniques. You can then remove these "known" parts of your project from your list of things you are really worried about, so you'll lose very little sleep over them. While there'll still be a portion of the project work that is not so well defined (possibly a substantial portion), at least the parts you can plan will be under control, lowering the amount of chaos and making your job easier.

Once the easily definable work is visible, turn your focus to the "unknown." Capture what you do know about the remainder of the work. Initial steps for even the most arcane efforts can be defined, and you can allocate the best, most competent, creative people available on your team to work on the most challenging activities.

Before accepting that your project must be a high-risk, scary excursion into uncharted waters, test all assumptions that impose new, untried methods. Explore options for delivering what is expected of your project using older, better understood technologies, processes, and methods.

Even with basic research projects, you can at least identify and list the key questions that your project must answer. Developing responses to these questions can be treated as elements of your WBS, and you can use them to control your project and assess progress. At any time, you can determine which questions are resolved and what you know about the others. If your overall rate of progress is not consistent with your stated project objectives, you can schedule a review to determine whether to revise the project objectives or shut it down. (For example, if a six-month investigation must resolve ten issues, then at the three-month point, you should expect substantial progress on at least five of them.)

If several approaches are available for uncertain work or a future decision could branch your project into one of several different directions, develop a breakdown for each of them. For your overall planning, include one of them— the largest, the longest, the most likely, or whichever it seems most prudent to use. This effort may reveal something about one of the alternatives that you were unaware of, and this knowledge may prove useful in planning, decision making, or discussions with your sponsor. Retain the other alternatives and treat them as contingency plans as part of your risk planning.

Work that is unknown to you may not be unknown to others. With that in mind, consider defining approaches that rely on outsourcing to experts, or arrange for help from specialized parts of your organization. Use your WBS to identify skill gaps on your team. Determine your needs and start looking for help.

Finally, split projects with excessive unknowns into two projects. The first project is chartered to complete the investigation and all feasibility work, and delivers a detailed proposal and plan for development and implementation. The second project can be undertaken to complete the deliverable, but only if it represents a prudent business decision.

Documenting Results

Capture the information for your project WBS immediately after you develop it. If you created it on a wall, take a picture with a digital camera (with sufficient resolution) or enter the items into a computer before you leave. However you initially capture the information, transfer it for posterity into a scheduling tool, a database, a document, or create a "WBS dictionary." Save it in a form that you can easily use for subsequent planning and store it where your team members can easily find it.

The most common place to save WBS data is in a project scheduling tool, such as Microsoft Project. The structure can be displayed there or in any document using the indented outline format to show where each item falls in the hierarchy. If you prefer a tree-structured version, specialized software exists for WBS charts, or you can use any general-purpose charting or presentation tool.

How and where you store WBS data matters less for project control than how you use it. It is the foundation for your project plans, so keep it visible, current, and handy.

Individual Goals

Defining the work is one challenge you face in controlling your project. Obtaining reliable commitments for each and every part of the work is the next. Your overall approach to gaining cooperation can be based on any of the ideas listed in the discussion on "getting through giving" in Chapter 3, but here we will focus specifically on defining clear objectives, discovering individual preferences, delegating responsibility, and gaining two-way commitment.

Defining Clear Objectives

Begin the process of setting goals while developing the project WBS. As your project's work takes shape, determine which member of your team is the most appropriate owner for the lowest-level activities in the structure. Some assignments will be easy and obvious; some team members have specialties and expertise that directly align with work that they identify and add to the project WBS. Other work will not be as simple to assign, but because each piece of the project requires an owner, you'll need to find a way to delegate responsibility to a willing owner. For each project task, but especially for any activities without obvious owners, verify that you have a thorough description that includes: a clear definition of the deliverable; all criteria that will be used to evaluate the results; any assumptions or constraints; role assignments (if the work is expected to be done by more than one person); and anything else that you know about how the work should be (or at least *could be*) done.

Personal responsibility, as discussed in Chapter 3, is a powerful motivating factor. Along with the work itself, ownership can be one of your most powerful tools for getting commitments for your planned project activities. Where there is an obvious owner who voluntarily accepts responsibility for a task with enthusiasm, most of your work is done. Document the commitment, and rely on the owner's desire to do the work to secure the deal. Ownership and the nature of the work will be more than sufficient to motivate contributors for some parts of your project, so you'll be able to easily satisfy the "getting through giving" criteria that a credible commitment requires.

Develop a list of all project activities, noting the commitments that emerge during development of your WBS. Use a simple list with names or develop a responsibility matrix, such as the RACI or DACI charts discussed in Chapter 5, listing activities one to a row with each project contributor in a separate column. To the list of activities that emerges from the WBS, add any other work that your project requires. Include all the ongoing efforts for reporting, keeping status and other project information up-to-date, and monitoring other project "overhead," particularly things that you expect to delegate to members of your team.

Project leaders who lack much authority can get around the problem by identifying activities that require more organizational clout and delegating them to their project sponsor. Document this work and either list it with all the other activities or make a separate "sponsor responsibilities" list.

Discovering Individual Preferences

When an activity has no obvious, eager owner, your work is cut out for you. There can be many reasons why no one seems interested in the work. Your first job is to determine, not just guess, why no one volunteered to take responsibility. In some cases, the work requires a skill no one on your team has. In other cases, the work may seem to be defined inadequately. Perhaps it is too high-profile, difficult, or risky. In still other cases, the work may appear boring, pointless, or thankless. There are other reasons people might avoid a commitment: They may already have too much other work, or they don't want to work with people no one likes, or they want to avoid work that depends on external factors out of their control.

If the main reason for no enthusiasm is that everyone thinks the work isn't necessary, test it and see if they're right. If the activity was listed simply because it appears on a planning template or because "we always do it," yet it represents no value added to the project, drop it. If the consensus is that the definition of the work is too "fuzzy," go back to the drawing board and work for more clarity in the WBS, then see if the newly defined activity might generate a volunteer.

Sometimes, though, you will need to roll up your sleeves and play "Let's Make a Deal." The overall process for gaining commitments using reciprocity starts with understanding what the people on your team care about and want, so that you can then offer something they desire in exchange for their commitment. Chapter 3 has many ideas about what you can offer as exchange capital, but some of the most useful are to:

- Identify team members who want to fill skill gaps or learn something new.
- Find out which activities are strongly desired by contributors and then use them as leverage or as part of a "package deal."
- Motivate contributors using project aspects they care about or a project vision statement tailored to their perspective.
- Find people on your team who thrive on challenges and like visibility.
- Find people on your team who like predictability and hate attention.
- Identify people on your team who are overloaded doing work that you might be able to shift to others.

Knowing what sort of offer you can make that would appeal to your team members will put you in a position to establish meaningful commitments for most, perhaps all, of the work in your project.

Delegating Ownership and Responsibility

The next step is to close each deal. List all the known and potential project work commitments for each member of your team. On your lists, strive to find a potential owner for all the unassigned work in your WBS, and consider options that you might use to convince people to accept responsibility based on what you know about them. Request your team members to make a similar list of known and possible project commitments. Ask them also to include any other responsibilities they have outside of your project, so you can discuss their situations as a whole and verify that the commitments to your project are realistic.

Schedule a one-on-one meeting with each person on your team to discuss and confirm goals. If there are particularly important unassigned activities that could be assigned to more than one person on your team, sequence your discussions so that you speak with your preferred choice first. Schedule a similar meeting with your sponsor last, to confirm the work you expect the sponsor to own and to explore options for dealing with project work that remains unassigned after you have met with each member of your team.

During these one-on-one meetings, begin each discussion by comparing your lists to verify commitments for all the work for which you believe the person has already accepted ownership. Add any new items where both you and your contributor have proposed ownership, and sufficiently discuss each item listed to validate that you both have a common understanding of the work.

Work down your list of potential additional assignments, using your best influence and negotiation skills to gain enthusiastic, or at least willing, acceptance for them, one by one. Deal with resistance using open questions that probe why the person is reluctant to take on ownership. Ask them to explain why they would rather not be responsible for the work, and explore if something about the work could be changed to make it more desirable. Also find out if there is any interest in taking on a portion of the work or teaming with others who could help. If there is a valid alternative for the activity that would be more acceptable (involving more "tried and true" methods for risk-averse contributors, or a newer, innovative approach for more ambitious team members), consider it.

Be persistent, but if no realistic option surfaces to secure a commitment, note it and move on to the next item.

Gaining Two-Way Commitment

When you have discussed all the items on your list, consider all the commitments you and your contributor have jointly agreed to as a whole. Be sure that the individual sees all the commitments, combined with his other existing responsibilities, as realistic. List these commitments, and express your confidence in the other person's ability to get them done.

The commitments made by your team are only part of the story. Also write down any commitments that you made to your team members, and schedule any work that you need to do to deliver on them. Remember, if you do not deliver on what you promise, your team members won't do it, either.

After you have met with all of your team members, update your overall planning documents and identify all of the gaps that still remain. You may be able to deal with some gaps by replanning, finding a way to make the work unnecessary. You can also potentially plug some of the holes by assigning the activities to yourself, but be careful—if you overload yourself, it will not be just a few activities at risk, it will be your entire project. Gather your information together, summarizing all the work identified for your project that you have no credible owner for, along with any thoughts you have about changes to the project that could resolve them.

Meet with your sponsor and get commitments for any activities that you plan to delegate upward. Never be bashful. A documented commitment to make a key project decision with a specified turnaround time never seems like a big deal early in the project, and it may prove very useful later in your project. Document your sponsor's agreements, and any commitments you have made in exchange.

End your discussion with your sponsor by asking for help and advice on unassigned work on your project. Explore options such as:

- Allocating additional staff to your project, at least part-time
- Delegating the work to others in the organization
- Outsourcing the work
- Modifying project goals so that they can be met with existing staffing

There are many other possibilities, but you need to develop support from your sponsor for alternatives that are realistic. Be clear about the consequences to your project if you are unable to resolve your staffing issues. Propose options that you have come up with, and ask your sponsor for advice and alternatives. Determine how best to deal with each gap, and end your discussion by summarizing your decisions and the actions needed for follow up.

Following your meeting, document all open staffing issues, along with any commitments you are not confident of to include in your analysis of project risk.

CLOSING THE DEAL

Patrick Schmid, a seasoned project leader who is managing director of PS Consulting in Germany, tells of a particularly difficult situation that he faced on one of his projects. To succeed, he had to depend on the services of an IT department team several hundred kilometers away in France. From experience, he knew that it would be easy to get a positive response to his initial request, but he also knew that follow-through was very likely to be late, not quite what he required, or both. The members of the support team were well known for doing what they wanted to do, not necessarily what was needed.

"I was concerned after my initial discussions that history was going to repeat itself," he says, "so I secured approval from my management to travel and spend time with the team in France. Getting approval wasn't easy, but the consequences of potential problems gave me a potent rationale for the trip." Over the course of several meetings with the IT team, he carefully described his project and what he needed. He asked for advice on how the team, and in particular his primary contact, thought it best to proceed. At the end of the day, Patrick asked his associate to join him for dinner, and during the meal they discussed a great deal, but neither of them mentioned the project.

When they met again briefly the next morning, he quickly secured an agreement for what he needed. The project was ultimately very successful, due in large part to the cooperation of the remote IT team. "In discussing it later," Patrick says, "I learned that I got cooperation because my associate did not feel that I was pressuring him; he appreciated that I gave him a say in the decision making."

Commitments offered willingly are much more reliable than forced commitments.

Collaborative Estimating

Of all the parts of project planning, estimating seems to be the one that project teams find most problematic. Whether doing assessments of duration or cost, project estimates are often too low, and the consequences of being wrong are severe. Estimating is one area where all the elements of control outlined in the initial chapters of this book come together. Processes and metrics matter a great deal, because estimates that aren't based on a good process and measured history are generally just wild guesses. There are also excellent opportunities to build teamwork and influence through collaborative estimating.

Some ideas for developing estimates that will help you to understand and control your project include using your plan details, learning from history, and approaching estimating as a team activity.

Developing a Detailed View

Much of the inaccuracy in project estimating comes from two related sources: estimating work too early, and estimating work at a level that is too high. A reliable process for estimating depends on the process for creating a thorough, complete WBS (as covered in previously in this chapter). If you lack enough information to develop a work breakdown structure, you will not be able to accurately assess the timing and cost of your work. One of the primary reasons for guidelines limiting activities at the lowest WBS level to "two to twenty days duration" or "eighty hours of effort" is to join the estimation and WBS processes at the hip. If you can define the work at a sufficiently low level of granularity, you can understand it and, consequently, accurately estimate it. If you can't, your estimates will probably be unreliable. Most people have a horrible track record of accurately assessing work that takes appreciably longer than about two weeks. Below this level, the single owner of the activity can take responsibility for the work and figure out what needs to be done. Based on estimates derived from knowledge of the work, your plan will be credible, realistic, and accurate enough to control your project.

If the estimates you develop for an activity seem to be overly large, further breakdown is one way to build higher confidence. Some activities may appear to be difficult to decompose into smaller activities, but there are a number of ways to make this easier. One of the most straightforward is to treat the activity as a project and apply your life cycle to it. Separate it into phases such as "thinking and analysis," "design and writing things down," "developing and creating the deliverable," and "testing and resolving problems." Other approaches include dividing the deliverable into subcomponents, thinking through a scenario for executing the work, or supporting the completion or acceptance criteria. Devise some basis, if only selecting a small portion of the work and doing it, to develop a solid understanding of the work that can support credible estimation.

The owners for each project activity are a good first source of duration and effort data. If their initial estimates are larger than your standards, press for further breakdown of the work to pull the estimates closer to numbers that will inspire confidence. If the initial estimates you collect seem unrealistically optimistic, probe for specifics. Ask what the estimate is based upon, and have the owners of project tasks describe how they plan to approach the work. Test each estimate you gather using what you know about your project's constraints and assumptions, available team skills and capabilities, staff availability and productivity, training requirements, and potential turnover. Be particularly skeptical of all estimates for project activities for which you have not yet been able to identify a named owner.

For each activity, collect an estimate of duration in workdays as well as an estimate of effort in person-days, engineer-hours, full-time equivalents, or some suitable combination of people and time. If the two estimates seem inconsistent (forty hours of effort in two days, for example), ask the activity owner to explain. Communications, meetings, and other interruptions consume time and affect the relationship between effort and duration. If the estimates you collect are based on shaky assumptions, adjust them to make them more realistic.

Finally, always probe for worst-case estimates. Get a sense of what the activity owners think might go wrong and collect this information to use in risk analysis later in your project planning. If the scenario that the worst case is based upon seems very probable, revise the estimates of effort and duration accordingly.

Learning from History

Accurate estimates are always derived, one way or another, from history. Actual results for project activity cost and duration are important project diagnostic metrics, which are discussed in Chapter 7. Historical measurements stored in databases or reported in the post-project lessons learned from previous projects are good direct sources for estimating data you can use; if available, this data can help you to validate the estimates for similar work you plan to include in your project.

Other potentially useful sources of information include your personal notes and recollections; consultations with experienced peers, consultants, and managers; and publicly available published information in magazines, presentations, and on the Web.

Historical information is also embedded in estimating guidelines and in parametric formulas that relate the size, volume, length, or some other aspect of a deliverable to effort and duration. All of this information is potentially valuable in verifying that your project estimates are credible and in the right range. Unfortunately, unless the historical estimates you have are for exactly the same activity performed by the same group of people, they will only be close, not precise.

Estimating as a Team

History is valuable, but it is not always written down in a form that is easily available. One back door into historical experience, which also serves to build teamwork and connection to your project, is the Delphi technique.

Delphi is a relatively high-overhead process, but it can generate credible estimates that your team will accept, even for activities where the owner lacks confidence and there is no applicable historical information. Delphi works on the principle that even when no individual is able to provide good estimates, you can rely on the wisdom of the team to give credible results. Delphi uses input from the team as a whole; as such, it enhances project motivation, buy-in, and teamwork.

Gather your team (a virtual meeting with distributed members works fairly well), including at least five people, all of whom have a good overall understanding of your project. Review what you know about each activity in your project WBS that lacks a credible estimate, but take care not to include any information or opinions on what you or others think the estimates might be. Ask each participant to provide a duration estimate, effort estimate, or both. In the first round of data gathering, ensure that each input is provided without any consultation and based only on each person's individual analysis.

Collect all the responses and then create three groups, one each for the highest, midrange, and lowest thirds. Reveal the results and explore with the group whether they find the average of the middle grouping to be reasonable. Also discuss the highest estimates and probe for personal experience that could credibly support these. For the lowest estimates, find out if someone has a clever, creative shortcut that could credibly allow the work to be done that quickly. Discuss the assumptions that outlying estimates are based on as a way to better understand them.

Following discussion, conduct more rounds of estimating, striving for convergence. For project estimating, one or two additional cycles are generally sufficient. In addition to providing believable estimates that would otherwise be difficult to derive for project activities, Delphi also delivers estimates that your team has had a hand in creating. Because the estimates are produced by the same individuals who will do the work, they are motivating, and contributors will generally do their best to deliver on them.

Outsourced Activities

Increasingly, projects are planned with work that will be performed by consultants, contract workers, and others outside of the organization. In analyzing your project, identify all the work in your WBS, including any portions that are likely to be outsourced. Outsourced work is particularly difficult to manage and control, and it is one place where all project leaders, regardless of their authority, need to work primarily through influence. Planning for outsourced work includes all the normal steps with particular attention on scoping, because getting it wrong can have very significant financial impact on your overall project. For better control, you also need to pay attention to your reasons for outsourcing, timing issues, sources of potential conflict and confusion (which you'll need to minimize), and the contractual arrangements.

Your Reasons for Outsourcing

Project work is outsourced for a number of reasons, including a lack of skills, expertise, or capacity inside your organization. It may be a strategic decision by your organization to outsource work not considered a core competency.

Cost may be the reason for outsourcing, or a desire to build organizational partnerships. If there are parts of your project that will be outsourced, or that you plan to propose doing on a contract basis, discuss them thoroughly with your sponsor and management to get full approval to go forward.

Identify both the benefits, such as not having to invest in building skills needed for a single project, and the risks of outsourcing for your project. If nothing else, outsourced work will probably consume more of your time throughout the project because of the additional administrative requirements. With your sponsor, carefully assess the issues, timing, probable costs, and other factors. Together, make decisions to outsource project activities based on solid business criteria. Outsourcing decisions made primarily to deal with a lack of available staff will weaken your project control.

Managing the Timing

Outsourcing takes time to set up, particularly if you are outsourcing work for the first time or working with a new supplier. Review your organization's process for procurement and discuss it with experts who know what to do. Verify that your project (and you) will have adequate time to deal with filling out forms, getting approvals, communicating, and negotiating.

If you don't have adequate time, work with your sponsor to expedite the process, or else find an alternative that will mesh better with your project timing.

Minimizing Sources of Conflict and Confusion

Control problems with outsourced work have many causes. There may be organizational differences, specification issues, or timing issues.

Organizational Differences. Different organizations have different working methods, terminology, and customs. When you are reviewing proposals and considering outsourcing options, insist on interviewing the people you would be working with. Get a sense of what the differences are between each organization and yours. If the processes and other aspects that you learn about are too dissimilar from yours, consider this a red flag. Building the trust and good working relationships that you need with people who think and work differently is very difficult. Seek to contract with organizations similar enough to yours to minimize the potential for misunderstandings and disagreements.

Specification Issues. Because it can be both expensive and time-consuming to make changes to work that you outsource, avoid contracting out activities where the deliverables are not fully defined or could change.

Carefully define detailed specifications of the deliverable, performance and measurement criteria, acceptance and testing requirements, interface specifications, standards to be followed, and all other relevant requirements.

Timing. Another common source of problems for outsourced work, or for any work done at a distance, is timing. When planning outsourced work for your project, define the work so that it includes ample opportunity for you to gather concrete evidence of progress. In addition to the ultimate deadlines, add checkpoints and milestones to review documents and prototypes and to participate in inspections, walkthroughs, and preliminary tests.

Contracting for Control

Work with the people in your organization to set up all contracts using standard forms or formats that include all the requirements your organization requires. For each contracted deliverable, ensure that ownership and timing requirements are clearly defined. If you can, structure the contract to be fixed-price and include tight, thorough specifications to minimize risk. If the contract is not fixed-price, include a "not to exceed" limit that will protect your project against excessive costs and force renegotiation of the contract before it breaks your budget. Also consider adding terms and conditions to the contract that will enhance your control, such as incentives for good performance or early delivery and penalties for poor performance.

Participate in the negotiations so that you can begin to establish an open, honest relationship during contract discussions. You will carry the relationship into your project, so playing hardball during contract negotiations will create large potential difficulties throughout your project. Finally, meet with the person who will administer the contract on the other side as you are signing the contract. Review the contract terms to ensure that all parties understand what the agreement means.

Interface Management

As you analyze dependencies for each activity in the WBS, pay particular attention to inputs that lie outside your project and deliverables within your project that are sent to other projects. Interrelated projects pose particular control problems, not unlike the challenges of planning outsourced work.

If you are managing one project in an elaborate hierarchy of projects that make up a large, complex program, you are likely to have many cross-project dependencies. Even in simpler situations, you will probably find at least some external interface linkages.

Begin your analysis by identifying all required outside inputs to planned work in your project that could impede or halt your progress. As your project's network and timeline take shape, document all your external input requirements, including both specifications and timing.

Approach the project leader you believe will be responsible for producing what you need so that you can discuss the interface between your projects, and request the other project leader's commitment to supply what you need in a timely manner. Use the same influencing techniques discussed earlier in the chapter for securing agreement with your project contributors. Ask for a formal written agreement, including a clear summary of the specifications and completion criteria for the deliverable. Also document and get formal agreements for all of the external deliverables for which your project is responsible, with commitments for periodic status updates. Treat these "memos of understanding" as contracts, using them to control and influence the work external to your project.

If you encounter resistance from another project leader who is part of your same program, escalate the situation to your program manager for resolution. If the other project is completely independent of yours, discuss the situation with your sponsor. If you are unable to resolve the problem, you may need to work through your sponsor to adopt an alternative that does not depend on the interface, or as a last resort, you may have to ask your sponsor to pull rank and force an agreement.

Your goal is to secure credible commitments to aid you in controlling work outside of your project. If you have what seems to be an excessive number of external interfaces, you should consider rethinking your overall approach. If your project is a piece of a larger program, encourage the program manager to revisit the initial program decomposition, looking for a program structure with lower interdependence complexity and risk.

Constraints and Plan Optimization

Collaborative planning begins with identifying the work as a team, and building on the WBS to add information about staffing and timing. Integrating these findings into an overall plan provides a picture of the project, bottom-up, that can be contrasted with the original objectives. It is about this place in the planning process when project leaders discover just how much trouble they are in. To gain control over your project, you'll next want to consider topics such as critical path, methods for minimizing schedule complexity, resource overcommitments and leveling, opportunities and plan optimization, and putting your project in a box.

Critical Path

Timing is important to any project. When you combine the project activities with their initial duration estimates and presumed logical dependencies, you can determine the minimum project duration based on that information. Although you can do the analysis manually (and everyone should do this at least once, if only to understand the details), there are many project management scheduling tools available, and even the least capable of these tools will do a much better job than you can of analyzing a project network. The rules are basic:

- Begin with as comprehensive a list of activities as you and your team can develop.
- Establish duration estimates that are as credible as possible.
- Set up logical dependencies to link activities together, avoiding fixed-date "must start on" constraints except in unusual cases.

Once entered into a scheduling tool, your network of linked activities will quickly turn into a gaily colored display of red and blue bars—a Gantt chart (named after Henry Gantt, the gentleman who devised it about a hundred years ago, with no help from any computer tools). The red bars line up in sequence across the calendar, with no gaps, showing the longest sequence of planned work for your project as it is currently laid out.

A Gantt chart display of your project tells you two things about control. The end point of the final red bar tells you the earliest date that the work on your project can be expected to finish, based on your detailed planning data. If, by some miracle, the date is on or sooner than the deadline specified in your project objective, there is hope. Most of the time, though, the initial critical path for a project is way past the expected deadline. In this case, control of your project depends either on optimizing your plan and finding a credible way to make it shorter, or convincing your sponsor to adjust the deadline. Both of these topics are explored later in this chapter.

The second thing the Gantt chart shows you about your project is how much flexibility is available in your plan. This is really not too useful initially, especially if the plan overshoots the deadline significantly. As your planning process approaches completion, however, you can see flexibility by comparing the relative proportion of red and blue bars on your Gantt chart. Red bars, by convention, are used for critical tasks and lie on the critical path. Your project can only be done more quickly if you change the estimate for one or more of these activities, one or more of their logical dependencies, or both. Blue bars, by convention, are used for noncritical activities—activities that can slip, at least a little bit, without lengthening the project. If most of your bars are red, you have little flexibility in your plan and control will be very difficult. If you have a single set of red bars stretching from the project start to the finish and a much larger number of blue bars, you have a chance, because you can shift the work represented by the blue bars somewhat when necessary to deal with issues and contingencies without effect on the overall project.

Minimizing Schedule Complexity

One potential source of confusion on projects that can threaten your control is an overly complicated plan that only you can read. One way to make project plans easier to read is to judiciously insert milestones to better show what is going on. Milestones are often used to show work leading into the end of a project phase, fanning into a decision or transition point where things are synchronized before the work then fans out into many parallel streams. Milestones can be used throughout your plan to show completion of sets of activities of any sort, and to untangle logic that would otherwise be a bewildering arrangement of "network spaghetti." Do use care not to add milestones that will unnecessarily increase project overhead, however.

For projects with multiple independent teams, or a high-level summary plan for a program, you can also make things easier on the various teams and subprojects by using milestones. Set up the plan with a set of milestones common to all the parts of the project, gathered under the heading of "Project Milestones." Define the milestones two to three weeks apart, and arrange them in sequence. Follow this section of your plan with a section that contains overall work that you are responsible for, followed by additional sections breaking down the work of each separate team, including any external suppliers. The detailed activities in each section will contain defined dependencies within the section, and external dependencies that link through the overall milestones at the top of the plan. The plan in Figure 6-1 is an example based on plans being used to manage a program responsible for a series of system deployments. The original plans contained about 400 activities, but when only one section plus the milestones are expanded, no more than about sixty lines are in view.

The plan can be stored with all the sections collapsed, except for the milestones cascading across the project timeline. Relevant parts of the plan can be easily read by members of any team, simply by expanding the work for their section of the plan with the milestones. Structuring the plan this way also simplifies tracking, because the milestones gathered at the top will shift and cause ripple effects throughout the plan whenever anything in the overall plan slips enough to affect one of the milestones.

FIGURE 6-1. A SEGMENTED PROGRAM-LEVEL PLAN.

ID	WBS	Task Name	Duration	Start	Finish	% Complete
1	1	**Wave N Key Milestones**	**199 d**	**Jul 4**	**Apr 6**	**0%**
2	1.1	Wave N Participants finalized	0 d	Jul 4	Jul 4	100%
3	1.2	Wave N Participant Configurations Documented	0 d	Sep 5	Sep 5	100%
4	1.3	Wave N Requirements Complete	0 d	Oct 10	Oct 10	100%
5	1.4	Wave N Scope frozen	0 d	Oct 31	Oct 31	100%
6	1.5	Wave N Scope changes prohibited	0 d	Nov 21	Nov 21	100%
7	1.6	Wave N Design Complete	0 d	Dec 22	Dec 22	100%
8	1.7	Wave N Construction Complete	0 d	Jan 16	Jan 16	100%
9	1.8	Wave N System Tests Complete	0 d	Feb 6	Feb 6	0%
10	1.9	Wave N Participant Tests Complete	0 d	Feb 20	Feb 20	0%
11	1.10	Wave N sign off and release	0 d	Mar 9	Mar 9	0%
12	1.11	End	0 d	Apr 6	Apr 6	0%
13	**2**	**Program Staff activities for Wave N**	**191 d**	**Jul 4**	**Mar 27**	**76%**
34	**3**	**Business Process activities for Wave N**	**194 d**	**Jul 4**	**Mar 30**	**71%**
76	**4**	**Participant activities for Wave N**	**199 d**	**Jul 4**	**Apr 6**	**67%**
121	**5**	**System Development activities for Wave N**	**179 d**	**Jul 4**	**Mar 9**	**79%**
153	**6**	**Output developmnt for Wave N**	**180 d**	**Jul 4**	**Mar 10**	**77%**
170	**7**	**Finance activities for Wave N**	**180 d**	**Jul 4**	**Mar 10**	**80%**
179	**8**	**Testing activities for Wave N**	**95 d**	**Nov 1**	**Mar 13**	**62%**
180	8.1	Develop Wave N test plans	20 d	Nov 1	Nov 28	100%
181	8.2	Communicate participant testing requirements	20 d	Nov 1	Nov 28	100%
182	8.3	Develop Wave N test scenarios	15 d	Nov 29	Dec 19	100%
183	8.4	All test data loaded	16 d	Dec 23	Jan 13	100%
184	8.5	Test Plans for Wave N validated	16 d	Dec 23	Jan 13	100%
185	8.6	Conduct system tests	12 d	Jan 17	Feb 1	0%
186	8.7	Conduct Participant tests	13 d	Feb 2	Feb 20	0%
187	8.8	Retest, following defect correction	28 d	Feb 2	Mar 13	0%
188	**9**	**Training activities for Wave N**	**110 d**	**Nov 22**	**Apr 24**	**33%**
199	**10**	**Support activities for Wave N**	**140 d**	**Nov 1**	**May 15**	**39%**
213	**11**	**Release activities for Wave N**	**17 d**	**Feb 7**	**Mar 1**	**0%**

Resource Overcommitments and Leveling

Activity timing, combined with effort estimates, provides another useful view of the work. Project scheduling tools can generate histograms to show this view of the work, if you enter the effort information for each activity into the database consistently with the tool's algorithms. You can also use spreadsheet analysis or visual inspection across your Gantt chart to determine where you may have parallel work scheduled that requires more hours of effort than the individuals on your team have to offer. Identify each period during the project where your preliminary schedule requires overtime or additional staffing to support what it calls for. To have any hope of controlling your project, you need to shift the work along your timeline so that the effort required is consistent with your team's available capacity. Scheduling tools all provide an automated function to level your plan resource loads. The function may work well for you, but before you try it, make sure you have a well-protected archive copy of your plan. The load-leveling function in most automated scheduling software is the project management equivalent of a food processor. After the software has sliced, diced, and pureed your plan, it isn't likely that you will recognize it.

Repeat your effort analysis for your whole project to see where the overall staffing is under or over what you need. This composite analysis will help you to determine whether you can manage your resource problems by shifting activities around or whether you will need to build a case for more staff with your sponsor.

Opportunities and Plan Optimization

Much of what you discover as your project plan detail comes into view is not good news. The initial schedule is usually too long. The staffing, resources, and budgets available are often far below what your cost analysis requires. One potential for good news in this scenario, however, lies on the third side of the triple constraint—scope. Following your analysis of the project and the work needed to get it done, you and your team will know more about the project than anyone on earth. The project that your sponsor and stakeholders have in mind represents the best option that they are aware of, but they know less about what is possible than you do. Inside many projects lie much better possibilities than what was originally specified.

As part of your analysis, test the assumptions on scoping to explore whether superior options are available. Technical possibilities that you are aware of may allow you to far exceed the specifications originally requested. You may find that you can deliver a core set of critical functionality sooner for a small fraction of the total cost. Investing in development of reusable components that can add value to later projects or improved processes that will make similar project work more efficient are also possibilities.

Spending at least a small amount of time exploring opportunities is both good business and one of your most potent levers for control, especially when your planning is at significant variance with the original project objective. The more alternative options you can develop for your project, particularly when the options are attractive, the more successful you are likely to be in negotiating needed changes to an infeasible project objective. Consider ways that you could add to the scope to increase your project's benefits, but without incurring enormous additional cost or taking more time.

Not all the options for possible alternative projects are going to be opportunities. Some realistic options reduce the overall project. For example, if you can't deliver everything envisioned in the original scope within the expected deadline and cost, extend your "what if?" analysis to explore what you could deliver on time and on budget. Consider possibilities for doing work in parallel (fast-tracking) to shorten the timeline. Determine if a larger investment or staff will allow you to meet the timing and scoping goals. Once you have a plan, spend some time trying to optimize it. Based on your project priorities, figure out how to meet the most important part of the scope-time-cost triple constraint by relaxing the least important factors.

Also review any intermediate milestones or target dates within your project and other constraints, such as resources available only during specific time windows. Look for alternative plans that solve problems with minimal overall impact, such as taking advantage of any periods where you find resource under-commitments or delaying noncritical work. If revisions to your plans require visible changes, select the ones that minimize your impact on your highest priority among scope, time and cost.

Once you have an initial plan, pushing around your assumptions to seek alternative better plans is not difficult. You'll gain knowledge about your project that will assist you in controlling it. In addition to supporting your negotiations and discussions, developing alternate scenarios gives you information you can use to react to project-threatening situations, and it will let you quickly and eloquently describe the adverse consequences of potential changes.

Putting Your Project in a Box

One additional way to view your project is to use your planning information to build a two-dimensional representation of your best assessment of possibilities for cost and timing. All project schedules and budgets based on planning have some measure of uncertainty, and there are many ways to assess the exposure. Collecting worst-case estimates of duration and effort is one approach, as are a number of commonly used risk assessment methods. Based on your planning, and using a method that you have confidence in, determine a pair of dates for your project: one that is aggressive but possible (that is, supported by a bottom-up plan that is not completely ridiculous) and another that represents a safe assessment that you think you can achieve even if a number of things go wrong. Generate a pair of budget numbers the same way—one that represents best-case funding (assuming everything goes well) and another that has some margin for error. Use these pairs of numbers to construct a "project box," as shown in Figure 6-2.

The space inside the box represents a continuum of credible project outcomes, ranging from barely possible in the lower left to reasonably straightforward in the upper right. As a planning tool, the project box will show that the deterministic-looking single date associated with the final milestone on your Gantt chart is only one of many possibilities, not a certainty. It will assist you in communicating your project exposure, developing plans to manage risks, and negotiating with your sponsor.

All the points inside the shaded box need to be supported by a detailed, bottom-up plan collaboratively created by you and your team, including the best-case point on your chart. Your project's initial objective may very well lie outside the shaded region, in the infeasible space well to the left and below your box. When the best-case and worst-case points on your graph are close together, you appear to have a well-planned project with relatively low risk. When these points are far apart, control will be difficult, and the credibility of the best-case combination is low.

The box idea will show you and your team what the effects of various

FIGURE 6-2. A PROJECT BOX.

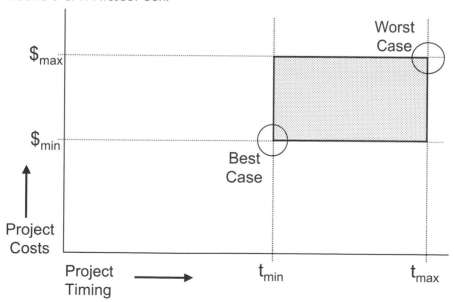

optimizing strategies will be. Compressing the project by adding resources will generally have two impacts: The costs (both minimum and maximum) will rise, and while the minimum time will drop, the time between the minimum and maximum date will expand. It will increase the overall size of the box, and in a quantitative way it will display the enlarged space of probable outcomes. Other optimizing options can similarly be compared in an objective, visual way.

The project box idea can also assist you in controlling your project through tracking trends. If you have done a good job planning, your initial box is as large as it will ever be. Over the course of your project, as plans and expectations are replaced by actual results and refined estimates, the box will contract in size with the shrinking uncertainty. If your periodic reviews show the box contracting in place, the best case stationary and the worst case migrating toward it, you are well in control. If the best and worst cases shift but remain inside the original dimensions, you at least have done a thorough job of planning and analysis. If, however, the box begins drifting up and to the right, you are probably in deep trouble. Tracking the center of the box over time is a reasonable assessment of whether your project remains in control. Ultimately your box will close in on the single point that represents your final cost and finish date—also ideally well within your original defined two-dimensional space.

Risk Identification and Assessment

Throughout your project planning maintain a list of risks that emerge. Some of these risks have been mentioned already, such as reluctant owners for activities in your WBS, worst-case estimates, and external dependencies. Others include:

- Complexity in scoping
- Inadequate specifications
- New or untried technology
- Activities lasting longer than two weeks
- Activities that depend on one key individual
- Communications or language difficulties

Risk identification, as with all of planning, is best done with your whole team. Brainstorm risks together, and let each person's concerns and potential issues prompt others to uncover related risks. Discuss project scenarios and consider what can go wrong. Problems in projects tend to recur, so also add to your list things that have gone badly for recent projects, including systemic organizational issues.

Again with your team, prioritize your listed risks based on their relative likelihood and potential for harm. Qualitative assessment, using ranges such as high, medium, and low for probability and impact, is generally sufficient to rank order the list.

With the most serious potential problems at the top of your risk register, work down the list and plan around the worst of them. Avoid or mitigate risks if possible through planning. If you and your team come up with no obvious or viable options for preventing a risk, develop a contingency plan for it to recover as best you can from its impact.

The value of risk management for control is pretty obvious, because it will allow you to avoid many of the worst of your potential problems. In addition, collaborative risk planning is particularly useful for cross-functional projects, because it allows your team to graphically demonstrate both the range of potential threats you all face and how painful it could get if the risks come to pass. Lack of awareness of possible exposure is a common root cause of project trouble on diverse teams; it is too easy to wander into disaster without being aware of its existence when you fail to discuss and communicate project risks.

Contingency plans are particularly useful for control because they are available at the onset of problem situations that you have identified and can be used to quickly recover your project. Without such plans, your project will enter a crisis mode, with significant distractions and the potential for symptom-based reactive actions that may lead to further complications and problems.

USING RISK MANAGEMENT TO BUILD A TEAM

In the closing days of December 1999, the government of the Netherlands decided to do away with the license fees charged to Dutch television viewers that it had collected annually for over fifty years. Returning the already-collected fees to millions of households would have been difficult to manage in any circumstances, but this effort had an aggressive goal, set by the politicians involved, to get it done in ninety days. To make matters worse, this project also coincided with the great Year 2000 (Y2K) panic in the IT industry. Karel de Bakker, an experienced project leader and consultant with deB Project & Risk in Delft, helped to organize and lead a diverse team to success on this project using what he refers to as "risk-driven project management." He explains:

> "The practical side of the project was not of particular interest to the ministers, MPs, or senators involved; in political decision making, the focus is rarely on efficiency or effectiveness. Nonetheless, even though the project had an adequate staff, the tight schedule meant that there wouldn't be enough time to perform all the activities necessary to deliver the required level of quality—the process had to be fully auditable.

"Not everybody likes taking risks, but some people really do. Perfectionists on the team were placed in charge of the production processes. Thrill seekers were asked to turn their creativity to the most uncertain project activities. Every team member became responsible for the overall project and actively looked for risks and ways to minimize them."

Karel used the differing comfort levels the project managers had with risk to align everyone with the project goal. All planning on the project was collaborative, with input from the entire team. Completing activities successfully meant reducing the project risk and improving the chances of overall success. He continues:

"In the end, the focus on managing the risks, performing at least three independent checks for every project deliverable, and the use of extensive testing and simulation throughout the project paid off. There were fewer than 1,300 incorrect calculations out of more than 6.5 million. Our diligent risk management and use of monitoring tools resulted in payment errors that totaled far less than a tenth of one percent of the 160 million euro total, and there were no underpayments. Everybody was more than happy, and we got official approval from the external auditors."

Doing a Plan Review

As your planning progresses, you will discover more and more information about your project. Although you are checking and validating each piece as you go, once you have all of your planning documents it is prudent to examine them all together. The purposes of a plan review are primarily to ensure overall consistency and quality, to identify and add anything your review reveals as missing, and to derive a high-level summary that you can use in discussions with your sponsor, stakeholders, and others with whom you need to discuss your project.

Involve your team in your plan review. This is another opportunity for team building, similar to a project start-up workshop, and it is an excellent way to ensure that all of your team members understand the project as a whole. Use techniques such as inspections or walkthroughs to carefully examine your project WBS, duration and effort estimates, dependencies, resource analysis, risk register and planned responses, and other project data. Search for inconsistencies, and then rectify them.

Bottom-up planning is about credibility, so at the conclusion of your review ask each team member if the contents of the project plan are believable. Approach the issue of credibility from two perspectives:

1. Does each person have high confidence that the plan is accurate and complete?
2. Are the individuals on your team confident that the plan can achieve the stated project goals—or, if not, does the plan achieve as much of the objective as possible?

If anyone on your project team doubts the overall thoroughness or believability of your plan, probe to understand why. In some cases, a better understanding of the existing plan will be sufficient to build confidence. In other cases, you may need to work further with your team to change the plan to boost its credibility. As Henry Ford said, "Whether you think you can do a thing or not, you are probably right." A team that believes in the plan will find a way to get things done; a skeptical team will usually fail.

The second question is even more subjective, but equally important. A credible plan that supports your sponsor's expectations is a desirable goal, but it may not be possible. Your team members need to believe that the course of action they are choosing is the one that makes the most sense, and you need to have a solid case for the plans you have developed, so you know they are the best you can do. If your plan shows you can meet your project objective, or there is only a small difference compared with the stated project objective, project control is feasible. If the differences are significant, use your planning analysis to develop at least two additional alternative projects, in addition to your team's consensus "best" version, supported by credible planning data. The more options you have that are backed up with compelling information, the more successful you are likely to be in negotiating necessary project modifications. Resolving differences between your bottom-up plans and your sponsor's top-down objectives when you commit to a project baseline is covered later in this chapter.

Conclude your project plan review by creating a high-level summary of your plans based on your detailed documents. Plan summary information should include:

- Scope (major deliverable definitions)
- Schedule (milestone charts with significant project dates)
- Cost (a budget summary)
- Staff (a project team roster with roles and responsibilities)
- Significant assumptions, issues, and risks

FLYING WITH YOUR EYES CLOSED

Reviewing information on projects is critical to catching and fixing defects and holes in a project concept before it is too late. "Les Sparks" (a close friend who wishes to remain anonymous) is a telecommunications expert and experienced project leader with a major managed services firm. Les tells of a very complex networking project where he was asked to help create a new global digital network.

"All of the initial planning and scoping was done by only one part of the eventual team, and only from their single perspective," he recounts. "The designers failed to involve any of the network management people, so operations and manageability were never considered." To make matters worse, well into the planning, upper-level managers inflicted a disastrous change on the project. As an indirect consequence of a recent agreement unrelated to this project, the new network had to include a large amount of equipment from a specific supplier. The mandated hardware was technically inappropriate, but it was designed in anyway, doubling the costs for the project.

The project went forward over loud protests and predictions that it could not work, and there was significant turnover on the implementation team. Completion of the work took three times longer than planned, and the initial attempts to use the network were unsuccessful; the network was largely useless. Operational problems continued though eighteen months of valiant but futile efforts to fix the network, and then it was abandoned.

But the company still needed the new network, so a redesign was quickly initiated. This time, there was broad cross-functional involvement in the design, and there were no inappropriate hardware constraints. The new project was completed in half the time, under budget, and the network was fully functional as soon as it was available. After his involvement leading portions of both projects, Les observes, "Wisdom is not found in just one place. Diversity is good; consensus is better. Getting opinions from more than one group and using multiple inputs results in better decisions. When you suppress dissension, the only opinion you'll get is your own."

To establish control, thoroughly review your plans with your team, and ignore what you hear at your peril.

▪ Measure Your Plan

Measurement is one of your fundamental tools for project control, as discussed in Chapter 4. Most predictive project metrics are based on planning data, and they serve as a distant early-warning system for your project. You can use predictive metrics to assess your project as a whole, identify unrealistic assumptions, uncover significant potential problems, and more clearly communicate what your project is up against. Because predictive measurements are primarily based on speculative rather than empirical data, they are generally less precise than diagnostic and retrospective metrics. Nevertheless, they can enhance your understanding and control over your project by:

- Determining project scale
- Supporting cost-benefit analysis
- Validating relative project priorities
- Quantifying unrealistic constraints
- Detecting faulty assumptions
- Identifying risk management requirements
- Justifying schedule and budget reserves
- Supporting successful project objective negotiations

Defining Predictive Project Metrics

Most predictive metrics are part of your personal review of the project plan, based on the planning information that you have developed and reviewed collaboratively with your team. Working by yourself or with assistance from key team members, examine the planning data to determine what it means. Even for predictive metrics that are based on more preliminary information, such as the ROI metrics (discussed in Chapter 5), you can revisit the assumptions and improve the quality of the information. Predictive metrics will help you develop a deeper understanding of your work and will support efforts by your management to compare, prioritize, and select projects. A number of examples of predictive project metrics follow, grouped into several categories. No project leader will find it useful or even necessarily possible to evaluate each of them, but you will find value in at least some.

Project Scale and Scope Metrics
- Size-based deliverable analysis (such as component counts, number of major deliverables, lines of noncommented code, function or feature points, blocks on system diagrams, volume of total output)
- Project complexity (interfaces, algorithmic assessments, technical or architecture analysis)
- Total number of planned activities
- Volume of expected specification changes

Timing and Schedule Metrics
- Activity duration estimates
- Project duration (schedule analysis of elapsed calendar time based on activity duration estimates—t_{min} for the project box)
- Total schedule exposure (schedule analysis based on worst-case duration estimates, contingency plans, or schedule simulations—t_{max} for the project box)
- Activity duration estimates compared with worst-case duration estimates
- Number of critical (or near-critical) paths in the project network
- Logical project complexity (the ratio of activity dependencies to activities)
- Maximum number of predecessors for any project milestone
- Total number of external predecessor dependencies
- Project independence (ratio of internal dependencies to all dependencies)
- Logical length (maximum number of activities on a single network path)
- Logical width (maximum number of parallel paths)
- Total length (sum of the durations of all activities, if they are executed sequentially)
- Total float (sum of total project activity float)
- Project density (ratio of total length to total length plus total float)

Resource and Financial Metrics
- Activity cost (or effort) estimates
- Total cost (the sum of all activity effort estimates, or budget at completion—$\$_{min}$ for the project box)
- Total cost exposure (aggregated worst-case cost estimates, contingency costs, or budget simulations—$\$_{max}$ for the project box)
- Total effort (the sum of all activity effort estimates)
- Activity cost (or effort) estimates compared with worst-case resource estimates
- Percentages of project effort planned in each life-cycle phase
- Maximum staff size (full-time equivalent team size)
- Number of unidentified activity owners
- Percentage of staff not yet assigned or hired
- Number of activity owners with no identified backup
- Anticipated staff turnover
- Number of geographically separate locations
- Value of expected project benefits
- Payback analysis (simple or discounted)

- Net present value
- Internal rate of return

General Project Metrics
- Total number of identified risks.
- Severity assessment of identified risks (percentages of your risks that fall into categories such as high, medium, and low).
- Survey-based risk assessment (summarized data collected from project staff, using a survey containing project factors).
- Adjusted total effort (project appraisal done by comparing your plan with completed similar projects and adjusting for differences).
- Cynical cartoonist correlation factor. (After developing your plan, collect thirty of Scott Adams's recent *Dilbert* comic strips and circulate them to your team. Ask people to mark each one that seems familiar. If your team average is below ten, control may be possible. If the average is between ten and twenty, work on your infrastructure decisions a bit more, and be very, very vigilant. If the average exceeds twenty, abandon hope for your project, but consider learning how to draw and make your fortune.)

Using Predictive Metrics

Useful metrics require a baseline, and baselines for predictive metrics are best set using retrospective information and metrics from recent comparable projects. Measurement baselines are used to decide whether things are "normal" (meaning, in the case of predictive metrics, that your project is controllable) or out of range.

Use these measures to further review your plans. If the measures that you choose to evaluate for your project are supported by thorough planning and they are consistent with completed successful projects, you are fortunate. If your planning metrics are more consistent with troubled or failed projects, changes to your project are in order. If your assessments significantly exceed what seems normal, assess the consequences of the differences. For metrics such as staff size, even relatively small increases above the norm may spell trouble. If the largest team you have previously led had ten people, taking on a team of twelve will be a big challenge. There will be more interruptions, longer discussions, more opportunities for miscommunication, and many more two-way relationships that can get your project into trouble.

Consider options for managing the potential consequences when these measures are out of the ordinary. Rethink your infrastructure decisions, and tighten up the processes you plan to use. When complexity exceeds the norm, explore older, more established alternatives for some of your work, or enlist technical assistance in your planning to better understand what you need to do to succeed. You will be able to turn down the heat on some metrics through replanning, but not without trade-offs. Consult with your contributors to enlist their help in thinking of ways to reduce problematic indicators.

If the adjustments you can make are only partially successful in resolving exposures, capture information on the remaining metrics and the consequences you anticipate. Use this data to support data-driven, principled negotiations when you discuss your project plans with your sponsor.

▪ Set a Realistic Project Baseline

If there are no substantial differences between your plans and the initial project objective, meet with your sponsor briefly to discuss your plans, commit to a baseline based on them, and skip this section.

All too often, however, even your most thorough planning leaves a wide gap between what your best plans demonstrate is possible and your sponsor's original expectations. The trade-offs in planning are not unlike trying to compress a balloon full of water—when you press one side in to decrease your duration, you create corresponding outward bulges on the other sides, representing increasing costs or diminished scope. All the alternatives you devise seem to fall short in some significant respect, resulting in a no-win scenario. You have two obvious choices: Commit to the original objective, knowing that you have no credible plan to support it, or tell your sponsor that the project is impossible and you want nothing to do with it. Neither option has much appeal, so you will need to create a third choice.

In the fictional Star Trek universe, Starfleet Academy poses a no-win scenario to cadets aspiring to command. In the Kobayashi Maru simulation, a ship full of people is stranded in space protected by a treaty. Two options are available, one where the people are abandoned to die and another where they are rescued, initiating an interstellar war.

James T. Kirk, role model for intrepid project leaders everywhere, did not like the options. He did not believe in no-win situations. So he cheated. He found a clandestine way to reprogram the simulator allowing him to "win" by rescuing the stranded victims *and* chasing off the Klingons to avert war. Your job, similarly, is to find a third way, to secure a commitment to a possible project that is acceptable to your sponsor and stakeholders.

Preparing Your Information

The first steps are described earlier in this chapter: planning, exploring trade-offs, and developing two or more realistic project alternatives to the best team-developed plan that you can come up with. Gather your summary planning information together, along with supporting detail to back it up. Focus on the quality and clarity of your summary data; too much detailed planning information can be more confusing than helpful.

For each plan, use your project box analysis, worst-case estimates, and other risk and contingency information to build a plan that has an appropriate reserve in it for time or resources (or both), so that for each of your options you have a reasonable chance of success and a solid explanation for the margin. This reserve in your plan is not "padding" to make up for bad planning or laziness; rather, it establishes a range of credible possibilities based on your assessment of the real exposures and risks your project faces. Be prepared to explain it with data from risk assessments or worst-case estimates, and be ready to defend your request with your sponsor. Successfully integrating schedule or budget reserves into your plan will enhance your chances of success and make your project easier to control. Even if you are ultimately unsuccessful in retaining a margin in your plans for risk, it is prudent to propose it in discussions with your sponsor. If you must surrender some or even all of it in your negotiations, your initial proposal will provide a negotiating point from which you may still wind up with a baseline that is not demonstrably impossible. Your initial proposals need to describe projects that are desirable to you and your team, not projects that are barely achievable.

Use your plan data and predictive metrics to build a strong case that shows why the initial expectations cannot be met. Even if you have some authority in your organization, sponsors have more, so you will need to do more than simply request a change. Your best course is to assemble your facts and use principled negotiation. If you depend on your worries, opinions, and assertions that the project will be "difficult," nothing will change. Collect quantitative information about your project based on your plans, and remember that however essential numerical precision may be for other aspects of your project, most predictive measurements and other planning information involve a good deal of uncertainty. Plausible numbers are more than adequate as long as you can explain them; after all, the numbers your sponsor and stakeholders will use are probably even less precise, having been plucked out of thin air.

If your plan shows that your project cannot be completed until a later date, document why the necessary activities cannot be executed as fast as desired. If your project needs more staff, money, or other resources than are committed, list the specific requirements that aggregate to support your proposal. If scope changes appear necessary, be able to describe why, and estimate the value of the modified deliverable. In each case, outline the results of not making the changes. Translate the consequences into monetary terms whenever possible; this is most effective for getting the attention of your managers. In addition to financial consequences, also determine potential impact on customer or user satisfaction, organizational reputation, or other concerns important to your sponsor and stakeholders.

Even with a strong case, you may not always prevail. If you are not making progress with your arguments with your sponsor, it may be helpful to refocus the discussion on exploring opportunities. This is when you present alternative project plans that could be capable of delivering demonstrably better results than initially requested. New potential benefits are particularly useful in nudging a conversation out of an "I can't deliver this . . . /Sure you can, you're the *best* project leader we have" rut. Develop ideas that will be seen as win-win. Consider opportunities that will both please your sponsor and stakeholders and create more breathing room for your project. Offer to expand scope in exchange for more time or resources. Find ways to break the project into smaller, sequential projects capable of delivering results—smaller results to be sure—sooner. Any plausible proposal that whets the imagination of your sponsor is capable of getting the discussion unstuck and refocused on the more important goal of setting up a project that is both worthwhile *and* possible.

If you are nervous or concerned about presenting a counterproposal to your sponsor, set up time with one of your team members to practice. Rehearse what you plan to say by laying out your case for change for a colleague who will play the role of your sponsor. Afterward, ask for criticism and suggestions to tighten up your arguments and improve your approach.

Negotiating

Schedule a meeting with your sponsor to set the project baseline. Request enough time to discuss your project and other issues and alternative project plans.

Begin your meeting by clearly explaining the principal reasons why the original project goals are not achievable. Then, describe what you can accomplish using your executive summary of the plan option you consider to be the best, followed by other good options you have developed. Explain that your proposals are realistic, based on solid planning and risk analysis. Highlight the value and attractiveness of each alternative.

Respond calmly and logically to sponsor demands that all the objectives are nonnegotiable and must all be met. Refer to the project priorities agreed to in the project charter, and point out that your proposed changes lean most heavily on the project parameters that are most flexible. Be clear and persuasive, and stand your ground.

Your influence and ability to negotiate modifications to the objective will never be higher than when you set the project baseline; after you commit to a plan you will be held accountable with little ability to alter it. Knowledge is power; remember that by now you are the world's greatest authority on your project, and your sponsor's assertions are based primarily on bluster. Display your enthusiasm for the project and remind your sponsor of your experience, technical knowledge, track record, and credibility. They are why your sponsor requested you to lead the project in the first place.

Try to avoid emotional or political discussions. Your sponsor is probably better at these things than you are, and has more clout. Keep your project and planning data front and center in the discussions; facts and figures are the one area where you are at least on an equal footing with your management. Use principled negotiation techniques:

- Focus on interests, not positions. Emphasize the reasons the project is being undertaken and show the value of what you can accomplish.
- Work together to brainstorm and explore options for mutual gain.
- Use active listening and open, honest communication.
- Insist on objective, fact-based criteria for discussion, analysis, and decisions.
- Focus on problem solving, not arguing about the project.

Where detailed planning data is a confusing and ineffective place to start your discussions with your sponsor, it does have its use. Faced with demands for faster execution or less resource consumption, hold up your detailed Gantt chart or WBS. Ask your sponsor to pick the activities you should drop in order to meet the objective. Most managers back off very quickly when confronted with such a request, and this will allow you to refocus the discussion on finding and setting a realistic baseline. If your sponsor does start selecting activities to drop, be prepared to explain the costs and other consequences of not doing those parts of your project.

Sometimes a sponsor will shift the conversation to how talented and clever you are, as if to say that you, of all people, certainly can find some way to get the project done as originally envisioned. If this happens, thank your sponsor for the compliment but point out that there are factors that not even you can overcome, your impressive capabilities notwithstanding. Drag the discussion back to the project.

Or the conversation may head off in the other direction. You may hear threats that your sponsor will "find someone who *can* do this," or demands to "do it because I *say* to do it." Again, stand your ground and point out that you have taken considerable time to understand the project and are working with a very capable team. What you are proposing is the best option available, and neither another project leader nor naked demands will result in anything very different.

Focus on options where both you and your sponsor get a good result. Caving in to unrealistic demands may look like a win to your sponsor, but ultimately everyone loses. You and your team will be stuck trying for miracles on an out-of-control, demotivating project, and your project stakeholders and sponsor will never get what they need.

Be firm, diplomatic, and persistent. Use all your influencing skills to build consensus for project goals that are credible, and do your best to justify and retain an adequate reserve in your plans so that your baseline is not an impossible project.

If your discussion leads you to a mutual conclusion not to go forward with the project, and it might, express regret but be philosophical. There are always more good project ideas in organizations than there are people to staff them, and canceling a doomed project early is much better than doing it much later or watching it fail. Early termination saves money and frees resources to take on high-value, realistic projects. Find out what's next and move on.

Conclude your discussions with a review of what you have agreed to, and commit to a baseline for your project. If you got what you came for—a revised objective supported by a credible plan—thank your sponsor. If you should find yourself forced to accept a project objective that seems likely to fail, convey your reservations to your sponsor, with a summary of the consequences of the decision. Either way, gather your notes and prepare to finalize your project planning documents.

Setting the Baseline

Planning and negotiating are the hard part. Complete your planning process by establishing the project baseline for tracking based on your agreements with your sponsor:

- Summarize and communicate the committed project deadline, budget, and deliverables for your sponsor, stakeholders, leaders of related projects, and your team.
- Revise your schedule if necessary, and set the baseline in your project scheduling tool.
- Freeze project scope and document all deliverable specifications.
- Make final versions of project documents available to all who need them, online if possible.
- Archive baseline planning documents in your project management information system.

GETTING THE LEAD OUT

"Get the lead out" is sometimes a command by a sponsor to speed up a project, but when Richard Simonds was a project consultant at Hewlett-Packard, he worked with one team where it had a very different meaning.

Some years ago a corporate team was charged with developing plans to convert all of HP to lead-free product manufacturing. Their initial progress was modest, so they asked Richard to help them with their project planning. "The basic plan was sound, but it was incomplete—the project was much larger than anyone had realized," says Richard. "I spent time with them reviewing the infrastructure for the project using a checklist. Much of what was missing became visible through these discussions. They made many important decisions that resulted in a much more robust project plan." (The list of questions Richard used was similar to the one in Appendix A.)

The project team presented a revised plan to the executive staff responsible for the initiative, with gratifying results: The sponsor commented on how well-thought-out the plan was, the team had ready answers for every question the executives threw at them, and the project budget was nearly tripled to meet the requirements demonstrated in the plan.

The project was baselined appropriately and proceeded as planned. The team met its goals for conversion to lead-free circuit-board manufacturing at HP sites worldwide, on schedule.

Use Your Plan

Once a credible plan is in place and agreed to, project control shifts to executing and tracking, which are the topics of the next two chapters. Transitioning from planning to execution primarily involves:

- Starting to collect status on milestones and deliverables called for in the plans and issuing reports
- Reconfirming all staffing and resource commitments
- Initiating a process (similar to the one described in Chapter 2) for managing changes following scope freeze
- Ensuring that all tools and facilities to be used for communication and tracking are available and working
- Reviewing and initiating all project processes needed for execution with appropriate team members, such as for quality management, contract management, and life cycles
- Arranging ready access for all who need project documents, plans, and data
- Reviewing project infrastructure decisions for execution and control using a checklist similar to the one in Appendix A

Once you set the project baseline, maintaining control now depends on keeping your plans up to date and visible.

KEY IDEAS FOR PROJECT PLANNING

- Plan your project thoroughly with your team, and integrate their inputs, suggestions, and perspectives all through your planning documents.
- Use planning data to set a realistic project baseline, negotiating required changes to initial objectives with your sponsor and stakeholders.
- Begin execution of your project with a credible, understandable plan that is available to all the members of your team.

CHAPTER 7

Maintaining Control During Project Execution

PERSEVERANCE MATTERS. All projects encounter difficulty, and most will undergo substantial change. Execution contributes to control through a steadfast focus on what is happening, what has been accomplished, and what is next. Dogmatic status collection sets the expectation that the 9th, 99th, and the 999th activities on the project plan are all equally important—because they are. To suspend status collection to solve a problem is to lose control; you must find a way to recover while continuing to collect the project data that you need.

Diagnostic metrics are the basis for status collection. They provide the information you need to assess performance and progress, and their visibility ensures that any issues will be addressed. They are the basis for ongoing communications, and they will support your efforts to control your project. Control during execution also demands teamwork, which you must maintain through your informal communications and personal interactions with your contributors.

▪ Deploying Status-Based Metrics

Initiation tells everyone what your project is doing, and planning shows how you intend to get it done. With everything clearly defined, project execution ought to be straightforward. As project leader, you should be able to relax while the project progresses on autopilot, feet up, eating bonbons and patiently waiting for it to finish. Unfortunately, even the best planned projects rarely run smoothly. Your plans are a merely a prediction of an uncertain future, and to maintain control you must stay abreast of what is happening all through your project. As outlined in Chapter 4, project metrics are central to staying in control.

Diagnostic metrics in particular can show:

- Critical activity slippage
- Excess resource consumption
- Adverse resource consumption and timing trends
- Unintended consequences of scope changes
- Staff performance problems
- Process efficiency or effectiveness problems
- Chronic issues
- The need to modify project plans or execute contingency plans
- Early signs pointing to potential future problems
- The need to trigger risk response or other adaptive action
- When to reset the baseline for (or cancel) the project

Defining Diagnostic Metrics

There are many more possibilities for measurement than will make sense for any one project. You need to select a small number of metrics that are likely be to useful enough to justify the effort it takes to collect them. Even for metrics that you do not intend to collect weekly, there is an ongoing cost for obtaining the information, analyzing it, and then doing something with it. Unlike predictive and retrospective metrics that are analyzed a single time, either at the start or at the end of your project, diagnostic metrics are an ongoing responsibility. Select metrics carefully, choosing ones that will provide useful data that you will use to guide and control your project, without inappropriate cost (or high potential for needlessly annoying your team).

The following list is not intended to be exhaustive, but it does contain the most common types of status-based diagnostic metrics, grouped into several categories.

Timing and Schedule Metrics
- Actual activity durations
- Actual activity completion dates
- Late activities and key missed milestones
- Cumulative project slip
- Early activities
- Number of added activities

- Activity closure index (the ratio of activities closed in the project so far versus the number expected)

Resource and Financial Metrics
- Actual activity costs
- Actual activity effort consumption
- Individual productivity
- Cost overruns
- Unplanned overtime
- Staff turnover

Earned Value Management (EVM) Metrics
- Planned value (PV), the cumulative expected cost for activities planned for execution in the project baseline by any specific date; also called budgeted cost of work scheduled (BCWS)
- Actual cost (AC), the cumulative actual cost for activities executed through any specific date; also called actual cost of work performed (ACWP)
- Earned value (EV), the cumulative expected costs associated with all the activities actually executed by any specific date; also called budgeted cost of work performed (BCWP)
- Cost variance (CV), defined as EV minus AC
- Schedule variance (SV), defined as EV minus PV
- Additional calculated metrics derived using EV, PV, and AC

Project Scope Metrics
- Number of submitted scope changes
- Number and magnitude of approved scope changes
- Results of tests, inspections, reviews, and walkthroughs
- Quality control statistics

General Project Metrics
- Issues opened and issues closed
- Impact on other projects
- Impact by other projects (cost, time, scope, other)
- Communication metrics (such as volumes of e-mail and voicemail)
- Number of unanticipated project meetings
- Risks identified after setting the project baseline

Control and Earned Value Management (EVM)

EVM is designed to enhance project control, and used properly, it can yield impressive results. It entails more overhead than many other diagnostic metrics, though, so unless your organization makes use of EVM mandatory, your decision to adopt EVM, either openly with your team or for your own analysis, needs to be based on the specifics of your project. Some considerations and trade-offs to assist you in making a judgment, along with a lower-impact alternative to EVM, are explored in this section.

Of all the diagnostic metrics, few generate more debate than earned value. There is a small camp of ardent defenders who cannot imagine running a project without full-bore EVM in use constantly. There is another small camp of rabid detractors who find EVM a complete waste of time and energy, professing a belief that it is a high-cost effort that generates huge amounts of meaningless project data. The truth seems to lie somewhere between.

What Is EVM?

Earned value is based on a simple idea. Every planned project has a schedule and a projected budget. By the time it is finished, the project will have another plan and another budget—based on actual data from the completed project. You can use information from these two schedules and two budgets to generate compound time/cost metrics for your project. EVM works equally well using effort data instead of cost data, but the monetary version is more commonly defined and will be the primary basis for the following discussion. For an effort-based equivalent, use the total effort (in person-months or some other suitable units) associated with the baseline plan and the final tally of effort consumed by the project as substitutes for the two budgets.

The two most obvious metrics are conceptually straightforward. Planned value (PV) is a curve charting the planned costs from zero at the start to the budget at completion (BAC) at the end. Actual cost (AC) is a curve on the same time scale that also starts at zero but winds its way up the two-dimensional graph based on actual expenses to eventually represent the completed project's actual outlays. (PV, like BAC, is actually a predictive metric; you can calculate it for your whole project when you set the baseline. It is often treated as a diagnostic metric, though, because it is generally calculated with the other metrics for a given date.)

The problem with these two curves is that when they diverge, you can never know why just by looking at the graph. The difference could be due to timing problems with your activities, or it could be due to cost issues. It could even be (and usually is) a combination of the two. As long as the curves are based on entirely different schedule and budget data, there is no way to differentiate.

Enter earned value (EV) to save the day. EV splits the difference because it is based on the planned budget combined with the actual schedule. EV is calculated by adding up the estimated costs (as with PV) for project work completed (as with AC). Now you can identify cost issues by comparing EV and AC; any differences between them are entirely due to variance between expected and actual cost. You can also identify that you have a timing issue by comparing EV and PV, because here the only source of difference is schedule variance. When all three basic EVM metrics have the same value for a given date, your project is considered under control—on time and on budget. The three fundamental metrics for EVM are shown in Table 7-1. (No one seems to have devised any use for a potential fourth EVM metric, combining the baseline schedule with actual expenses.)

Should You Adopt EVM?

Two requirements of EVM make it controversial. The first requirement involves creating credible cost estimates for each activity, or at least apportioning 100 percent of the project budget, bit by bit, among all of the lowest-level activities defined in your work breakdown structure (WBS). The second requirement is that you must collect actual cost data for each activity from the beginning to the end of your project. These two requirements, particularly the second one, can represent quite a bit of additional management overhead for projects where use of this data is not already common practice or mandated. On the plus side, when using credible data, EVM will reveal irreversible project cost overruns well within the first quarter of the project's timeline.

EVM includes a somewhat bewildering alphabet soup of calculated variances, indices, and projections for the project that are calculated using the three base metrics, EV, PV, and AC. Because the basic data used for EVM is primarily financial, the cost variance (CV, or EV minus AC) information is the most straightforward to interpret. Because CV is the difference between the value you have "earned" (that is, the cost of the work expected by your plan) and what you have actually spent, it reveals the cumulative inaccuracy of your cost estimates for your project so far. If you begin with a thorough WBS and credible estimates, are working true to your plan, and are able to collect verifiable cost data for each activity, CV can be quite useful. This is, however, a rather long string of "ifs."

Also potentially useful is schedule variance (SV, or EV minus PV), which

TABLE 7-1. BASIS OF EVM METRICS.

		Budgets	
		Planned Expense	Actual Expense
Schedules	Planned Schedule	Planned Value (PV)	
	Actual Schedule	Earned Value (EV)	Actual Cost (AC)

is the difference between the estimated costs of the work you have *actually* completed minus estimated costs of the work you *expected* to have completed. A negative variance will indicate that you are not keeping pace with your plan, but since the calculated metric is in monetary units, it can be hard to interpret. ("My project appears to be $3,000 late.") Adverse schedule variance requires further digging and root-cause analysis to pinpoint what your schedule problems, if any, might be. Variance analysis of metrics directly related to critical activities on your schedule is a more accurate indicator of your schedule performance.

EVM also includes definitions for both schedule and cost indices. The cost performance index (CPI, or EV divided by AC) is the ratio of the cumulative estimated and actual costs for completed activities. The schedule performance index (SPI, or EV divided by PV) is also a ratio, but of the estimated cost of all the work completed and the estimated costs of the work you hoped to complete. As with negative values of CV and SV, values of these indices below one represent adverse variance. Additional EVM metrics continue to build on the three fundamental measures, EV, PV, and AC, using increasingly complicated formulas to calculate the estimated remaining project cost, total expected budget, expected completion date, and other project information.

The project in Figure 7-1 is about halfway to its deadline. It is significantly over budget, and it is probably somewhat behind schedule.

FIGURE 7-1. GRAPH OF EVM METRICS.

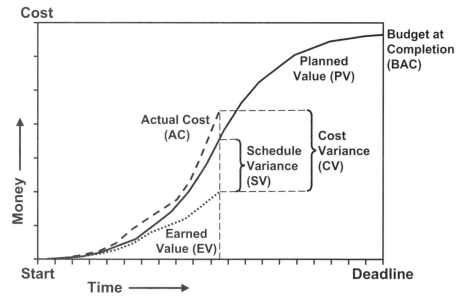

Ensuring Useful EVM Results

Partly as a result of its apparent complexity, EVM is relatively easy to game, especially early in a project. When these metrics are used in ways that are viewed as punitive, this can be a serious flaw. EVM can be gamed by establishing a schedule that front-loads a lot of relatively easy work and associates costs with it that are overly generous. Rather than enhancing control, this will result in projects that, after apparently running smoothly, suddenly develop huge difficulties sometime after their midpoint. EVM can also be gamed for some projects by including all expenses for the project in what you track, not just those associated with effort. The distortion created by including nonlabor costs in some projects can be huge, and by timing them to land near the end of the project they can effectively mask a lot of problems. (This is one reason why EVM analysis based on effort rather than money can provide more useful control information. It also gives you a good reason to collect actual effort data that might otherwise be lost to support future project estimating.) Yet another way to bias the metrics is to work on things out of sequence. Starting activities early grants either 50 percent or prorated credit for EV, so if you report initiating activities that are not yet scheduled, you can distort the EVM variances and indices in your favor. All these sources of bias are under your control as the project leader, and of course you would never consider them; it would be wrong.

Your team can also undermine the usefulness of EVM by misreporting costs (or effort) for activities or reinterpreting what "done" means. There are ways for you to verify the data, of course, but with geographically distributed teams especially, it may not be easy.

The best defense against gaming with all metrics is to avoid using them to criticize or punish people. For EVM, this means that when adverse results surface, everybody involved, including sponsors, managers, and stakeholders, focuses on resolution, not affixing blame. If the cost variance is negative, the discussion should be about whether the project needs additional resources or staff. If EVM indicates schedule variance that is an actual problem (adverse variance can be due to slippage of noncritical activities that do not threaten the project objective), discuss adjusting the project's deadline. If the normal response to negative variance is problem solving, good data will be reported. When the more typical response is abuse, EVM will operate with "garbage in, garbage out."

Gaming can also be minimized by asking people not to do it, and confronting data credibility problems whenever you suspect them. Discussing the metrics you plan to use and getting buy-in from your team is crucial in avoiding problems with data quality.

An Alternative to EVM

EVM is fairly elaborate, will consume a good deal of your time, and can be confusing to implement. There is a way to enhance your control that is similar to EVM with a good deal less overhead.

If you implement EVM using the simplifying assumptions that all activities have the same cost and they are spread out linearly across your timeline, you will surrender a good deal of precision, especially initially. As more and more of your project completes, however, even fully implemented EVM is increasingly about averages and general trends. This simplified approach is based on the "activity closure index" listed with schedule metrics. The basic idea for the index is that halfway through your project you should have half of your activities finished. At any point, you can assess whether the fraction of the work you have completed is above, at, or below the fraction of the timeline you have consumed. This ratio approximates EVM's schedule performance index (SPI), the ratio of EV to PV. The accuracy of the activity closure index as an indicator of your project's performance will improve as your project completes more and more work, and it provides a very good prediction of potential schedule overrun following the first third of your planned project duration. Determining whether the overrun is primarily due to insufficient resources or execution problems will require some additional analysis, but this easily calculated index will cue you to investigate.

Selecting and Setting Baselines for Diagnostic Metrics

Some of the metrics that you will collect for your project will be defined either by standard practices of your organization or by decisions that you made with your team in reviewing a list of infrastructure questions (see Appendix A). You may decide to add other measures, based on discussions with your team, or you may also decide to measure some things about your project on your own, to better understand how it is proceeding.

Metrics that will be collected and reported publicly will affect behavior. Consider the impact that the measures you intend to use could have on your project, as discussed in Chapter 4. If a metric might lead to potential adverse behavior, explore balancing it with another measure to provide tension or think about possible alternatives.

You also need to establish a baseline for each diagnostic metric you plan to use. Without a baseline, there is a "compared to what?" problem that makes interpretation and use of the data difficult.

Typically with diagnostic metrics, baselines are set using data from the first several collection cycles. A range based on empirical data is useful in establishing what is "normal" for the process being measured, both in terms of magnitude and variation. Use this information to define the values that are within an expected range and the limits above and below which you need to act to bring things back under control. Resist making decisions and changes before determining the baseline; you will not be able to tell what, if anything, you have accomplished without a pretty good understanding of what you started with. Individual productivity is an example of a diagnostic metric that requires baseline data. If you have a severely time-constrained project and your plans call for installing new equipment or modifying a process to improve how quickly you will be able to get things done, begin by measuring the status quo. Measuring it again following the change will let you verify the results, to see whether your expected estimates were credible.

Not all diagnostic project metrics have baselines derived from data collection, at least not directly. Much of what you will collect will be compared with information from the project baseline that you set with your sponsor. If the project baseline is set using bottom-up analysis that is well grounded in historical experience, using the project baseline for your variance analysis is perfectly valid. If your project baseline is rooted more in wildly aggressive or optimistic fantasy rather than reality, variance analysis will tell you more about what your sponsor does not understand than it will tell you about how you are doing. In EVM, planned value (PV) is the baseline for both earned value (EV) and actual cost (AC). If it is credible, the variances and indices will tell you how you are performing against reasonable norms. If PV is based on top-down demands for budget and schedule, your analysis will tell you how much trouble you are getting into, but not very much about how well you are managing your project. In general, when the baseline for a diagnostic metric is a prediction that is not supported by any data (such as a guess, a hope, or a demand), interpretation will be difficult.

Calculated metrics have baselines derived from the baselines of the measures used to calculate them. Most variance metrics have a baseline of zero and the index metrics have a baseline of one, including those associated with EVM.

THE FIRST ONE IS JUST FOR PRACTICE, BUT TAKE CAREFUL NOTES

The baselines for innovation projects are often suspect, but they provide an opportunity to measure and learn. Arun Swamy of Hewlett-Packard in Bangalore had responsibility in 2000 for implementing a complex Web portal with several colleagues. The business, functional, and technical requirements, along with a high-level timeline, had been completed by a consulting firm, but the team still needed to coordinate the efforts of a number of external parties based in Europe and the United States to complete the analysis, create the application architecture, develop detailed project plans, and write and test the software. Because this project was unprecedented, there were many reservations about the expected one-year project baseline. Due to these concerns, they selected a number of metrics to collect before beginning the work.

"As anticipated, not everything went smoothly," Arun recalls. "There were many escalations of unmet dependencies stemming from the multi-vendor environment. Disagreements on design with the original consultants were also common. After a lot of hard work, the portal successfully went live, though it was three months later than planned." The post-project retrospective focused on data collected during the project, which led to a number of important recommendations for process improvement, including:

- Assess deliverable size accurately (in terms of screens and program logic).
- Normalize all productivity data for the project's initial baseline using the established organizational baseline.
- Predict defects to be caught using size, and then determine the number of test cases needed to catch the defects.
- Track defect trends throughout the project phases to ensure product quality.

Once the first release of the portal was accomplished, Arun's team continued to track and use data during ongoing enhancements. They collected data on schedule performance, defect management, effort variance, and productivity over the next five releases. "The key for the business was going live as planned," says Arun, "which was achieved using the metrics to improve our schedule performance." In addition, the metrics helped them execute more efficiently, with a dramatic reduction in effort variance, significantly improved productivity, and improved defect management. Overall confidence in the team grew to the point where the sponsors' high confidence in the India team eliminated all need for outside consultants—the Bangalore team now had sole responsibility for the portal.

"It's clear that the discipline the team showed in collecting metrics was largely responsible for the process improvements and consistent results we achieved," concludes Arun. "And that wasn't the only benefit. Metrics also let us demonstrate and communicate significant business benefits that pleased our customer."

▪ Status Collection

One of the most important and visible jobs of a project leader is communicating project status. This depends on a repeating cycle of information collection, analysis, response planning, and outbound reporting. This tracking cycle repeats throughout your project, typically weekly. The focus of this chapter is on surveillance and analysis, which will keep you informed. In Chapter 8, on tracking and monitoring, the focus shifts to the remainder of the cycle, response and reporting.

Status collection begins the cycle and involves implementing your diagnostic measures, collecting inputs, verifying the data, and using project variance information.

Implementing Your Diagnostic Measures

Most of the predictive metrics discussed in Chapter 6 are based on planning, which is primarily your responsibility. You can develop predictive measures you feel are appropriate and you directly control many of the inputs. Diagnostic metrics related to project status are another story, both because using them requires ongoing work and because most of the data must come from others.

You should collect basic schedule and resource metrics routinely every tracking cycle, including the data for earned value analysis, if you plan to use it. Other metrics such as those associated with scope may be collected only as needed. For a typical project, collect information concerning:

- Activities started, delayed, or completed, with actual start and finish dates
- Milestones completed or missed
- Effort and/or cost for completed activities
- Adjusted duration and effort estimates for problem activities
- Deliverable tests
- Data related to current issues and risks

If you are a project leader without a great deal of authority, you will need to work to obtain meaningful commitments from your team to provide the information that you need. To do this, you will need to discuss with each individual on your team how the information will be used and what the benefits are. You may need to employ influencing skills to get buy-in, relying on things that you can provide as a project leader in exchange for the information that you need.

Frequency is important. Determine how often you need each input to be effective. Work with the members of your team to establish when you will collect each measure that you define for your project. (Determining the frequency for data collection is included in the infrastructure checklist in Appendix A, along with other parameters of your project tracking cycle.)

Most project leaders collect routine project status weekly, as this is a good compromise between the currency of the data and the overhead required to assemble it. For adequate control, it is rarely necessary to collect data more than once a week unless you are in crisis mode working to solve a particularly urgent problem. Getting status less often can cause serious control problems, however. A lot can happen in two weeks. Weekly collection also allows you to establish a specific day and time that people can easily remember and become accustomed to. Your project staff members will have many other things to worry about during the project, and they will respond best to inquiries that they expect and understand. Work with your team to set up a process and frequency that everyone accepts.

How you collect the data also matters. Devise ways to simplify the process; the easier you make it for people to respond to your status requests, the more likely it will be that you will promptly get back what you need. Providing each person with a list or table of current activities that they are responsible for and including any information from the prior cycle is one way to make it simple. If you list activities that each person owns that are scheduled to begin in the next two weeks, you can also use your status requests to remind people of upcoming commitments. Updating a few cells in a spreadsheet or table that are well identified is quick and easy, and most people will supply the information as requested.

Project leaders successfully collect status using many methods. Whatever mechanism you select, it is good practice to do it the same way throughout your project. A very common technique is to use e-mail. E-mail provides a simple, unambiguous way to collect status, and it leaves an audit trail for your records. It works well even for distant team members, and people can send it to you at the same time that they are responding to other communications, with no need to do something unusual on their part. If it is common practice in your organization and you are using a Web- or server-based project tracking tool, it is also possible to collect much of your status information by having your team members update their progress directly in the database of your scheduling tool. For cross-functional teams, though, resistance to learning a specific system and dedicating the time for weekly updates may pose insurmountable barriers. Direct online data collection also may create data integrity issues with your tracking; when more than one person enters data into a scheduling tool, inconsistencies are difficult to avoid. Other status collection methods include conversations, meetings, and online or printed forms. Any method that works for you and your team should provide what you need for project control.

You may find it necessary in some cases to use alternative methods for gleaning current status that shift more of the burden onto you. If you are unable to get a credible commitment from a team member to submit regular status, explore other options for finding out what is happening. Some of your team members may be part of other organizations or teams that routinely collect much of the data that you need, and you can collect your status by gaining access to their reports to extract what you need. If it is easier for some members of your team to establish a document containing their project work that they will periodically update on a server or knowledge management system, encourage them to align it with your plans and use the information on it to keep your overall status up-to-date. Consider any option that will maximize the timeliness and quality of your status information.

Collecting Inputs

Once you have determined what measures will be useful for project control and how you will collect data for them, you need to routinely gather the information. Be consistent and timely in every cycle. Follow the frequency and schedule you and your team have set as dependably as you can. If your team suspects that you are not taking status collection seriously, they will begin to ignore your requests and reminders.

Provide adequate time for people to reply to your status inquiries or to update their online status documents, but establish deadlines for the status requests and follow up promptly when people fail to provide the information. Be particularly vigilant when collecting status relating to past issues or problems that may have impact on particularly urgent current work. Managing problems requires increased intensity in status collection; it should never be a rationalization for skipping a cycle. For complex projects, out of sight is nearly always out of mind. This situation leads to small control problems cascading into much larger control problems.

One of the most difficult project situations, especially for new project leaders, is dealing with bad news. When someone reports a delay, a cost overrun, or other problems, experienced project leaders clench their teeth and say, "Thank you for the information. I appreciate you letting me know promptly." Human nature in this situation is to find a chair to break over your team member's head (or worse), but the consequences of "shooting the messenger" who delivers bad news will destroy your project. In a heartbeat, all the effort you have put into building trust and a good working relationship will evaporate. Worse, the next time you ask for status, the reply will be, "Um, fine. Everything is going just fine. (Please don't pick up the chair. . . .)" Reacting to bad news with abuse or punishment, as with misusing any metrics, will shut down honest reporting and leave you without credible project information. To control a project, you need to know what is happening, so smiling and acting grateful for bad news is something all effective project leaders learn to do.

Particularly for extended members of your team, thank people for sending you status. Acknowledge the time and effort that it takes, at least once in a while. Ensure that people know that you care about the information you receive and that they know how you are using it to manage the project. If you are perceived as apathetic or just collecting data "because you can," your contributors will stop providing it or will start sending you slapped-together, inaccurate status.

Work as hard as required to collect status inputs from distant team members and from outside contractors. If any team member fails to provide status on time, send additional requests and reminders. If all of these are ignored, call the person on the telephone to collect the status verbally. Call them when they are at work (regardless of what time it is where you are). If the problem persists, discuss the status reporting commitment your team member made and work to resolve the problem by renewing or adjusting it. Remind any delinquent contributors that the work they are responsible for will show up in your project status report as behind or incomplete if you do not have their input; accurate reporting is your responsibility, even when it reflects badly on individuals. If even this fails to resolve the problem for some unresponsive members of your team, enlist the assistance of the individual's manager or your project sponsor. Failure to report status is a leading indicator of more significant performance problems (see Chapter 8), and the earlier you recognize and deal with them the easier it will be to keep your project under control.

Verifying and Analyzing Project Variance

If any of the status information seems inconsistent with other inputs or past data, too good to be true, or otherwise unreliable, discuss it with the person who supplied the information. Validate the reliability of the information by asking open questions that require a detailed explanation of what the situation is.

Take all the status data you have collected in each cycle and compare it with your project baseline. Identify all the differences you find. Most variances on projects tend to be negative, but note any positive variances as well. Even small variances may signal potential opportunities or major future problems. Problems are easiest to deal with while they are small.

These variances are diagnostic project metrics—numbers and facts—the hard data about your project. The variances you find allow you to differentiate the parts of your project that are under control from the portions that are causing (or will cause) problems. The hard data for your project reveals the existence of problems, but it may not tell you much about where those problems stem from or help you find a way to resolve them. Informal communication provides a second kind of status—soft data. Stories, rumors, concerns, and other nonempirical information about your project and your team will help you discover the root causes behind the status you collect, as well as alert you to potential future project trouble.

Before spending much effort working to analyze, resolve, or report on your status, investigate each variance that you do not already understand. Determine if an unexpected status is a single event or if it (or something similar) is likely to recur. Strive to uncover the reasons for productivity and execution problems. If other project work is interfering with your project, verify the relative priorities. Find out why delays are happening and how long they are likely to persist. Pay attention to impending changes outside your project that could impact your work, such as building construction, system upgrades, network maintenance, or other services and facilities that you depend upon.

In statistics, two types of errors are identified. Type-I errors are "false negative." Investigating the underlying soft data for reported status that seems questionable may reveal adverse project variances that are in fact on track. Type-II errors are "false positive," and they are more common and more difficult to root out. Project status reporting, especially at a distance or when the project leader has not developed much of a relationship with the team members, is potentially chock-full of this type of error. Many contributors find it much easier to report what they are expected to report, even when there are problems. At a minimum, they will avoid the potential annoyance of a long conversation with you discussing what comes next. Other motivations for unreliable reporting include criticism or punishment. Sometimes incorrect status results from inappropriate optimism: "The first half of this assignment took two weeks to complete, but I think I can finish it in a day or so." Whether you characterize this response as gaming the metrics, inaccurate assessment, or just plain dishonesty, you will need to screen status inputs with a particularly skeptical eye whenever you are dealing with people with whom you have not established sufficient trust. In such cases, follow up on status reports to get some verifiable support, such as documentation, test data, or other tangible evidence of progress. Participating in reviews, tests, demonstrations, and other meetings can also give you better insight into the progress of work that you can't monitor directly. Project control requires timely, accurate information.

Having validated your status data, analyze your schedule variances. For delayed activities that are critical, determine the impact on your project schedule and on important intermediate milestones. For all continuing activities that are expected to finish late, determine the cause. Projects are filled with similar activities, so a current delay even for a noncritical activity may be a result of something that could impact your project significantly in the future. Also explore any positive variances, probing for possible replanning opportunities that could enhance your flexibility and chances for success.

Next, analyze any resource variances. Identify reasons for all overruns and consider the possible impact of work scheduled later in your project. All resource overconsumption for the project is cumulative, so every little bit hurts. If you are using earned value analysis to track your project, calculate the values for earned value, planned value, and actual cost, including appropriate portions of work in progress and scheduled to be in progress. Compare any adverse variances that are associated with EVM with other project indicators and determine the cause of any differences that you discover. Then determine if any positive resource variances indicate opportunities to complete future work at lower cost or effort than estimated.

Note all other significant variances, in areas such as individual productivity, project changes, or metrics derived from elements of your project scope.

Periodically, take a longer view with your analysis of status data. About once a month, at life-cycle phase exits or during project reviews, examine the trends in your data. If schedule or resource consumption problems are growing and you do not see a realistic way to reverse the trend, you may need to propose resetting the project baseline with your sponsor. Detecting the need to make adjustments to the project objective early makes it much easier to generate support for change proposals; conversely, waiting until the latter portion of your project to raise an alarm will result in little sympathy, excessive criticism (or worse) directed at you, and probable cancellation of your project.

Saving and Using Project Variance Information

The most immediate uses of project status analysis are making adjustments to control your project and generating project reports (which are topics in Chapter 8 on tracking and monitoring). Diagnostic project metrics can also be useful for assessing and improving your processes, motivating your team, and providing real-time information about your project for meetings, presentations, and discussions.

Status metrics are also part of your project management information system (PMIS), as discussed in Chapter 2. Store the project metrics where you and your team can access them, and use them to support your project reviews, presentations, and post-project lessons learned.

MIRACLES HAPPENED ON TUESDAYS

Status collection can be a very powerful motivator. Nancy McDonald, most recently a senior executive with Accenture, was responsible at one point for installing all of the voice and data networking for a new data center project. This data center was to be one of the largest ever built at the time, and about thirty different technology companies were involved in the massive project, including major computer systems vendors, telecommunications equipment manufacturers, and a number of networking companies.

Nancy was responsible for the hundreds of circuits within the data center, point-to-point modem connections to local and more distant sites, and a bewildering array of other requirements. She engaged a large group of suppliers and delegated the necessary implementation to them. "Due to the enormous size, the project was exceedingly complex," she says. "To be successful the project would require close cooperation between companies that were direct competitors. Each company had responsibility for installing its own equipment and services, and each had an incentive to do a good job in order to secure additional work as the already-huge data center grew."

The executive sponsor of the data center project designated the first Wednesday of the month for all thirty suppliers to jointly report on their progress and to raise any issues. Many of the suppliers initially objected to meeting in a combined session with competitors, but ultimately they all agreed to participate. With so many participants, no meeting room was sufficiently large, so the monthly meetings were held in the still-empty data center itself. Nancy continues:

> "At the first status meeting, using folding chairs on the data center's newly installed raised floor, the largest computer vendor highlighted an issue: Dirt under the raised floor was hampering their installation and might affect reliability. In response, a team immediately sprang into action, quickly found a contractor with a very large vacuum cleaner, and the dirt was gone. The executive sponsor of the corporation's largest-ever IT project was not about to let dust bunnies become a showstopper. The senior representative who had raised the issue was asked to inspect under the floor to verify it was clean."

It became obvious to all the suppliers that raising an issue at these status meetings would result in immediate action, but these actions might be embarrassing or painful. "On Mondays, two days before the Wednesday meetings, all the suppliers would call me to review their status," Nancy says. "When they asked me to assist with problems, I advised them to raise the issues at the Wednesday status meeting."

Soon, miracles began to happen on Tuesdays. Problems that were impossible to resolve on Monday were consistently being fixed by Wednesday. Because they had already discussed the issue with Nancy, the suppliers couldn't just sweep issues under the rug (or even the raised floor) and hope that no one would notice. They had to actually resolve the issue, or at least have a credible plan of attack. The initially unwieldy project meetings became an extremely effective tactic for managing the overall project.

Nancy has come to realize, after many projects, that the right plans, processes, and project controls are important, but they're not enough:

> "Project success always depends on the people involved. And while having the right skills is necessary, they aren't sufficient, either. For projects, you must understand the group dynamics. Multisupplier and cross-functional projects can easily deteriorate into finger-pointing and the blame game. To nip this in the bud, you have to work to establish an environment where everyone is motivated to accomplish the overall goal. This can be a consequence of everyone buying into an overarching vision, or it may simply be a desire to avoid embarrassment in front of others."

Whatever the motivation, for a project to succeed, everyone must push each other to excel—and make miracles happen.

▪ Informal Communication

Status collection and metrics concern facts and figures. Control of your project depends on more than this hard data, however. You need to know the stories behind the data, and the more you know, the better you will be able to control your project. Communication is one of the most, possibly *the* most, important jobs for any project leader. This section focuses on informal communication and "soft" project status. (Project reporting, meetings and more formal communication are addressed in Chapter 8 on project tracking.)

For project leaders who don't have a great deal of actual authority, informal communication can be more critical to project control than formal communication. Whereas formal communication provides information and context, informal communication—conversations, social exchanges, even nonproject interactions—forms the basis for the trust, teamwork, and durable relationships that are essential for efficient project execution and prompt resolution of difficulties.

For project teams composed of strangers, any problem can easily become a crisis. People who don't know each other tend to be suspicious of one another, so problems are assumed to be someone's fault, and much energy can be poured into accusations and finger-pointing. Project teams that know and like each other are much more likely to approach problems simply as problems and put their effort into resolution, not struggling to affix blame. In addition, teams with good working relationships tend to watch out for each other, and frequently can detect and avoid potential problems before they occur. Many risks and problems initially surface through informal communication, long before they are visible through formal status collection.

Management by Wandering Around

The idea of management by wandering around, or MBWA, originated during the early days of Hewlett-Packard. In David Packard's book *The HP Way,* he traces the practice back to his experience as a young manager with General Electric. He found that working with people directly and getting to know them was essential to resolving difficult problems with manufacturing on the factory floor. Identifying and correcting inadequate, incomplete, and sometimes incorrect documentation required a level of interaction and trust that was impossible except through one-on-one discussion and personal involvement. The main agenda of MBWA is that it has no agenda. It is not about collecting status or solving a particular problem. It is about interacting with people and informally talking to strengthen interpersonal connections. Packard stresses the need for "frequent, friendly, unfocused, and unscheduled" interactions to seek out people's thoughts and listen to their opinions. He believed that anyone could do it; they just had to make the time for it and do it willingly.

MBWA can be done remotely, using the telephone, but it is much more effective face-to-face. The same principles apply for remote MBWA as for in-person interactions; it is about building a long-lasting relationship based on trust, openness, and mutual respect. Some people begin or extend telephone calls to inquire generally about the other person and to catch up. Others prefer to call periodically "just to talk," but this can be difficult for busy people, particularly with global teams. MBWA can also rely on technology, all the way from exchanging casual notes, pictures, and postcards to using full-motion videoconferencing. Even with all the technology available these days, relationships between people who are colocated and interact directly are deeper, more meaningful, and more durable, so it is important to take full advantage of any time available during trips or meetings where you are together, even if only for a short time.

These principles will help you to use MBWA effectively:

- Be unpredictable and spontaneous. If being inconsistent isn't natural for you, leave yourself reminders if necessary.
- Ask general, open questions, not "yes or no" questions. (Examples: What do you like best about your work? What have you done recently that you are most pleased with? Are there any changes that you would like to see? How is your family/pet/hobby/club?)

- Listen attentively. Let the discussion go wherever it goes and allow the other person to do most of the talking.
- Avoid confrontation or arguments. Foster an open, trusting environment.
- Focus on matters that have nothing to do with your company, organization, or project. Get to know your team members personally.
- Wander even if you are shy. Practice and persistence will make it easier over time.
- Seek out all of your team members equally, not just the people who are easiest to find or with whom you are already friends.
- Wander without any specific objectives, armed only with a few general questions to use if necessary.
- Do it often. MBWA is not a waste of time.

Joe Podolsky, an experienced manager at HP, says: "In the end, we each instinctively know that our most precious asset is our time. Investing that asset in face-to-face contact will always be appreciated as our most sincere and visible sign of caring."

Conversations

Conversation is a central part of management by wandering around and of informal communication in general. It is easy to overdo conversation; if you initiate conversations too frequently, it will contribute to a loss of productivity. You will also undermine your control if you interrupt contributors doing urgent work, so keep your conversations and stories brief. In general, though, the converse is not true. Project leaders who fail to suspend what they are doing when team members need to talk do so at their own peril. Responding promptly when team members have something they need to discuss is one of your primary responsibilities, and it's an important source of your influence within the project.

As with all communication, conversations are most effective when they are face-to-face. Studies vary on the precise breakdown, but there is general consensus that about half of the meaning we convey in conversation is nonverbal—body language, facial expressions, posture, and so forth. Roughly another third of meaning is carried in intonation, leaving a small minority of meaning (less than 10 percent, by some accounts) left for the basic words to convey. Because formal communication is almost entirely written, it is usually less influential and meaningful than person-to-person informal communication. Conversing regularly and effectively is key to project success, so it is essential that you exploit every opportunity available to meet and converse face-to-face with distant team members. You will have to exert additional effort to overcome the barriers and disadvantages that your project faces when distance makes one-on-one interaction infrequent or impossible.

Conversing well is a critical skill, particularly for project leaders who have little formal authority. In effective conversations:

- Each person's ideas are heard in the context of a two-way dialogue.
- Questions arise naturally out of the discussion and active listening. Questions intended to lead to predetermined answers are avoided.
- All parties show genuine interest in what each speaker is saying, and wait until thoughts are complete without interrupting.
- Each person speaks a roughly equal portion of the time.

The environment for effective conversation also matters, and it includes location, timing, and other factors. Conversations that take place in the office or "turf" of one person, especially when that person has more organizational power, can be intimidating and may limit what people are willing to say. The best environment for conversation is neutral, not belonging to anyone in the conversation. The setting for effective conversation needs to be comfortable and allow people to face each other on the same level. If some participants are sitting, all should be seated, facing one another in the same type of furniture. Overly formal settings can constrain conversations, so choose a casual environment that will allow open, friendly discussions.

On the telephone, timing is important. Conversation is best when the participants are awake, alert, and not distracted. Be sensitive to time-zone issues when setting up telephone meetings and teleconferences and avoid conflicts with mealtimes, any other commitments you are aware of, and the middle of the night. It is unfortunate but true that you will have more influence and get better feedback and other information if you call others to talk with them during their business day, even if it falls at an awkward or inconvenient time for you. (Project leaders do tend to lose sleep to 5:30 A.M. and 11:00 P.M. meetings, at least occasionally.)

It is easy to see how conversations, or any information delivered through speaking, can lead to misunderstandings. Referring to Figure 7-2, each original idea that you convey begins as a thought inside your head and must be translated into a message in spoken language. The words you chose can be many or few, and regardless of how you chose to construct your message, it always seems perfectly clear and complete, as far as you are concerned. The spoken message is sent out into the no man's land between you and the person you are speaking with, and in addition to the words you have chosen, it also includes your choices of nonverbal communication (such as emphasis and body language), some of which you aren't even be aware of. Listeners who receive the

FIGURE 7-2. COMMUNICATION OF IDEAS.

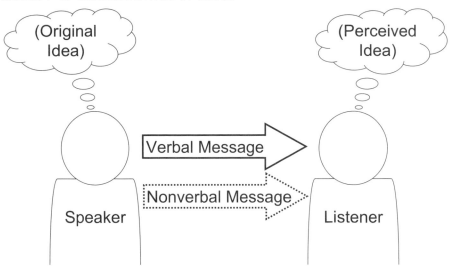

message repeat the process in reverse, reassembling the idea using the verbal and nonverbal bits that they happen to be paying attention to.

The original idea and the message that you create are both a product of your own unique perspective, so there may be portions of it that are completely opaque to your listener. The perceived message is a product of the listener's perspective. In addition, it may also be subject to selective editing; listeners tend to hear what they want to hear. (People who live together for a long time are well aware of this phenomenon. Their perspectives generally converge through shared experiences and mutual regard, but the selective editing of spoken messages seems to increase over time.) The chances are low that there will be a perfect match between the original idea that the speaker had and the idea that the listener perceives.

You can improve the odds by carefully considering what you say and how you say it. Avoiding jargon, idioms, acronyms, and other potentially confusing terminology will help. Speaking slowly and clearly, particularly when on the telephone or speaking to people who are not native speakers of the language being used, is also a good practice.

Active listening is also a valuable technique for detecting and correcting misunderstandings. Active listening requires listeners to paraphrase the idea in their own words, reversing the communications process. If there are differences between what the speaker had in mind and what the listener conveys using different words, there is a good chance that it can be detected and corrected. Use active listening to ensure what you think you are hearing from team members is in fact what they mean. When you are conveying important, complicated ideas through conversation, ask the people you are speaking with to express back to you what they heard you say; do not simply ask, "Is that clear?" For critical project information that you communicate verbally, it is also a good idea to follow up in writing to reinforce your message.

Conversations are carried on differently around the world. In North America and northern Europe, conversational etiquette is for speakers to take turns, speaking when the other person finishes. In Latin America and southern Europe, conversational patterns are similar, but there is a tendency for speakers to overlap, with transitional periods when both people are speaking. In Asia there is often a respectful pause after one person speaks before the next person begins to talk. When conversing with people from the same cultural background, this all works fine, most of the time. But when people with different conversational patterns converse, it can result in frustration or, worse, being perceived as rude. The safest course of action for project leaders is to do their best to fall into the pattern of the other person, with some bias in favor of the Asian model. Speaking too soon after another person completes a thought can be a result of not really listening. Some "conversations" are little more than two monologues—each being delivered in spurts, interrupted by the other—with neither person paying much attention to what the other is saying. Project leaders need to listen well, which will be appreciated by others and help build a relationship of trust and respect.

Notes and E-Mail

Your informal written communications are also important for building influence on your project. Even though you will typically create and send notes and e-mails quickly, you need to take enough care with each of them to avoid problems. Few things will erode your influence faster than creating confusion. Don't force the recipients of your notes to guess what you are trying to say; don't send incomplete information that will require them to seek clarification.

Your influence improves when you communicate well, so reread all of your notes before you send them (or scribble and leave them stuck to someone's computer screen), checking them for possible misunderstandings, poor grammar, or anything that could be read differently than you intend. Read each of your notes from the perspective of the recipient, keeping your eyes open for questions that could imply unintended criticism or statements that could be wrongly interpreted as complaints. Take full advantage of spell-check software, but don't put all your trust in it. One of the most common errors in hastily written notes is omitting the word "no" or "not"—with potentially catastrophic results. Carefully read what you write to make sure it actually says what you mean it to say.

Written communication is flat; there are no good ways to incorporate the equivalent of nonverbal spoken language. You can use typographical conventions such as all capitals, bold, or italics to indicate emphasis, but there is no guarantee that the reader will pick up the emphasis you intended. "Emoticons" such as the sideways smiley face :-) are also a possibility, but again the exact meaning may not always be clear to the reader, and some people think they're silly. Always follow up any written news that is complex or might have negative connotations with a conversation to ensure that your message is not misinterpreted. Better yet, have the conversation first and then follow up with a written confirmation.

Tailor your written communications, particularly notes that you send to only one recipient, by including a personal sentence or two at the start or the end. Make your informal written communication part of your "management by wandering around" strategy, building your relationships with those you work with and reinforcing personal connections. Even though it is more effort, for important messages and requests, consider sending individual notes that include a personalized comment or two instead of a single standardized e-mail message to a long distribution list. This tactic makes it much more likely that your message will be read.

Informal communication on projects invariably includes a lot of "ad hoc" e-mail exchanges that may volley back and forth for quite a few cycles in a small group. If the ongoing discussion at some point requires new participants, you will do everyone a favor by untangling the story by providing a short, high-level summary of the exchanges to date in the note you forward to anyone new. Also, when appropriate, you should go through the pages and pages of attached e-mails and delete any notes that are no longer relevant. This will make it easier for new participants to catch up quickly while also ensuring that important points are not buried a dozen pages deep in endless replies.

Finally, be careful to scan all e-mail notes you create and eliminate, or at least tone down, anything that you would prefer not to have widely circulated. Double-check the distribution list before you "reply to all" so that you know who will read your reply. When you do for some reason need to communicate sensitive or private information by e-mail, make it as clear as possible to all recipients that the information is for their use only and not to be shared. If you are upset by an e-mail or other communication you receive, never reply immediately. When you are ready to reply, write what you wish to say and file it away for at least an hour, better yet a day, and go do something else. When you return to the note, decide whether what you have written is more likely to make things better or make them worse. Edit the note as needed to ensure that what you are writing will not damage your project, your relationship with any of your stakeholders or team members, or your overall influence. Remaining calm and rational (or even appearing to be calm and rational) when everyone else is stressed and begins to panic will invariably increase your control of your project. E-mails can live forever and they are very easy to forward, so be mindful of what you write and send.

A BLINDING FLASH OF "INSIGHT"

Informal communications are often what separate a frustrated project leader with a failing project from a successful one. Peter Vogel-Dittrich, a manager and consultant with Hewlett-Packard in Germany, tells of a large cross-functional project called "Insight" that he was part of some years ago to revamp a program for new first-level managers worldwide. The team was global, with assignments for people in India, Europe, the United States, and other countries. He remembers, "In the three months leading up to the pilot for the program, rigorous weekly telephone meetings were used to discuss progress and deliverables, and the program manager based in the United States kept things on track, by being perceived as tough."

During the pilot in Spain, many of the members of the virtual team met face-to-face for the first time. In the preceding months, most of the interactions among the team had been somewhat stiff and formal, and the impression many had formed of the program leader was that she was "all business." In person, she and everyone else relaxed, and as issues arose during the pilot they were quickly resolved. There was a great deal of flexibility and cooperation. Cultural issues and differences, which were central to the success of this program, could be seen and felt, not just described.

Subsequently, within the project after the pilot, there was an entirely different environment. People operated differently following their interactions in person, and they had much more positive perceptions of each other compared with the first phase of the work, when the team was just virtual. Peter credits the solid relationships that were formed for the success of the program (and the dinners in Spain probably didn't hurt, either). As the program was being established, the open sharing and interaction among the members of the distributed team were essential to gaining acceptance and widespread success of their efforts.

▪ Maintaining Relationships

Establishing good relationships with your project team depends a great deal on your ability to exert influence (the topic of Chapter 3). Establishing trust and a good relationship with each of your contributors is one of your main objectives during project initiation and planning, as discussed in the previous two chapters.

Continued influence and control depends on your ability to maintain those solid relationships with all the members of your team throughout project execution. There are a number of things that you can and should do to maintain good relationships for the remainder of your project. Ways to maintain good connections with your team include building on common interests, using team activities, tailoring your interactions, staying positive and loyal, interacting socially, and using humor.

Building on Common Interests

Some of your informal communication with individual team members should concern topics other than your project. There are a great number of possible interests that you share with your team members, such as your academic background, professional affiliations, hobbies, sports, literature, movies, travel, food, earlier projects, or other employers. Identifying what you share with your team members will give you things to discuss and solidify your relationships and ongoing teamwork.

Using Team Activities

Projects that are successful function together effectively, and secondarily focus on their own individual concerns. Throughout the project effective team behavior patterns can be encouraged and sustained through effective use of team-oriented activities. It may also be helpful in fostering teamwork to establish a communal space for the team to call its own, either an actual room (such as a "war room") or a virtual space such as a website. Even for distributed, global, and virtual teams, it is useful to bring people together in person at the start of the project and again about every six months throughout the project.

The most effective way to begin a new project is to assemble the team for a project start-up workshop (discussed in Chapter 5). When people know each other, they tend to like and trust each other, and they will be able to work together smoothly. It is human nature for people who have never met to be suspicious and to quarrel with each other, especially when they come from different backgrounds. Start-up workshops are most effective when conducted face-to-face. If this proves impossible, schedule at least a teleconference meeting to allow your team members to interact with each other at the same time.

One way to strengthen interpersonal connections right at the beginning of a project is to work as a team to name your project. Forging a project identity will serve to draw the team together by providing an easy, shorthand way to refer to the project as a whole. If you do decide to select a project name with your team, ensure that the name makes sense and that it is culturally appropriate for everyone on the team. (But don't, in an attempt to please, name it after your sponsor's dog. Dogs don't live forever. It's hard to run a project named for a dead pet.)

Throughout project planning there are many opportunities for the entire project team, or at least portions of the team, to work together. Your role will be to take full advantage of these opportunities to reinforce and maintain effective teamwork. Many planning processes benefit mightily from team collaboration.

There are many opportunities to work as a team throughout the execution of a project. Structure your work so your whole team, including members who are geographically distant, has integration, interfacing, and coordination requirements that ensure collaboration at least once a month during the project. Other chances to work as a team include variance analysis and replanning; change management; risk monitoring and review; conflict and issue management; collaborative problem solving; and project reviews. More details on collaborative approaches for these activities are outlined in Chapter 8 on project monitoring.

The final opportunity for teamwork on most projects is capturing lessons learned during a post-project retrospective meeting. This is primarily done to improve processes for future projects by uncovering things that went well and should be repeated and things that did not go well that need to be changed. However, it also serves to bring the project to an orderly conclusion and recognize the team's successes. A retrospective is also an excellent opportunity to reinforce relationships developed during the project. Building teamwork on a project that is ending might seem like an odd thing to invest time in, but it's a small world and people who have worked together once are very likely, sooner or later, to work together again. Chapter 9 on project closure further explores the subject of capturing lessons learned for your project.

Tailoring Your Interactions

The people on your project team will each have individual preferences for how they like to work, communicate, and interact. These unique preferences result from all of each person's experiences, learning, culture, and background. When you share a substantially similar history with one of your team members, you should have little difficulty interacting in ways that you both find familiar and comfortable. However, on today's project teams, the backgrounds of team members from different cultures, educational backgrounds, parts of the world, and age groups vary a great deal. Discussing communications options when reviewing the decisions for your project infrastructure, as described in Chapter 2, is a useful way to set expectations and establish appropriate methods for interacting.

Some people may be naturally team-oriented and accustomed to working within a defined, structured hierarchy. Other people may be more independent and good deal more comfortable working in an environment where they have a high degree of autonomy. Cultural differences even affect how time and deadlines are perceived. Some people are scrupulous about making and meeting time commitments, while others have a less precise approach to deadlines. Preferred communication styles vary a great deal, with some people preferring informal interactions to be verbal and others who prefer more distance and communications to be in writing.

Uncovering these preferences is an important part of establishing a relationship with each of the members of your team. This can be a challenge, especially when the interpersonal differences between you and a contributor are significant or the team member is located far away. Nonetheless, to the best of your ability you need to minimize the effects of your cultural and other differences. This is easier said than done, but one tactic that helps is never to pass up a chance to visit distant team members, to see for yourself where and how they work. Going alone is most effective, because traveling with other people can result in a "bubble" that creates a barrier to really understanding the places and people you visit. Also, when your attention is on your traveling companions, it is not on the people you are visiting. Study can also help in understanding other cultures; there are many references and classes available on languages and cross-cultural relations. The most effective way to understand others and build relationships, however, is through personal interaction, which is after all your main objective. In most cases, simply trying to meet people partway will be rewarded with significantly increased cooperation and improved relations.

To some extent, it may also be effective to partition project work in ways that minimize the need for frequent interactions, which will make differing preferences for communication and variations in working styles less significant to the project. Even when this solution is helpful, though, you remain responsible for the project as a whole and must interact with everyone on the team. The burden of conforming to styles, time frames, and modes of communications that are effective for each member of your team falls squarely on your shoulders.

Staying Positive and Loyal

When everything on your project is going well (don't laugh—it does happen), it's easy to be positive. But even when things aren't going very well, good project leaders remain resolutely positive. Depressed, unhappy project leaders who are convinced that their projects are doomed invariably infect their teams with this belief. Pessimism is contagious, and it is disastrous to projects. Even when you begin a project with good relationships between your team members, an impression that the project is a death march will quickly undermine them.

One of your most essential tools for maintaining trust and team cohesion is unflagging loyalty. Your loyalty to each team member must be unwavering throughout the project. As things go wrong on your project (and they will), you will start to hear complaints and criticisms of your team members from outside your project. You may even be tempted to be critical of team members yourself when discussing your project with others. Publicly criticizing members of your team, or even remaining silent while others heap abuse on them, can be extremely corrosive to team cohesion. You need to listen to complaints, problems, and issues, and commit to looking into them, while steadfastly expressing support for your team members until you can investigate further.

If a member of your team has performance or other problems, it is best to deal with the individual one-on-one, with sensitivity to the overall situation and generous offers of support and assistance. Loyalty, trust, and good relationships on your team are essential, and your team members will tend to follow your lead on loyalty to others on the team and to the project. Throughout the project, as difficult as it may be at times, strive to serve as a good example. Remaining loyal to your team will contribute much to team success.

In the midst of problems, work to keep the focus on problem solving and recovery, not on personal attacks and "blame-storming." Don't focus on problem areas to the complete exclusion of things that are going well; always mention things that are on schedule and going well in project discussions. When reporting on problems, focus on the progress you are making toward recovery.

Interacting Socially and Feeding People

Team cohesion is about more than just the project. Non-project-related activities, such as going to a movie, a sporting event, or some other type of outing, can be a significant boost to building team relationships. This tactic works best if the activities are selected by the team and are not too frequent. The context of a face-to-face meeting such as a start-up workshop or project review provides a good opportunity to schedule some kind of event that will involve the whole team, including distant team members.

Armies are said to travel on their stomachs, and so apparently do most project teams. One thing that all humans have in common is eating. Things we have in common tend to draw us together, which helps in team building, and sharing a meal fills this need. It also serves as a socializing event. With a little research and creativity, you can find a menu that can be enjoyed by even the most diverse team members. Teams can share snacks of some kind in the course of normal meetings. They can share meals together before or after a meeting or work, or integrate food into special events. One project team I worked with was particularly fond of dark chocolate. This global team held twice-yearly meetings that were attended by team members from all over the world. During these meetings, a competition developed where all attendees were challenged to bring local chocolates or something made with chocolate to the next meeting. During the breaks, we all gorged on chocolate. It was the best kind of competition, because in the end, everyone won. (The energy in the room did tend to dip about an hour or so after each of these chocolate breaks.)

Take advantage of the power of social events and food to build camaraderie, but do so sparingly and in ways that your team will respond to.

Using Humor and Having Fun

Projects can be difficult, long, and stressful. Breaking away from a monomaniacal, relentless focus on the work, at least occasionally, will help everyone survive.

Project leaders who are liked by their teams have more influence and control over their projects, and cultivating an appropriate sense of humor is one way to increase your likability. You don't need to be a natural-born comedian to share a short, humorous story appropriate to a meeting, or to include a relevant cartoon in a presentation or an e-mail. Getting people to laugh, or at least smile, is an excellent stress reliever and can be of great help in maintaining morale and working through difficult situations. Showing you are not overly serious all the time is a good way to connect better with your team and improve relationships. Use humor in moderation, and work to stay within the boundaries of decorum, taste, and cultural sensitivity.

BEING SENSITIVE TO GLOBAL CULTURAL DIFFERENCES

Emphasizing the importance of maintaining good relationships, J. D. Watson, a manager with many years of experience at DuPont, shared this story about a project critical to divesting a part of his organization that was being sold to another company. The project involved establishing a new global telecommunications infrastructure for a hundred locations in sixty-five countries. In addition to the significant costs, they had to manage all the technical difficulties, including application changes and data center consolidations, on the very tight timetable required by the divestiture agreement.

Quickly, all the telecommunications managers involved realized they would not succeed without face-to-face meetings. Regular meetings in person were the only way to ensure that none of the hundreds of the necessary tasks would be overlooked. While e-mail and teleconferences were frequent across all time zones, they could not substitute for face-to-face meetings. In person, language and cross-cultural difficulties shrank, "turf battles" were rare, and problems were quickly solved. J. D. observes:

> "Success for this complex global project was dependent on thousands of details, many of which only came to light through the individual discussions and interactions made possible by our face-to-face meetings.
>
> "The nature of project team relationships is increasingly ephemeral. When I worked major projects in the past, relationships with internal experts and external contractors were well established and long lasting. These days, you're lucky if there are any people you know on your team; the group you work with from Texas on one project may be from India on the next, and from Guangzhou for the one after that. Because people don't trust people that they don't know, it has become more and more essential to meet in person."

KEY IDEAS FOR PROJECT EXECUTION

- Define diagnostic project metrics that will enhance control of your project, then get buy-in for them from your team.
- Be dogmatic and disciplined in collecting project status.
- Use informal communication to collect "soft data," and work to maintain relationships and trust within your team.

CHAPTER 8

Tracking and Monitoring for Project Control

M OST STATUS CYCLES bring at least some unwelcome news. Sorting out the problematic from the merely annoying is the initial step in overall control. Seeking ways to adapt or shift the plan to deal with bad news means recovering from problems, not succumbing to them. To do this you will need to have a full complement of techniques for control of schedule, cost, quality, and other potential problems. Managing scope changes is essential to project control, as are dealing with individual performance problems, managing issues, and monitoring risks. To control long-duration projects and programs, you'll need to rely on periodic project reviews to ensure that the objectives continue to make good business sense and to make needed plan adjustments. On occasion, control actions also may require, as a last resort, canceling the project.

▪ Scope and Specification Change Management

Project control depends heavily on a stable scope for your deliverables. Failing to manage scope change is about the most common reason for loss of project control. When scope is allowed to drift and move easily, the results aren't good. You'll no doubt recognize the old adages:

- Projects quickly get to 80 percent complete, then stay there forever.
- The first 90 percent of a project takes 90 percent of the time. The remaining 10 percent takes the other 90 percent.

This sort of overall performance rarely results from laziness or stupidity. It happens because of unconstrained scope change. When the rate of specification change exceeds your rate of progress, you can never reach your moving target. Nailing down project scope relies on freezing your scope when you set the project baseline, as discussed in Chapter 6. Avoiding unnecessary changes through the remainder of the project requires an effective process for managing proposed scope changes that empowers you to say "no" most of the time. The particulars of your process will vary as appropriate for your project, but overall it needs to operate much like the typical change control process described in Chapter 2.

If you don't have a great deal of formal authority, a robust process for managing scope changes may be all that stands between you and complete chaos. If a good process exists in your organization, adopt it and use it. If not, write one and get your team to provide feedback on it. Draft a process that has a default answer of "reject" for changes, with all changes treated as unnecessary until proven otherwise. Also include explicit criteria to be used in making a decision for each change. The more specific you make the criteria, the more useful they will be in helping you to control project scope. Develop and include a criterion for characterizing each change as either mandatory (addressing an execution problem, regulatory or legal changes, shifts in relevant standards, new competitive offerings) or nonmandatory (enhancements, new technology, opportunities, meddling management). Design your process to strongly discourage changes that are not mandatory.

Your team can be one of your most insidious sources of scope creep, so asking for and implementing their advice when you establish your change control process is essential to securing their buy-in and support. The other players you need to get approval from include your sponsor and key stakeholders, who are also potential sources of frivolous change.

Before you set your project baseline, get everyone who you think might come up with project changes to sign off on a well-defined, documented change management process. Most people you approach will willingly offer support if you ask early enough in your project. If you wait until they have thought of their first change, though, their enthusiasm for the management process will drop quickly.

Whatever the specifics of your exact process, there are several things that you can do to minimize project changes. During initial consideration of any change, quickly assess what it will do to the project objectives. Especially consider the likely impact on your highest priority. If you have a severely time-constrained project and a change would inject a significant delay, point this out. If resources are strictly limited and the change will require significant additional effort, let people know.

Always answer two questions about every proposed change:

- What does it cost?
- What is it worth?

Be thorough with the first, and remember that only you and your team are really in a position to assess the impact of proposed changes—it is your project, after all. Be very skeptical of answers to the benefit question, especially for changes that seem to be enhancements rather than proposals aimed at resolving legitimate project problems. If the cost exceeds the potential value, that's a good argument against the change.

Finally, always consider all four possible decisions for any change: Rejected, Approved, Approved with modifications, and Deferred for future consideration. When you are unable to muster an outright "no," "not yet" is almost as good. When you are not able to avoid changes, be thorough in exploring any alternative changes that might meet the need with lower impact. Validate each aspect of each change that appears inevitable, and strip out anything superfluous before approval. A disposition of "Okay, in part" may allow you to avoid much of a change's impact on your project.

When changes are approved, communicate them. Notify your team and others who need to know, and promptly update all affected project plans and documents.

A VIEW FROM THE EDGE

With large, multisystem programs, even managers with substantial authority sometimes have too little. Ron Askeland is currently an R&D Master Engineer with the Hewlett-Packard Inkjet Products Group in San Diego, where scoping problems frequently cross organizational boundaries. The complexity arises because different HP businesses are responsible for the printer, the "pens" that carry and eject the ink for printing, and various printing media for specialized applications. Differing charters and motivations within these businesses make resolving technical problems particularly difficult, because a solution that fixes a problem for one division can, and often does, create problems for the other divisions involved.

Shortly before the end of one new printer project, serious integration problems arose. Changes were going to be required to meet the scheduled introduction date for the printer. No single project team working alone would be able to "own" the entire problem, and the lowest-level manager that everybody reported to was on the corporate executive committee. Clearly, they needed to quickly find a pragmatic solution that considered the system as a whole. Ron says:

"To deal with this situation, we developed the concept of a 'seam team.' We established a cross-divisional work group chartered to develop the best overall resolution, considering all trade-offs within the system as a whole. Led by a senior engineer, with core team members from all of the affected businesses and functions, the seam team was set up to facilitate rapid development and streamline the normal build/test/fix cycle. The engineers were given decision authority and asked to develop a system solution while ensuring that no important issues fell between the cracks."

Working together, ink chemists, pen designers, system test engineers, media chemists, and printer design engineers made rapid progress on the problem, taking into account all the components of the overall system. The team got this problem resolved in the required time, including obtaining approvals for modifications in nearly all the subsystems.

Seam teams are responsible for evaluating problems and optimizing solutions at the system level, exploring all options without regard to where the ideas originated. They are led by engineers, not managers, to give the teams independence and avoid tying them too closely to the priorities of a specific division. To move quickly to closure, seam teams have both the authority and responsibility to address their issues. Seam team recommendations carry weight because the management of all the affected organizations is committed in advance to accept their decisions. All seam team recommendations are communicated widely and put into effect with very little interference or debate.

Ron observes, "These projects lived and died by their seam teams. Seam teams are essential for promptly resolving difficult issues in parallel."

▪ Overall Control

Project scope control involves an element of choice, so managing it requires a specialized decision process. Most other project control issues are a result of unavoidable circumstances or events that have already occurred. Maintaining or reestablishing project control in most situations involves minor adjustments, replanning, or substantial changes to the overall baseline, depending on the severity of the problem.

To stay under control, effective project leaders can use their assessment of variance against a credible baseline plan to detect control problems. Early detection is essential to control, because problems uncovered while they are small can often be resolved with minor adjustments. You can easily arrange such actions as working late, shifting the timing of a noncritical activity, or having other team members pitch in to help someone who is having difficulty. Easy fixes do not always work, though. Tactics that bring your project back into control need to focus broadly on the entire remaining portions of your project. What is important is delivering on your commitments. If the most straightforward action you can take to restore a credible likelihood of overall success involves making changes to some part of your project that is not directly related to the immediate problem, then that's the action that is most appropriate.

Regardless of the source or magnitude of a control problem, approach resolution using the Deming "Plan-Do-Check-Act" cycle:

• *Plan.* Using the variance analysis of your project status or other information about a situation that you need to control, work with your team to develop options for response. Consider the costs, other impacts, possible unintended consequences, and risks associated with each proposed response. Review all proposed ideas for consistency with your project infrastructure decisions. Conclude your planning by using a decision process (such as the one outlined in Chapter 2) to select the best option.

• *Do.* Get any approvals needed from your sponsor, management, or other project stakeholders. For proposals that impact project scope, get approval through your scope change process. For any major changes that affect your project's goals, work with your project sponsor to renegotiate and reset the project baseline. Update all affected project plans or documents and implement your chosen action.

• *Check.* Use status metrics and other information to verify either that you have resolved the problem or that a control problem persists. Check for unintended consequences and impact on other work or projects.

• *Act.* Loop back to "Plan" for situations that require further attention. If you have successfully resolved your control problem, take any steps necessary to minimize recurrence later in your project or in the future. Document your actions and results in your project management information system (PMIS), for later project reviews and analysis of lessons learned.

Now, let's look at specific ideas that may be useful in managing these common project control situations: performance problems, schedule control, cost control, quality control, outsourcing and contract administration, risk monitoring and control, issue management, loss of a project sponsor, and taking over a project.

Performance Problems

In planning, you assigned ownership of all project responsibilities and all of the lowest-level activities in your work breakdown structure to some individual on your team (or, by default, to yourself). Whenever you identify a variance from your plan or other problems, there is always some a chance that if the individuals doing the work could be at fault. When investigating the source of a variance, start with the assigned owner. Meet, face-to-face if possible, with the individual to explore the situation. Discuss the consequences to the project (in terms of additional cost, schedule slippage, or other issues) of missing a commitment. Emphasize aspects that affect your contributor personally.

Work to understand why your team member failed to follow through. Some reasons may be:

- Your team member does not know how to do the work.
- Delegation of ownership was not clear.
- Conflicting priorities represent more work than your contributor can finish.
- Your team member requires help or more resources.
- A required input for the work is delayed.
- Your contributor has too little authority to do the work.
- Necessary information for the work is unavailable.
- The individual was directed to do something else.
- Your contributor sees little personal benefit or reward in achieving the goal.

Don't guess what the reasons might be or jump to conclusions; ask your contributor to describe the reasons in his or her own words. Probe to uncover the root cause, not just an excuse.

Ask your team member for possible solution suggestions. If the root cause is something that your contributor needs but does not have, consider options for addressing the need. There are opportunities for influence in situations where, for example, your contributor needs help or training. Arranging for a mentor, coaching, or training may solve the problem while also helping to establish a stronger relationship. Don't promise what you can't deliver, but do commit to removing barriers and helping in any way that is appropriate.

When a possible resolution requires additional project expense that you may not be in a position to approve, you'll have to approach your sponsor or other manager to secure the money. If you need a way to justify the training, consider this story: Responding to a training request, the approving manager observed that it would be expensive and asked, "What if I approve this request and he quits?"

The project leader replied with another question, "What if you don't approve it and he *stays*?" The manager promptly approved the training expense.

With your team member, look for solutions that address the root cause of the problem. Examples include a problem escalation to expedite a delayed input, or discussion with your sponsor to resolve a resource shortage. After your team member has made proposals for resolution, bring up any ideas you have as well. (You will find suggestions for specific types of project control problems further along in this section.) Work together to select and document the path forward that appears best to both of you. Ask for a commitment to follow through, and express your confidence that your contributor will be successful.

For performance problems that persist despite your repeated attempts at one-on-one resolution, involve the individual's manager, your sponsor, a manager responsible for personnel problems, or others who are responsible for such situations. Turn things over to those with experience in handling chronic performance cases to protect your organization, the individual, and yourself. Unless you are the individual's direct manager, limit your role in dealing with serious performance problems to that of a concerned participant.

WALKING IN SOMEONE ELSE'S SHOES

Ashok Waran, currently managing operations for SupportSoft in India and a veteran of many complex projects, recalls a performance issue he encountered in Bangalore when he was working for a small company that manufactured computer devices for the Indian public sector. This was before the economic liberalization in India, and all the components they used were made locally. He remembers:

> "I was a project manager working on developing data terminals, statistical multiplexers, and word processors, among other devices. I was a young manager then and had not learned much about influencing my coworkers.
>
> "For one particular project, I was a designer, developer, and manager rolled into one. I believed that everyone involved with my project would do whatever it took to get the job done—just as I would have. One of my responsibilities was to get the electronics working and tested, and that was easy. I had people I had worked with before for that, and of course I could do that by myself, if needed.
>
> "I was also responsible for getting the final product out of the factory. We had a workshop that did the sheet metal and fiberglass work, and they were responsible for getting all

the components assembled and ready to ship. The factory workers were very skilled in their own areas, but different in their behavior and approach from the engineers who were responsible for the electronics.

"As a project manager, my job included bringing everything together—the electronics, the power supply, and the final assembly. Everything else was proceeding well, but I had a great deal of trouble motivating the factory workers. They ignored some of my orders. Others they would pretend to obey, but then produce only what they wanted to. They were intelligent people, but they didn't look at the world the way I did. The packaging—the metal cages, the fiberglass covers—all had to all be made by hand, then painted and finished. I could never predict when this work would be finished. This made my overall task of bringing everything together very difficult, and I was frustrated.

"This is when I began to visit with the factory workers to get to know things more intimately. I spent time and energy at the workshop getting to understand what it took to do their work and learning about their work environment. Most importantly, I got to know the people. I couldn't do any of what they did myself, but I was there with them when they had problems and showed interest in trying to solve them. I found that my work with them earned me such huge gratitude that after a short time, they would have done the impossible for me. As a result, we easily achieved our desired results and met the delivery schedule that I had been so concerned about.

"This experience taught me humility, and it taught me a lot about people and giving them respect. The big difference between the factory workers and the engineers [like me] was complete loyalty: They wouldn't even hesitate to lay their lives on the line, had I asked for it. I was moved beyond words for who they were and what they could do. I learned to respect them enormously. My approach to project work was profoundly influenced by those folks. It made me a better manager, far better than I might have been otherwise."

Schedule Control

Most schedule problems are detected during the plan variance analysis portion of your project tracking cycle. Determine the impact on your project's key milestones and completion date. Investigate the root cause of each variance, initially with the activity's owner. Determine whether the timing problem is a single event or the result of a longer-term chronic situation. For problems that are likely to recur, assess the potential impact to later project work.

As with all planning, the more brains and perspectives the better, so involve your project contributors in brainstorming approaches that could restore your project schedule. Focus on addressing root causes, particularly with potentially recurring problems. Consider alternatives such as:

- Using responses that have been effective in similar past situations
- Consuming schedule reserve (if you negotiated some)
- Implementing a contingency plan developed as a risk response
- Delaying the start of one or more noncritical activities to let other team members assist in catching up
- Revising the sequence of remaining project work
- Decomposing future project activities for faster parallel execution
- Shifting resources away from activities where you can tolerate longer durations
- Personally helping out, where you can, with slipping activities
- Identifying innovative shortcuts for remaining project work
- Borrowing resources temporarily from other projects or organization efforts
- Working overtime on non-workdays
- Proposing removal of lower-priority requirements from the project deliverable
- Getting approval from your sponsor for the resources and expense required to "crash" upcoming project activities
- Documenting a compelling case and using it to negotiate a later deadline with your sponsor
- Proposing other major changes to the project baseline

Test rescheduling ideas you are considering using a copy of your baseline schedule. Explore possible "what if?" scenarios thoroughly, looking for realistic possibilities for getting back on schedule. For each schedule problem you encounter, also consider whether upcoming project work could run into the similar difficulties. Treat these as new project risks, and modify your schedule as necessary to minimize potential future problems.

The earlier you deal with significant threats to your deadline, the less painful it will be. If you get to the scheduled end of your project and a great deal of work remains, no one will be happy with you or your team. At that point, cancellation is more likely than approval for a timing adjustment, with dire consequences to your career and reputation. Be proactive and address problems as soon as you detect them.

Cost Control

Like schedule problems, most budget problems surface while assessing variance in your tracking cycle. Financial variance is cumulative, so every adverse variance is always "critical" to your project budget. Use root-cause analysis to understand why your costs are too high, initially through discussion with the activity's owner. Determine whether each variance might be a recurring problem or part of a dangerous trend. For chronic problems, determine the expected overall impact on the rest of your project.

Brainstorm with members of your team to develop approaches to deal with project costs.

Many of the same tactics that applied to schedule control, including pitching in yourself, applying contingency plans, and using solutions that have been used before, may lower overall expenses. Consider as well alternatives such as:

- Consuming budget reserve (if you negotiated some)
- Locating people you can temporarily borrow without cost from other projects or organization efforts
- Leveling resources
- Lengthening the schedule
- Documenting a compelling case and using it to negotiate additional resources or funding with your sponsor, or proposing other major changes to the project baseline

Verify that the ideas you develop will address your expense and budget problems, either by bringing overall expected expense in line with your plans or through a well-documented proposal for a larger budget. The earlier you can address a cost overrun situation, the less painful it will be. If problems accumulate and you run out of money well before your project is complete, you will get little sympathy and your proposals for adjustment are unlikely to be approved.

Quality Control

Scope-related variances also may arise from your analysis of project status. Begin your diagnosis of the situation through discussions with the owner of the activity, test, inspection, walkthrough, or other source of the problem metrics. A cause-and-effect ("fishbone" diagram) analysis will help you to understand the root causes. When needed, involve the rest of your project team in uncovering process issues or other potential sources of your problems.

Quality control begins with planning. It's often said that quality is "planned in," never "inspected in." Quality planning is tightly coupled to the scope planning and deliverable definition processes discussed in earlier chapters. Reliability, performance, usability, and other aspects of your deliverable that are critical to your project's success all must be reflected in your requirements and defined acceptance criteria, so your plans are structured to deliver what is needed. Quality management will also generally involve industry standards and specific policies adopted by your organization.

Project quality control and quality assurance are tightly linked. Examining work results throughout your project to detect quality control problems will show you whether your processes for quality assurance are providing adequate structure and guidance to achieve your goals for quality. Quality problems you may detect in your status metrics include deliverable-related measurements that are outside of defined limits, nonrandom in unexpected ways, or exhibiting unacceptable trends. You can use statistical tools such as Pareto charts, scatter diagrams, control limit graphs, and histograms to help you to understand problems and resolve them.

If you can solve a quality problem by adjusting a process owned by you and your team, work to improve the process. Other situations may result from hardware or equipment problems, requiring recalibration, replacement, or repair. If scope changes will be required, initiate the required change requests. If the process that you need to improve is beyond the authority of your project team, document what the owner of the process will need, then use your data and influencing skills to sell your sponsor on the need for a change. Offer to help with any necessary modifications.

Significant quality problems may also involve escalation. There can be quality problems for which you are not able to find any realistic solution. Projects are unique, and you may find that the quality your project has achieved is the best that it is possible to deliver. If so, document the situation and meet with your sponsor and important stakeholders to explain the constraints you have discovered. Quality problems can be showstoppers; if the differences between what you can deliver and your goals are too great, project cancellation can sometimes be an inevitable result. However, if the project quality that you are able to achieve does deliver sufficient value, negotiate project changes, update your project scoping documents, adjust your acceptance criteria, and get on with your project.

Outsourcing and Contract Administration

Most of what applies to any other control issue applies to work done on a fee-for-service basis. Schedule problems are not uncommon, and they often occur without much warning after a long series of "doing just fine" status reports.

Precision, performance, and quality issues can also arise without much warning. Depending on the contract terms, cost problems can also quickly spin out of control.

When problems arise, contact your contract liaison or the individual who is on your team to discuss the situation. Response and resolution ideas include all those listed previously, so explore options that can result in a credible commitment to get things back on track. Seek to resolve or at least minimize the project impact from the variance. For timing problems, arrange for expedited execution of upcoming work whenever possible to compensate for the problems.

If there are penalty clauses in the contract, use them in your discussions as leverage. In general it will be a lot better for your project if you can work together to find a way to resolve problems instead of invoking penalty clauses. Price reductions and other adjustments that are built into the contract will not generally help you successfully complete your project.

When you encounter scoping changes that affect team members who are working on contract, they may present significant cost issues. Before initiating a change that would modify any contract terms, discuss the proposed changes with your supplier liaison. Review the terms of the contract regarding amendments, and get an estimate of what the financial or other impact of the change would be to the contract. Avoid amending the contract whenever possible, but whenever you encounter unavoidable contract changes, work to minimize the incremental expense or other adverse consequences. For all contract changes, quickly amend or rewrite the contract, get all parties to approve it, and get your project back on track.

Risk Monitoring and Control

Risk control is a bit different from the other items in this section, which all deal with issues, problems, and other project certainties. Risks are tied to future probabilities, so there may or may not be much that is necessary to do at any specific time.

Risk monitoring has three aspects that relate to control. One is ongoing surveillance of the trigger events associated with each risk on your risk register. The second is regular review of project risks, to identify new risks and reevaluate the identified items on your risk register. The third is periodic review of contingency plans, schedule reserves, and budget reserves to determine if changes are needed.

Ongoing monitoring means regularly scanning project status to detect risk trigger events or thresholds. You also need to be on the lookout for overall risk, and ensure that those team members who own the risk response plans remain alert. Status-cycle monitoring is usually sufficient for minor risks, and it will also reveal unanticipated risks that may arise. For more significant risks, the risk owners will need to respond more quickly and diligently monitor for trigger events so that they can react promptly with their contingency plans. Many risks identified have specific time windows when they are most likely to occur, so be particularly alert during the times of maximum exposure. When you detect a problem that is a result of a risk you have not foreseen, or your established contingency plans prove ineffective, deal with project risks using appropriate schedule and cost control techniques. If a risk represents a material change to your project baseline, discuss the situation with your project sponsor and appropriate stakeholders. When facing the consequences of a major risk, escalate promptly; risk-related problems tend to go from bad to very bad in a hurry. Some risk responses may even require renegotiating a new project baseline.

Every day of your project, you learn more and realize new things. About once a month, get out your risk register and review it in light of your new knowledge. Add any new risks that are now apparent. New risks arise from changes in or around your project, so think about anything that has shifted since your last review. You may also discover additional risks by reviewing recent and upcoming work, looking for previously invisible exposures that are now obvious. Assess the impact and probability of all new risks, but also adjust your assessments as appropriate for all the risks you already have listed. As you reassess existing risks, remove any that no longer represent a threat or that have already occurred. Using the new and revised assessments, reprioritize your risk register. Develop and implement mitigation and avoidance strategies where possible for significant new risks, and establish owners, triggers, and contingency plans for all significant risks that you are not able to prevent. After each review, circulate a summary of your work. Between reviews, store the risk register where it can be easily accessed, discuss new risks in project team meetings, and work to keep the most significant identified risks visible to your team.

As your project progresses, changes will occur. Work with the owners to review contingency plans periodically to ensure that the response you are planning for a risk remains your best option. Periodic review also will serve to keep the risk, and its consequences, more visible. Monitor trends in your status data for signs of overall project risk exposures. Earned value and other diagnostic metrics can reveal how your project is doing as a whole; these measures may also signal project-level risk problems in advance.

Not all project risks will be listed on your risk register. Some will be "unknown" risks, arising from external factors you are not aware of or from unique aspects of your project. The only effective mitigating technique for unknown risk is establishing management reserve for your project—*schedule reserve* to deal with unanticipated timing problems and/or *budget reserve* to deal with expense overruns. If you have established reserve for your project, monitor how much of it is consumed by your contingent actions and unexpected problems. If your project is half done and 80 percent of your reserve is used up, you have a situation that you should discuss with your sponsor.

Throughout your project, archive the risk registers. Track your risk history in your PMIS for future planning, project reviews, and analysis of lessons learned at project completion.

Issues Management

Issues arise throughout projects. Your control relies on visibility and on prompt resolution. Managing issues is important for project control, and it requires a process similar to the one outlined in Chapter 2. To maintain control:

- Recognize issues promptly.
- List issues with owners and expectations for resolution and keep them visible.
- Escalate, but only when all else fails.

Issues are problems that don't yield to trivial resolution. They can arise from a significant project variance, a meeting action item, a risk that has occurred, or from many other sources. Be proactive; monitor your status data and use informal communication to detect project issues as early as possible. Controlling an issue begins with catching it while it is small and resolving it before the situation grows unmanageable. Ignoring issues hoping that they will go away is never healthy for your project.

Increase the visibility of current issues for your team by creating a list and maintaining it in a public place. A list that is part of your PMIS that you regularly review with your team is usually sufficient. On the list, assign an issue identifier, note the date you opened the item, and unambiguously describe the issue. Work with your team to identify an appropriate owner and a target completion date to each item. Include a status for each item, such as Open (unresolved), Done (resolved), Obsolete (resolution is no longer required), or Replaced (superseded by a newer item).

Project team meetings are a good opportunity to review open items and to discuss owners and dates. For urgent items, however, you will need to initiate action as soon as you uncover the problem without waiting for the next meeting. Use a process for setting goals, like the one described in Chapter 6, to get a commitment from the assigned owner of each issue and an agreement to the resolution deadline. Track open issues and follow up on items on your list that are approaching (or past) their due dates. Use issue status reporting to publicly recognize prompt resolutions and to highlight any delays. Publicizing a lack of follow-through can be a very effective motivator.

As a last resort, when resolving an issue is beyond your team's capacity, prepare to escalate to someone outside of your team who will have sufficient authority to deal with the issue. Develop a detailed summary of the problem, including your attempts to deal with it. Outline possible approaches for resolution that might be used by others with more authority than you have, and document the costs and other consequences of each alternative. Before you escalate, also quantify the consequences of failing to resolve the issue quickly.

Inform your sponsor (or another decision maker that you have identified for this escalation) that you have an issue. With this person, review the escalation process you established during project initiation and get a firm ownership commitment from them and a due date for resolution.

Continue to track the status of the issue in your list with the new owner, and include its status in your project reporting, explicitly assigned to the decision maker. Track the issue through to resolution. If it looks like the resolution will be late, warn that you plan to report the status with a big, red stoplight indicator. If that doesn't bring things promptly to closure, issue your report and name names.

Loss of a Project Sponsor

If you find yourself in midproject with no sponsor (due to reorganization, retirement, a medical problem, or other circumstances) locate a new one. Projects without a sponsor—particularly projects managed by project leaders with limited authority—are very likely to encounter difficulties that they may not be able to recover from. Resources will be at risk, you may have no one to escalate problems to or seek help from, and you might have a hard time getting stakeholders, and even your team, to take you and the project seriously.

Make finding a new sponsor a high priority. Consider managers in your organization that would be good candidates. One option is to identify the person in your organization (besides you, of course) who would suffer the most if your project is not successful. Another option is to find the manager closest to your level who is capable of canceling your project. Whether you can convince this person to assume sponsorship or not, it is an excellent idea to ensure that the manager has a good impression of your work.

Before you make an approach, investigate what your prospective new sponsor cares about. Develop a presentation that connects the value of your project and the potential consequences of failure to interests that are relevant to your potential sponsor. Use your influencing skills to sell your project, and reestablish the management support your project needs to navigate through difficulties and remain in control.

Taking Over a Project

Almost as traumatic as losing a sponsor is the loss of a leader. When you are asked to assume leadership for a project that has already begun, proceed with caution. While the plans, team, and infrastructure could be excellent, it's risky to assume this is the case. The safest thing to do is to follow the maxim: "Trust, but verify." Use the existing plans to monitor ongoing work while you begin to sort through all the available information for the project and get to know the team. As with any project, control and success originate in understanding and preparation, and even a perfect plan will not help you much until you understand the project.

As a naïve young project leader, I learned this the hard way. I had a team of about a dozen systems programmers who were extremely good at what they did, which was remotely managing a few dozen midsize systems at sites throughout the United States. They worked together well, and as a team we were very productive. One day, while we were minding our own business, I was told that we were to apply what we knew to the installation and support of a major mainframe system. The system was already configured and the hardware was on the way, and they handed me a plan. I was assured that the "experts" had reviewed the details and signed off on it, so we should expect little difficulty. Even as inexperienced as I was, I was skeptical, but who was I to question the experts?

The more we got into the project, the more I realized that the planning had been done primarily by salespeople who knew almost nothing about the specifics of how this particular system would be used. In fact, no one knew much of anything about it; we were flying blind without anyone we could approach for advice or help. We continually ran into problems and roadblocks, and progress was slow and erratic. One critical element of the system we had to configure was a specialized interface unit. After several hours of unsuccessful attempts to get it running, I noticed a half-dozen people in navy blue suits, white shirts, and striped ties watching us from the edge of the data center. When I asked why they were there, I was told that they wanted to watch the installation because we were the first team *in the world* to install their hardware in production.

Long days, weekends, and holidays were consumed getting things set up and running. Ultimately we were able to get the system operational, more or less on schedule. It was hard to call the project a success, though. The teamwork we had worked so hard to build was frayed by the pressure, resulting in arguments and short tempers on the project. I did learn never to rely on a plan that wasn't mine, though.

Treat any project you inherit much the same way you would a new one. Validate the charter and scoping documents, and thoroughly review or rewrite the project plan. If the project plan you develop will miss the stated objective, approach the sponsor and propose a more realistic baseline. You can't take a great deal of time to do this, but for your own sake, *do it*. (The original project leader did leave for some reason, and it may or may not be exactly what they told you.) You have at least a little initial leverage; the project sponsor needs to get a commitment from *someone* to run the project.

A change of project leader is a useful time to schedule a project review, using a process such as the one discussed further along in this chapter. Most of the planning you need to do can be integrated into the review, and it can be a good place to start building the relationships and trust you will need for project control.

▪ Formal Communication

Control throughout most of your project depends heavily on the tracking cycle of information flowing inward through data collection, analysis of project metrics, plans for response, and outbound reporting to inform people what is happening in your project. The first two portions of this process cycle—status collection and variance analysis—were explored in Chapter 7. Control strategies for response are found earlier in this chapter. Reporting is the final step of your repeating tracking cycle, and project reporting is the most widely distributed form of formal communication. Formal communications include project status reports, project meetings, and presentations.

Project Status Reports

Status reporting pulls together all three strategies for control outlined in this book. Reporting is a central part of your information management process; done effectively, it will enhance your influence and it is the primary conduit for conveying project diagnostic metric analysis.

Maintaining control of your project requires that you be seen as the leader. When you have little formal authority, being the source of project information gives you crucial leverage. When no one on the project has specific formal authority, the individual who takes the initiative to manage the flow of project information will be drawn into the leader role by default. Your role as the principal source of project information can be an effective substitute for formal authority.

Issue project status reports with the frequency you committed to in setting up your communications infrastructure, generally weekly. Never skip cycles when there are problems; you might even need to intensify your status collection and reporting frequency to regain control. If you say that you will send a project report every Friday, send one every Friday. Distribute a detailed status report every cycle to your team, and at least a summary to your sponsor, stakeholders, and the managers of related projects.

For written project reports, always strive to be clear, concise, and honest. Stick to the truth, even when your report contains bad news, but always balance trouble reports with a summary of how you plan to resolve it. One of your most powerful control levers is the power of the pen. When you collect status information from your contributors, summarize and clarify it. Emphasize what you want and need people to know. Never issue reports that are nothing more than a concatenation of individual reports from your team members; although the information that your team and others need may very well be in there, somewhere, no one will ever find it in the confusing mass of chaotic data.

Always begin your project status reports with a short executive summary, containing about five to seven main points. Focus on important accomplishments, current issues, and significant next steps. Lead with a clear digest containing the headlines for your project, and make it fit on the first screen for recipients. For some people you send your report to, the summary will be all that they actually read.

After the summary, include more detailed information in sequence of declining importance. Write for your readers. For sponsors, stakeholders, and managers, avoid technical jargon and complicated language. Summarize information and include analysis to emphasize what the information means. Use graphs and charts to illustrate important metrics, statistics, and other quantitative information. For your team and technical peers, include text, tables, and more detailed information, but work to keep things as clear and simple as possible, even for this audience. No one has time to decipher an overly complicated status report. The precise content for your report will be determined by what is customary in your organization and specific decisions you make in determining your project infrastructure, using a list similar to the one in Appendix A.

Contents of a Typical Status Report
❏   An executive summary
❏   Project issues
❏   Scope changes (if any)
❏   Schedule status
❏   Resource status
❏   Detail on recent accomplishments
❏   Planned work for the next reporting cycle
❏   Project variance analysis
❏   Current and newly identified risks
❏   Additional detail as required by audience

Whatever format you adopt and topics you choose to include, be consistent. Make it easy for people to find the information in your reports that they need by putting it in the same place every cycle. One technique that simplifies the work of customizing reports sent to different audiences takes advantage of including project information in sequence of importance. For your team, you can probably get away with sending the whole, rather lengthy report. For those needing less detail, you can whack off some of the material at the end and transmit a moderate level of detail. For your sponsor and other managers, you might chop off everything but the summary and some information on issues and accomplishments. Customizing by truncation is a good deal less work than writing a completely different report for each part of your project's constituency.

Clear language increases your influence, so monitor your writing to eliminate any confusion that might erode it. In written reports, avoid jargon, acronyms, and any potentially ambiguous or confusing terminology. Never assume that all recipients will understand everything in your project. Project teams are dynamic, ebbing and flowing as the work progresses, and everything you write and transmit in electronic form could be forwarded to almost anyone. Acronyms, which may seem like useful shorthand, can be opaque and annoying to all but a small circle. Particularly with global teams, don't use idioms; they often don't translate across cultures.

Your power of the pen also involves making decisions about what to include or exclude. With definition documents, project plans, and project reviews, the requirements for thoroughness are such that you really should do very little filtering. For periodic status reports, though, it is neither necessary nor appropriate to put in everything that you know. It's not helpful to include project detail only relevant to the project team in reports that will be broadly distributed; in fact, it may obscure important information. The amount of attention you give to newly identified project risks and problems that arose and have been successfully resolved between status reports are judgment calls for you to make. There is a trade-off between demonstrating your professionalism and diligence on the one hand, and scaring the pants off your managers and sponsors on the other. Filter what you communicate to maximize the visibility of the most essential information.

Set the sequence of information in your reports to lead with accomplishments and emphasize the positive. First impressions are lasting, and you will increase the impact of your reports if the people reading them clearly understand what you and your team have achieved. Leading off with problems, issues, and other negative news can cause a loss of confidence in you and your team and severely interfere with your future influence.

In all written communications, never miss a chance to recognize contributions by individuals and teams of contributors, both within and outside of your team. Recognition is motivating, so naming names and making contributions visible will substantially improve your chances of getting cooperation and commitments for the remainder of your project and beyond.

Not all project news will be good. You also need to report situations that are not going well on your project. Yet reporting on issues and problems can be an opportunity to expand your influence, if you demonstrate that you are in control. Reporting project difficulties without any proposed solutions will leave the impression that your project is doomed. Before providing formal status on a problem, always work with members of your team to develop a response. In your reports, include a description of your problems with a summary of how you will address it. Explicitly outline how you plan to recover from the problem, or at least demonstrate what you are doing to minimize the impact on your project.

One last strategy for effective reporting is to proofread. Write your report, then set it aside for at least a few minutes while you do something else. Your project status report underpins your control, so before you send it, read it over, carefully. Clean up any spelling, grammar, or other errors, of course, but primarily focus on your message. Try to misinterpret what you wrote. If there are parts of your report that can be read with more than one meaning, rewrite to make them unambiguous. If your project involves confidential or proprietary information, read your report carefully to ensure that you are handling it properly; you can never tell where a status report might be forwarded. Read for tone; remove any unnecessarily pessimistic or negative thoughts. What you think about your project can be contagious. If you communicate confidence, people will share it. If you communicate doubts, people will become depressed and look for a cliff to throw themselves over. Also scan your report for personal information or criticism concerning your team members. If you find you have included any, remove it. Confine your broadcast status reporting to verifiable facts and figures about your project; deal with interpersonal and performance problems privately.

FLATTERY CAN GET YOU ANYWHERE

In the late 1980s, I was part of a large program created to consolidate hardware into a new state-of-the-art data center being established in a new European headquarters building in Geneva, Switzerland. We were to gather computer systems and other equipment from a half-dozen older sites all over the city, and my part of the program was to manage moving all the telecom equipment and packet-switching hardware used for worldwide data communications—while ensuring, of course, uninterrupted network access to all systems over the several months that it would take to relocate all computers.

A central part of the new data center design was a massive patch panel through which all the internal and external communications were to be routed. As the time to begin installing my networking hardware approached, I grew concerned that the patch panel was behind schedule.

The empty panel frame had been erected in the data center, but the hardware that would fill it up was still sitting in the manufacturer's boxes. I dropped hints a few times to the team responsible for assembling this hardware, to no avail. On a program like this, there are always many competing priorities and tasks.

A week before my first installation was scheduled, I approached the leader of the patching hardware installation team. Rather than complaining about the looming deadline, I asked if he would show me how the panel worked, so I could verify that everything was compatible. Together, we started opening boxes and he showed me how the parts fit together. I continued asking questions and opening boxes while he started snapping things together and screwing the components in place. After about forty-five minutes, he had installed about a dozen connections and wired them up. I was able to test my cables and fittings and verify there were no mechanical mating problems or electrical faults. I thanked him for his help, and we both returned to other work.

While I was grateful that some of the hardware I depended on was now installed, my real motive was to collect data for my weekly status report. In my summary for the beginning of my next report, I mentioned that I was now confident we would meet our schedules, based on the capable and effective efforts of my partner project leader. I praised his cooperation and expertise and publicly thanked him for his efforts.

Because of the attention the status report generated, the patch panel infrastructure was fully installed in plenty of time. In addition, throughout the rest of my project, whenever I saw the other team leader in the data center, he always asked if I needed anything done.

Project Meetings

Meetings are another important type of formal project communication. Controlling your meetings is crucial to controlling your project, because most people will assume, with justification, that if you cannot run a meeting well, you probably cannot run a project, either. If it is run well, your weekly project meeting will be one of your most useful control tools.

Unfortunately, on many projects the weekly meeting does not accomplish much, is only sporadically attended, and is primarily a time sink. Too many projects hold weekly status meetings with no agenda, and the meetings are best described as random conversational meanderings that terminate only when the scheduled time for the meeting is over. There are at least two potential problems with status reporting in meetings. One is the amount of time consumed reporting on things that are proceeding just fine. When there are no problems, particularly for parts of the project where many on your team may not be directly involved, listening to details is not an efficient use of your team's precious time. The second potential problem is to detour during the meeting into problem solving or a side topic that is of intense interest to a few participants but of little interest to others, and would be better dealt with outside of the meeting.

An effective project meeting should focus on three things: noting significant accomplishments and recognizing the people who were responsible; conducting a quick review of what lies ahead for the project (including discussion, as needed, of current issues where the involvement of the whole team is warranted); and giving each participant an opportunity to *briefly* comment on matters involving the team. In setting up the meeting, you should prepare a list of accomplishments and items to review, but also use your informal contacts with your team members to find out what each of them has on their mind. If someone has a topic that requires team attention, don't relegate it to just a quick comment. Ask the contributor who raised the issue to prepare it for the meeting (or help with it), add it to the formal agenda, and assign an appropriate amount of time for discussion.

Even with a formal agenda, important side topics will arise. While there are cases where the urgency is high enough to justify hijacking your meeting, the best course is to capture it as an action item and assign it to a subset of the project team to address outside of the project meeting. Extended excursions into problem solving that break out in team project meetings rarely involve everyone and are a poor use of time.

Your team will find project meetings useful and will willingly attend them if you:

- Obtain credible commitments from each team member to attend.
- Begin meetings on time and keep them short.
- Run the meetings efficiently with an agenda that you distribute in advance.
- Set ground rules for team meetings that everyone agrees to and diligently enforces.
- Minimize unnecessary conflicts during the meetings.
- End early whenever possible.

As part of your overall project documentation, be disciplined about documenting all of your project meetings so that team members who are unable to attend can keep up with your project. The minutes of the project team meeting are also an additional piece of communication that you can use to maintain people's awareness of your project. Use them to let your sponsor and key stakeholders know of your accomplishments, alert them to issues and potential problems, and make sure they do not forget about you. The set of minutes for your meetings will be useful in reviews, preparing for presentations, and will help ensure a thorough post-project analysis of lessons learned.

While it is difficult to imagine a project with no meetings, most projects can easily manage with fewer. Enhancing your control through meetings requires you to carefully consider the reason for each meeting you schedule and avoid calling a meeting whenever you have other effective options. For the meetings that you do hold, keep them as efficient, organized, and short as possible.

MINUTES TO PROVIDE CONTINUITY (AND SAVE HOURS)

Terry Ash, presently a director of information technology at Hewlett-Packard, is a veteran of many worldwide projects and virtual teams. "When running a global project," he says, "one of the most important things is communication, and I've found that it's impossible to overcommunicate. You need to communicate more than you think is necessary." He uses periodic teleconferences at workday-friendly times for all the time zones involved. The calls are weekly when his projects are running well; when in crisis mode, he holds teleconferences daily. Terry explains:

> "One key to doing these teleconferences successfully is making sure to take good notes, document the action items and confirm them over the telephone, and then follow up with an e-mail to ensure that everybody has understood them the same way. This is especially important when dealing with different cultures and team members whose native language is different from the language used by the project team. Reflective listening and double-checking what you heard and what is being committed to are key to avoiding confusion. When you come around to the next meeting, be it the next day or next week, you immediately use your meeting minutes as a reference point to get started. That way you can measure your progress since the last teleconference before moving on to any new issues you have."

For Terry, dealing with distant team members is all about disciplined, frequent interaction. "Communicate, as much as you can. Think of every way that you can to get messages and information back and forth between separated teams."

Presentations

Formal communication also includes project presentations. Presentations are often opportunities to directly capture the attention of your sponsor and stakeholders, and by influencing them you can improve your overall project control. They are also an excellent way to remind your sponsor, stakeholders and team why the project matters—to keep your project vision front and center. Presentations are also a good way to get attention for project issues that you need addressed and to recognize the accomplishments of your team members.

Most of what applies to meetings is also true of presentations, but because they are usually more formal and all of the objectives must be entirely achieved during a single meeting, planning and preparation need to be more rigorous. Because the purpose of this kind of meeting is unique, it may involve activities and items that you do not do very often, so prepare and review the agenda in detail.

Begin by clearly defining your objectives for the presentation. Identify the motivation for the presentation and align your objectives with the reason for the meeting. You may be convening this meeting to address the start of a new project, a project review, problem escalation, phase exits or stage-gate transitions, or a major change or other significant news.

Determine the people who should attend your presentation and outline the aspects of your project that matters most to each of them. Identify issues and questions that they will want you to address. Schedule your presentation to maximize the participation of your target attendees. Invite participants well in advance, and request that each person confirm their attendance beforehand.

Start your presentation with introductions if they are necessary, and lead with a high-level summary of your project objectives; don't assume that everyone knows as much about the work as you do. In your presentation, tell the audience what you're going to tell them, then tell them, and then tell them what you told them.

For presentations associated with phase or stage-gate transitions in your life cycle, prepare material that explicitly addresses all of the deliverables required for transition forward for your project. With any presentation, include updates on progress, accomplishments, and next steps to demonstrate the competence of your team and your effectiveness as the project leader. Also include a summary of issues and risks, with your specific efforts for managing them. In presenting information about remaining project work, be positive and use the information to motivate and renew enthusiasm and support for your project.

▪ Rewards and Recognition

Recognition and, where appropriate, rewards for your team will make controlling your project during execution a good deal easier. The principal of reciprocity—giving and getting—operates throughout your project, so you can increase your influence through public recognition of successfully completed work and secure commitments in exchange for specific rewards.

The easiest and cheapest (and most underused) form of reward and recognition is the simple thank-you. Contributors on complicated technical projects complete difficult work all the time, and often the only thing that they hear is, "Good—here's more work." When team members do a good, or even satisfactory, job on a project activity, don't miss the change to express your appreciation. Personal thanks will improve your relationships with your team, and it is an excellent excuse to manage by wandering around (or by telephoning around). Including thanks to individuals or teams working on your project in status reports can be very motivating. Thanking people for their work in an e-mail, and copying their managers when they do not report to you, is also a powerful way to strengthen your project influence and control. And, of course, it is something you should do anyway—you are genuinely grateful for every piece of your project that you can put behind you that brings you one step closer to successful completion.

Project leaders who don't have a great deal of formal authority may feel that they aren't able to do much about rewards and recognition. Even so, you can always request, propose, cajole, and use your influence to *recommend* these things to the people who can do something. This is a case where trying will be appreciated almost as much as succeeding. Whatever might come of a suggestion that you make for rewards, at least the individuals involved will appreciate your efforts.

Rewards and recognition work best when you know your team and can successfully predict what they'll appreciate the most. Public recognition can be either motivating or demotivating, depending on the individuals involved, cultural factors, and other circumstances. Public team rewards can do more for your project control than individual rewards in most cases, because they avoid the inevitable consequence of identifying one "winner" and, by implication, many "losers." Individual rewards, particularly those with significant value, may be of more help to your project when kept private.

Rewards and recognition fall into two broad categories, tangible and intangible. While granting tangible rewards may require more authority than you have as a project leader, intangible rewards are fair game for anyone.

Intangible Rewards and Recognition

Many ideas for recognizing contributions cost nothing but a little of your time and perhaps a negligible expense. These ideas work best when used unexpectedly. If you become predictable and your behavior begins to look insincere, your efforts may reduce overall morale and team cohesion.

- Thank people personally. (There, I said it again. Do it.) Write them a note and send a copy to their managers.
- Print out an e-mail thank-you note, then handwrite a personal comment (legibly) and sign it. Give or send it directly to the person.
- Highlight individual and team results in team meetings and include them in the meeting minutes.
- Give credit where credit is due. Use team member's names in your presentations, reports, reviews, and other project documents when discussing project accomplishments. Be specific about results, and describe why their contributions matter.
- Ask your project sponsor or other high-level manager to personally thank individuals on your team. (And thank them for doing it.)
- Communicate with the managers of your team members. Thank them for their cooperation and support for your project, then give them feedback on individual performance, particularly for each individual's annual performance appraisal.
- Organize brief gatherings for self-congratulation (always with snacks) when you pass significant milestones. Find a way to involve distant team members in a similar mini-celebration at their location.
- Recognize significant accomplishments of people and teams in public meetings (but only when you know it will be welcome and culturally appropriate).
- Put up a big sign that everyone at your location can see when you complete your project.
- Take individuals to lunch or send them a small, unique, and edible gift. (Be careful of food items that melt, though.)
- Offer project team members an opportunity to attend meetings with your sponsor, management, or key stakeholders.
- Delegate more responsibility for project work.
- Provide time off for work that requires personal sacrifice.
- Devise awards to acknowledge performance: small items such as buttons or a trophy that circulates among the team to recognize the "star of the week." Keep a public list, perhaps with pictures, and find plausible reasons to ensure that all team members are included sooner or later.

More Tangible Rewards and Recognition

Use tangible rewards with care, especially if they are given in public. When rewards or recognition are inconsistent with personal preferences or are unwelcome, they can be very demotivating. Most monetary rewards are private, and as with any positive reinforcement they are most effective when awarded randomly. When monetary incentives are routine and automatic, they are no longer seen as rewards. Some potentially motivating ideas that you might employ (or propose) are:

- Events and celebrations planned with members of your team
- Nomination of individuals or teams for award programs, either internal or external to the organization
- Approval to attend desired training or professional conferences
- Performance awards that have monetary value, such as gift certificates
- Promotion or explicit expansion of responsibilities
- Salary increases
- Bonuses or stock options

You can doubtless come up with your own long list of possibilities. Be creative, and discuss anything that you plan to do with your team to ensure that it will be welcome and motivating. No one enjoys forced merriment or being embarrassed.

▪ Project Reviews for Lengthy Projects

If you have a car, you probably don't do very much for it most weeks except add more fuel and perhaps wash it, look at the oil level, and check the air in your tires. While this works fine in the short run, if you never do more than this, the car will soon fail. Automobiles need periodic maintenance to run properly, so it's a good idea to take it in about twice a year to have it thoroughly checked. After six months you should replace the oil and repair anything that is wearing out, to restore it to good working order.

Longer projects present a similar challenge. The planning horizon for most complex projects is about three to six months, so a periodic review is useful to ensure that you have the information you need to control the next parts of your project. In addition, keeping the work on a very long project fresh and interesting is a challenge. Revitalizing the vision for lengthy projects is essential to maintaining team motivation. Reviews are often synchronized with life-cycle or stage-gate transitions, other significant milestones, completion of a major deployment, a substantial project change, or the close of a fiscal period.

Planning Your Review

Project reviews are similar to project start-up or planning workshops since they use much of the same material and agenda items, and you are focused on the project overall and developing an understanding of upcoming work. Also similar is the role a project review plays in reinforcing relationships and trust among your team members. Project reviews are most successful when you are able to meet face-to-face, so work with your sponsor to justify the expense of meeting in person on a regular basis throughout long projects.

One difference between early project workshops and a project review is that you'll have the opportunity to also look backward, similar to a post-project retrospective analysis (discussed in Chapter 9). A project review also lets you celebrate. (Long projects never seem to have enough parties.) A typical agenda will include:

- Review of the overall project objective and vision
- Recognition of significant accomplishments
- Revalidation of project constraints and assumptions
- Overall plan review, with detailed focus on the next phase of work
- Revisions to activity duration and effort estimates
- Review of resource and staffing plans
- Reassessment of project risks and risk responses
- Evaluation of project metrics and processes
- Adjustments to project infrastructure, based on experiences
- Review of contracts and outsourced work
- Planned team activities

Prepare for the review by assembling project documents and plans. Be sure to obtain updates for any materials that may have shifted since the start of the project or your last review because of changing market factors, user needs, or external factors. Schedule sufficient time to cover the items on your agenda (typically a day or longer is needed for complex projects). Set a date when the people you want to attend are available, and get a firm commitment from each of them to participate. If you are unable to meet in person, break the review up into smaller segments that are more appropriate for a teleconference and schedule them to minimize time-zone inconveniences.

Conducting Your Review

Begin your project review with a summary of major accomplishments and things that have gone well. Spend time reviewing why your project matters and the differences that your results will make, to revitalize your team and maintain motivation. Throughout your review, focus on how you plan to succeed with the next phase of the work, not why you might fail. Review new information and potential changes to the overall project objectives and develop course corrections in your plans to deal with them. Use the collaborative planning ideas from Chapter 6 to involve your whole team in updating schedules, estimates, dependencies, and other project data using your best current information.

Collect decisions, recommendations, and action items in writing throughout the review, then at the end, identify all the items captured that require more work and follow up after the meeting. Close the review with overall comments from participants about their expectations for the next phase of the project. Review all the action items and recommendations, and assign owners and due dates for each one.

Following Up After Your Review

Summarize the findings and recommendations from your meeting and send a report outlining your results to a distribution list, based on the one you use for your project status reports. Update all project plans and other documents as needed, and put the current versions in your PMIS, archiving all obsolete documents

Take action on recommendations that are within your authority, and submit any change requests necessary to your change control process. Discuss recommendations and major changes with your sponsor, negotiating modifications to your project baseline when needed. Implement changes as soon after your review as you can obtain appropriate approvals and agreements.

A review is a great opportunity to schedule a general update presentation about your project. Invite your stakeholders and leaders of other, related projects. Include your team in the presentation and offer to have members of your team prepare and present parts of it, if they want to. Use your presentation to summarize your project and its accomplishments and update people on your plans for the next stage of your work. By making your presentation positive, you can use it to enhance your overall influence in the organization and build your team motivation.

During or soon after the review, find opportunities to reward and recognize your team. Thank contributors for significant accomplishments and consider other options for expressing your appreciation. A review is also a good time to schedule a celebration of some sort to recognize your interim accomplishments; one party at the end of a multiyear project is not enough.

▪ Project Cancellation

Some projects that seem like excellent ideas, even through initiation and planning, ultimately prove to be poor uses of resources. As you progress you learn more and more, and barriers, risks, and challenges that were hidden at the outset emerge from the shadows to threaten your project. When the obstacles prove to be too great, cancellation may be inevitable.

Projects are canceled for many reasons. Some are stopped because they are unable to meet their goals. Watch for trends in your status metrics showing:

- Quality or other scope issues that fail to meet requirements
- Inadequate schedule progress
- Excessive resource consumption
- Inadequate staffing or other resource shortfall

Before you conclude that you should abandon your project, do at least a quick project review to verify the magnitude of your problems. Revisit the expected benefits and consider whether there is still be a credible business case to be made for continuing your project. If your project's current costs, timing, and value no longer make sense, investigate other options for scoping; opportunities that you were not aware of initially may now be apparent. Just because your project will not be able to achieve its original objectives does not necessarily mean that you should recommend canceling it. If you believe that your project is viable with modifications, discuss it with your team and stakeholders, set up a meeting with your sponsor, and negotiate a realistic new baseline. If it is clear, however, that the current prognosis for your project is dire, or if you are unsuccessful in setting a new baseline, prepare to bring your project to an end. One of the worst reasons to continue a project that extends well beyond its deadline or runs over budget is: "We're almost done." Throwing good money after bad, especially on projects with a history of chronic problems, is rarely a good business decision.

Healthy projects are also sometimes terminated, generally for reasons external to the project, such as:

- Loss of interest by the sponsor
- Shifts in business strategy or organizational priorities
- Actions by competitors or changes in market demand or user requirements
- Recognition, by the organization, that the projects running are exceeding capacity

In these cases, there may not be much that you can do about it. It's still useful, though, to verify assumptions and discuss alternatives for continuing with your management. Know the value and vision for your project, as it is or with modifications. New sponsorship, reprioritization, a major shift in scoping, or other changes might be a better proposition than cancellation.

However, when it's clear that your project must be canceled, accept it, and don't prolong the process. The longer a project runs, the more invested everyone gets in it. No matter when you pull the plug it will be difficult, demotivating, and stressful, but it is far less so after only a few months than it will be after everyone has invested a year of their life on the project.

When it is inevitable your project cannot be rescued, verify the decision to cancel with your sponsor and report it in writing to your team, your management, and your stakeholders. Write a final status report, summarizing the situation and describing any alternatives that were considered. Let people know the results that your project achieved and recognize your team's contributions, and include a summary of your plans for project closure.

Complete the shutdown of your project by updating your documents in the project management information system. If there is a possibility of resuming the project in the future, leave sufficient information to make continuing the work as easy as possible. Terminate any project contracts that you have using the terms set out in the contract. Document all the work that was completed under contract and determine any financial or other consequences of early termination. Complete any paperwork required for ending the contract and approve final payments that are due, including any penalties. Complete your other project closure activities, as outlined in Chapter 9, particularly the post-project analysis of lessons learned—there is generally a lot more to learn from things that go wrong than from success. Strive to keep things as positive as you can. Focus your retrospective analysis on what went well and things to change, and minimize recriminations, "blame-storming," and personal attacks. Thank people sincerely for their work and help everyone transition from the project to whatever they do next with enthusiasm.

▪ Control Challenges

Many of the challenges faced by project leaders who work with matrix, distributed, cross-functional, and global teams arise because of the "other" factor. It is easy to work with and gain the cooperation of people with whom we are friendly and we know well. From a distance, whether literal, intellectual, functional, cultural, or some other type, the situation reverses. People don't trust others they don't know.

To meet these challenges you need to use your influence to establish relationships and trust with your team members, as described in Chapter 3, and maintain good team cohesion through your loyalty, personal interactions, good humor, and other ideas, as outlined in Chapter 7. Most control problems are easiest to resolve (and to avoid in the first place) face-to-face, so meet with your contributors as frequently as practical. On longer projects, bring the team together at least twice a year for project reviews or other collaborative activities. Mistrust will develop over time between virtual team members who have little or no personal contact with each other. To remain in control, you will also need to manage barriers and conflicts.

Dealing with Barriers

Project teams often face barriers that block progress, such as inadequate resources, timing conflicts, or insufficient priority. Individuals on your team may face difficulties in their work that they cannot control, and often these issues will also be beyond your control. You need to confront and manage the obstacles.

Team cohesion depends on a "one for all, all for one" attitude across the whole team, and this starts with you as the project leader assuming each team member's problems as your own. If a problem is a result of a failure to fulfill some earlier written commitment, you may be able to resolve it by intervening, reminding the others of the promise, and mentioning that you would prefer not to have to widely circulate a detailed summary of the situation in your next status report. Communication (or even threatened communication) can be an effective way to deal with a wide range of issues and project problems.

In other situations, you will be able to use your planning and other project data to clearly show the consequences of not resolving an issue to the people responsible for the problem. A compelling, data-driven case should give you sufficient leverage to get things in your project back on schedule.

In the event of especially serious barriers, you may be unable to resolve them solely through your own efforts. In these more extreme cases, you may need to escalate to get help from your project sponsor or others with more authority. If you have successfully maintained good relationships with your sponsor and stakeholders, escalation will generally lead to a quick resolution (which is one reason, among many, to keep your project sponsors involved and supportive). Reserve escalation as a tactic of last resort, after exhausting all the options you have to influence and resolve the situation on your own. Frequent escalations will annoy your sponsor and undermine how you are perceived, and they will also alienate people that you need to work with and make project control more difficult.

Resolving Team Conflicts

Sometimes the barriers are within your own team, where one team member's progress is impeded by another. Team conflicts often arise from the different perspectives that diverse team members bring to the project. Since interpersonal conflicts can be so corrosive, dealing with them effectively is essential. The best approaches for dealing with conflicts among team members rely upon confrontation and compromise.

Other techniques for conflict resolution include autocratic forcing, using authority to mandate the leader's preferred solution, ignoring the situation for a time by withdrawing and moving on to other work, hoping that the conflict will diffuse, and smoothing over the situation by encouraging team members to be nice to each other. For project teams that need to cooperate over the course of a lengthy project, forcing, withdrawing, and smoothing over are not effective because they fail to deal with the conflict's root cause, which will likely recur and cause bigger troubles later in the project. Confrontation, pulling the issues causing the conflict into the open, and compromise provide a basis for long-term solutions that everyone involved will be able to live with.

Interpersonal conflicts are especially common in projects with cross-functional, virtual, or geographically dispersed teams, and when the project leader has limited authority. In these situations, dealing with project conflicts well and in a timely way is essential. Work with your team members to establish consensus for a conflict resolution process for diffusing disagreements throughout the project. Whenever a conflict arises among team members, work to promptly resolve it within your team by:

- Reviewing documented information for the project and resolving all portions of the disagreement that you can, using defined, validated data
- Setting up a face-to-face meeting (or a conference using a suitable technique) that includes all the people involved
- Establishing an environment where everyone will treat others with respect and be comfortable discussing matters openly
- Verifying that everyone wants to resolve the conflict
- Taking each issue of the conflict one at a time, starting with the ones that seem easiest
- Probing for information using open-ended questions and active listening, seeking to understand the source of the disagreement
- Letting people present their side of each issue
- Allowing everyone to ask questions of each speaker, but discouraging criticism and negative comments
- Avoiding outbursts of emotion and personality by maintaining a focus on facts and data
- Quantifying the matters discussed in terms of time, money, or other numerical units that will permit objective comparisons
- Brainstorming alternatives and combinations of ideas to find resolutions that are win-win—allowing all to agree with, or at least accept, a common solution
- Confirming closure of each issue as you reach agreement and documenting what you decide in writing

If a consensus solution proves impossible, you may find it necessary to "pull rank" and impose your decision. If so, support your position with as solid and logical a case as you can develop. Ensure that everyone understands why you believe your decision is best for the project and begin working to repair any bruised relationships.

For some conflicts, resolution within your team may not be possible. In these more serious cases, escalate the situation to your project sponsor or others with more authority. Problem escalation should always be your last resort, but sometimes a solution imposed from outside the team may be the only option possible. As with all escalations, use this tactic sparingly; it can generate resentment and malicious compliance on your team that can destroy your control.

HOLDING A DISTRIBUTED TEAM TOGETHER

Revathi Muruvanda Muthanna is a veteran of many projects for the Systems Technology and Software Division of Hewlett-Packard in Bangalore, India. On a recent project she faced a number of significant challenges. Her team was supporting the tool used to conduct peer reviews of development work in progress; it was used by three business units in India, working with four partner business units in the United States and elsewhere. She had scheduled several maintenance releases that depended on contributions from people in the business units involved, from her team, and from outside contractors. Most of the contributors were only available part-time to her project, with other priorities they were responsible for within their own organizations. Revathi recalls:

> "My biggest challenge was keeping the team together, ensuring that our schedule did not slip and that we could successfully deliver a quality product.
> "Because I did not directly manage any of the people on the distributed team, I set up regular weekly meetings with the contributors involved, face-to-face at their site whenever possible. This helped to connect the team, and we met our milestones with quality. I heard about problems and issues firsthand during my weekly interactions with the team members, and we were easily able to resolve problems working together."

Her investment in thorough communication even allowed her loosely coupled team to deal with a significant unanticipated change for a key release. With short notice, Revathi learned that the operating system version in current use was to be upgraded, posing a new and significant requirement for through testing of the production application in the new environment. To deal with this, she borrowed several extra computers to accommodate the additional testing, and she convinced her team to take up the challenge of meeting their existing milestones. "The success of the project was entirely due to following good project management principles," she says, "and staying connected to all of the people involved on at least a weekly basis."

KEY IDEAS FOR PROJECT TRACKING AND MONITORING

- Manage scope changes with a disciplined process that accepts only mandatory, business-justified modifications.
- Develop and take adaptive actions promptly whenever problems arise.
- Use reports and other formal communication to keep people in sync with your project and aware of its progress.
- Motivate your team using frequent thanks and recognition, and rewards when appropriate.
- Periodically review longer projects to validate objectives and plans, and to revitalize the project vision.
- Deal with barriers to progress and promptly resolve project conflicts.

CHAPTER 9

Enhancing Overall Control Through Project Closure

CLOSING A PROJECT WELL involves some time and work, but it is essential to the control of future projects. Getting agreement from your sponsor and all of your stakeholders that your work was satisfactorily completed is necessary before you can transition to new projects. Retrospective metrics contribute to longer-term control by guiding needed process improvements and validating predictive project metrics. Completing and archiving your final project documents will provide information necessary for defining and planning similar future projects.

And speaking of future projects: It's a small world, and it's safe to assume that you will work again with some of the people on your current project. So there are two more things that you should schedule with your team to reinforce your relationships and enhance control of future projects. The first is to celebrate your accomplishments and recognize and reward the contributions of your project team by thanking people for the work they did. The second is to conduct a post-project retrospective analysis, which will improve your control through standardizing the practices that worked well and improving processes that did not.

▪ Delivering Your Results and Getting Sign-Off

As important as it is to stay in control throughout your project, it is even more essential to bring everything to a successful conclusion. The whole point of your project is to create an appropriate deliverable so that when all the activities are complete, you are able to deliver what you have produced for evaluation and final approval. Getting written acknowledgment that you have delivered a satisfactory result is always a good idea, but it is particularly important for project leaders who lack much authority because the evidence may be useful at a later time.

If you defined your scope well during project initiation, including clear, quantified acceptance criteria, and you were able to minimize scope changes throughout your project, ensuring that your deliverable meets the required specifications should be straightforward. Whenever any changes are accepted during your project, make any necessary adjustments to acceptance criteria, testing plans and processes, and equipment you will need for testing. Before requesting final customer certification that the work is satisfactory, complete an even more stringent evaluation with your project team. Work to design your tests and checks so that what you produce will exceed, at least slightly, all the stated requirements. If your team's tests reveal defects or problems, develop plans to resolve them before user acceptance tests.

Deliver what you have produced as planned, and then inform your sponsor. Work with those who will approve your results to verify that you have met your project goals. Obtain approval for each in-scope requirement, one by one. If all requirements are accepted, get formal sign-off and notify your sponsor and other stakeholders. Sign-off varies for projects of different types, but it is generally coordinated with a project milestone event such as final life-cycle phase transition, release to shipping or manufacturing, customer or user acceptance, or final test. If your project was done under contract, promptly initiate the final customer billing.

If there are any exceptions noted where your project doesn't meet one or more requirements, document them and address any deficiencies by:

- Extending your project to accommodate additional work necessary
- Renegotiating project scope to be consistent with what you produced
- Obtaining conditional sign-off and committing to resolution at a future date

Even when there are deficiencies, get a written acknowledgment of what you did deliver. Distribute a summary of the results of acceptance testing in your next project status report, and archive it with the outcome of each of your tests in your project management information system.

▪ Employing Retrospective Project Metrics

In general, the role of retrospective metrics is to evaluate a process following execution. Retrospective measurements are especially useful for a project leader who has limited power and authority. These measures can provide the additional data you need to successfully negotiate with your managers and future sponsors on matters where you were unpersuasive in the past. These metrics are also useful on projects in determining how efficiently and effectively you worked during the project. Whether your project ends successfully, with difficulty, or even if it is canceled, backward-looking project measurements will reveal much about what you did well and what you need to improve. Specific uses of retrospective project metrics include:

- Validating the accuracy of predictive metrics
- Deciding when to improve or replace current project processes
- Providing guidance for fine-tuning your project processes (such as estimating)
- Assessing the effectiveness of your scope and change management
- Identifying significant individual or team accomplishments
- Uncovering new sources of risk and recurring problems
- Empirically forecasting the magnitude of "unknown" project risk
- Establishing standards for schedule reserves and budget reserves
- Tracking long-term trends

Defining Retrospective Project Metrics

Many retrospective metrics are after-the-fact actual measurements that correspond to plan-based predictive metrics. Others relate to the efficiency and effectiveness of your processes or other quantitative data for evaluating your project and comparing it with similar projects. Retrospective metrics will assist you in diagnosing your overall project; they will also help you to detect trends over time, both positive trends that you wish to continue and negative trends that you need to reverse. All of these objectives—setting better baselines for predictive project measures, improving project processes, and tracking overall trends—will equip you with the information you need to improve your control over future projects that you undertake. Examples of retrospective project metrics, grouped into several categories, are listed here. No project leader will find it useful or even necessarily possible to evaluate each of them, but you will find value in at least some of them.

Project Scale and Scope Metrics
- Actual "size" of project deliverable (such as component counts, number of major deliverables, lines of noncommented code, function or feature points, blocks on system diagrams, or volume of total output)
- Number of submitted changes
- Number of accepted changes

- Number of defects (classified by severity)
- Final performance and quality measures for deliverables compared to project objectives

Timing and Schedule Metrics
- Actual activity durations
- Actual project duration
- Number of missed major milestones
- Assessment of duration estimation accuracy
- Performance to standard duration estimates (for standardized activities)
- Number of new unplanned activities

Resource and Financial Metrics
- Actual activity costs (or effort)
- Actual total expense at project completion
- Total project effort
- Final earned value assessments, such as cost variance (CV) and schedule variance (SV), or other evaluation of effort or cost estimation accuracy
- Cumulative project overtime
- Added staff
- Staff turnover
- Actual life-cycle phase effort percentages
- Performance to standard effort estimates (for standardized activities)
- Variances in travel, communications, equipment, outsourcing, or other expense subcategories
- Measured value of the delivered benefits

General Project Metrics
- Late project defect correction effort, as a percentage of total effort
- Number of project risks encountered
- Project issues tracked and closed
- Actual measured return on investment

Deploying and Using Retrospective Metrics

Baselines for retrospective metrics are often based on retrospective measures from similar past projects and trend assessments. Be wary of making changes to processes based on the measures from only a single project. Another common issue with retrospective metrics is the "compared to what?" problem. Some adverse-looking variances and indices may derive more from unrealistic initial assumptions than from anything in your overall project process. (These measures will provide you with ammunition to better highlight faulty assumptions and to better manage expectations on future projects, however.)

As with predictive metrics, most of the data collection will fall to you. The choice of which metrics you evaluate, in addition to any that are required within your organization, is largely your personal choice. Metrics that relate to particularly problematic forecasts (such as project estimates), processes that you are concerned about, and aspects of your project infrastructure that need improvement are reasonable places to start.

Retrospective measures are a significant source of information for post-project lessons learned, and the preliminary assessment of these metrics will be one focus of your project reviews. Process improvement is an important use of backward-looking measures. Retrospective metrics have a role (along with trends in diagnostic metrics) as a trigger for initiating a focused effort to modify poor processes; they are also your primary means of evaluating process changes. Retrospective measurements from your previous, inadequate process can be compared with retrospective measurements from your modified process to verify whether you have met your process improvement goals. If you have not, the measurements will tell you that you need to seek other modifications, and the specific numbers may help you find the best opportunities to investigate.

▪ Administrative Closure

Closing out a project involves several administrative activities to finish up the project paperwork and say thank-you to your team. These steps include closure (if necessary) for any outsourced work and issuance of final project reports.

Closure for Outsourced Work

If some of your contributors are working under contract, verify that all of their work is satisfactory and all deliverables, documentation, reports, and other outputs have been received. Review the contract to ensure that all parties, including you, have met the terms of the agreement, including any approved revisions or amendments.

If you find any deficiencies, discuss them with your contractors or the supplier liaison for that contract. Whenever possible, resolve all variances involving project requirements by successfully getting the work completed. If any part of the work you contracted for can't be finished, determine any consequences, such as penalties or payment adjustments. If there are any other significant differences between the terms of a contract and the actual performance of your contractors, determine their consequences as well and what you need to do to deal with them. If necessary, escalate to others with sufficient authority to resolve all outstanding contract issues.

Complete the financial obligations of each contract by reviewing the payment histories and approving all final payments required by the terms of each contract. Also complete all of the paperwork and reporting required within your organization to account for contracted work, and verify that all the necessary project accounting you are responsible for is finished accurately and promptly. After all final payments are made, terminate the contract, or at least the portion of the contract that relates to your project.

As a final step, evaluate the overall performance of each service supplier you worked with during your project. If any of your contract work was terminated before the end of your project, thoroughly document the situation, especially if it was due to performance issues. Add the document to your project information archive along with all accounting reports, contract communications, status project reports, contract change history, and other relevant documents. Forward a copy of your supplier evaluation information to your peers who are responsible for similar project work, since they may want to consider using comparable services in the future.

Final Project Reports

Write a final project report, including all of the information that is customarily reported at project end within your organization. Use your final report to communicate to your team, your sponsor, and your stakeholders that the project is over. A final project report is generally very similar in structure to the periodic status reports that you send throughout your project, but it focuses on the project as a whole, not just on current events. It also is an excellent place to recognize specific accomplishments achieved by your entire project team and to formally highlight significant contributions made by individuals and by groups of contributors to your project.

As with all of your project status reports, it is best to begin your final report with a high-level summary, a small number of points that include your project's most significant accomplishments, and thanks to all of your contributors. Structure the rest of the report to supply details and project retrospective metrics on important aspects of your project. If you have completed your post-project analysis of lessons learned by the time you issue your report, also include your most important recommendations, placing them near the beginning of your report. Include your final report in your project information archive.

▪ Celebration and Team Rewards

One of the best (and certainly the easiest and least expensive) things that project leaders can do to motivate people and reinforce their influence is to thank team members for their contributions to the project. Express sincere gratitude to each of your team members for the help, support, and hard work provided during the project. Thank people face-to-face if possible. For distant team members, at least make a personal telephone call. Find at least one thing in particular to comment on for each individual as a way to reinforce your appreciation. Also express your thanks in writing, and send the notes to the managers of contributors who do not report to you. Chances are that you will work with at least some of the people again who were on your team, and how you exit this project will make a difference when you meet again. (And even if you don't ever work together again, thanking people is still the right thing to do. It can't hurt, and it might help.)

Rewards and other types of recognition (as covered in Chapter 8) are another important way to positively reinforce the contributions of individual contributors and groups of people on your team. Be generous in giving credit for project accomplishments to your team members in presentations, discussions with management, and in other conversations.

As project leader, you have another final task: arranging to commemorate the end of your project with some sort of event. If your project was highly successful and you can get approval to hold a party or take your team out to dinner, find out what your team would prefer and then organize it. If you are not able to do anything significant that might involve additional expense, at least set up a small get-together to end your project on a positive note. Even if your project didn't end exactly as planned or there were problems along the way, you will be able to identify a few achievements to commemorate that you can all be proud of. Effective celebrations don't need to be elaborate; simply getting together to share some snacks that you provide or having a potluck meal together, with food contributed by everyone on your team, can be a great way to end a project. If your team is distributed across several sites, consider options that will allow each location to have a comparable event. Find a way to let everyone join the party.

▪ Capturing Lessons Learned

Some project teams break up and scatter immediately, so the only chance to meet and reflect on the project as a whole will be right at the end of the work. If that's your only chance to capture lessons learned, schedule time with your entire team that coincides with delivering your results. However, if you can wait a week or so after your project work completes and schedule a separate activity for this purpose, you will generally get a more useful outcome. Waiting will give people a chance to reflect on the project as a whole, rather than just on the last part of the work, which tends to be stressful and will adversely affect how people feel about the project. Never delay more than two weeks, though, because you may have difficulty getting people to participate, and memories, especially bad memories, can fade quickly. Whenever you do it, a post-project retrospective analysis will give you an opportunity to discuss all aspects of the project and allow you and your team to put it securely in the past and move on to whatever is next. If you have difficulty persuading any of your team members to participate, then tell them it's an opportunity to bring things to emotional closure and to give voice to their feelings about the project, both good and bad. That may convince them to attend.

The overall process is structurally very similar to a project review, except that the focus of a review is primarily forward looking, designed to address the remaining project work, whereas a retrospective analysis is, as the name suggests, primarily backward looking. Your tasks are to prepare for the retrospective, to meet to review project results and processes, and then to document and follow up on recommendations.

Preparing for the Retrospective

The value of a retrospective relates to improving long-term project control, and you accomplish that by identifying good practices to keep and bad practices to change. The first task is not very difficult and is likely well within your authority as a project leader. The second can be somewhat tricky, because change is difficult and recommendations from your post-project analysis might be ignored. Some organizations faithfully do retrospectives, and still project after project reports the same problems, over and over. The documents are written, distributed, and filed, yet nothing ever changes. For a retrospective analysis to be worth the time and effort, you need a commitment to take action on the results. In advance, request support from your sponsor for a minimum of one recommendation produced by your analysis. Remember, one definition of insanity is doing the same thing again and again, hoping for a different result. You can use this commitment as another good reason to encourage your team's participation.

Before the meeting, send each participant a template or survey to get them thinking about the overall project. Collect information about your project in categories such as project management processes, project infrastructure, communications and information management, and tools and techniques. Solicit thoughts about what went well and what could use improvement, and challenge people to develop recommendations to address anything that they do not believe went as well as it might have. At minimum, collect the input of any participants you invited who won't be able to attend, then compile all the input you collect to seed your discussions.

Arrange to have the current project documents and retrospective metrics available for reference during the actual meeting, including your final report, if it is complete. And establish an agenda for the meeting that includes:

- Discussion of things that went well in the project
- Identification of processes or other project aspects that need improvement
- Prioritization of recommendations
- Action plans and summarization of lessons learned
- Thoughts about the project from each contributor

Meeting to Review Project Results and Processes

A retrospective analysis is just a meeting, so structure it to be effective. Start the meeting promptly, review of the agenda, come to agreement on ground rules (especially one prohibiting personal criticisms), and assign a recorder to keep track of what happens. Open the discussion with a focus on what went right, for two reasons: It will start things off on a positive note and if you fail to discuss the good outcomes first, you may never get to them. Keep track of processes that were particularly effective and of any things that your project did differently from earlier projects that were useful. When you have listed and discussed most of the positive things people have identified (including the data you collected from those unable to attend), begin to identify potential changes.

For changes, look for processes to modify or eliminate, practices to simplify, and opportunities to standardize work or develop a new process. Focus on the work, not on "blame-storming" and identifying scapegoats for things that did not go well on the project. Use measurements from your project to quantify the need for changes. If arguments arise concerning what happened during the project, resolve them using your project reports and other documents. When you have identified specific suggestions for areas of improvement, prioritize your list and focus on the top two or three items.

Use root-cause analysis to understand the source of each item, and brainstorm possibilities that could potentially deal with each identified situation. Consider all the recommendations as a team, and select the best options for implementation.

If you can implement a recommendation working with your team, identify an action item and plan to do it. If any recommendations require more authority than you possess, assign yourself an action item to develop a proposal and take it to your sponsor or other management.

As you close your meeting, collect all the issues and action items and verify the owners and due dates. Summarize what you have learned and ask all participants to write down something that they plan to do differently on the next project. End the meeting by offering each person a chance to quickly comment on the project and to share personal plans for future work. End with yourself, and use the opportunity to reinforce your thanks to everyone for their contributions.

Documenting and Following Up on Recommendations

Document your retrospective meeting and summarize the recommendations you and your team have made. Include details of the meeting as well, such as the lists of what went well and what should change. Send your summary to the members of your team who participated in the analysis and add it to your project management information system.

Follow up on your key recommendations. Implement the changes recommended where you can, and work to convince your management to approve more significant changes using metrics, your project team's input, and other supporting data. For process changes that you implement, use metrics to verify that you have achieved the results you expect, and carefully watch out for unintended consequences.

MEASURING SUCCESS

When projects encounter trouble, post-project analysis usually turns up the same issues that plagued other, earlier projects: "We didn't fully understand the requirements" or "We didn't spend enough time planning" are the common reactions. Esteri Hinman, currently a manager in the Corporate Program Management Office at Intel Corporation, relates a different story from an experience before she joined Intel, when she participated in a project retrospective analysis for a project:

> "My personal experience has taught me the value of thorough planning. A former manager of mine 'bet his career' on project planning. He was convinced that by applying more rigor to our processes, particularly the up-front processes, he would gain high productivity dividends. For his software development project, he did everything by the book, with a great deal of discipline. His team was still defining user needs when parallel projects in the same program were closing up their requirements. When everyone else was well into coding, his team was still meeting weekly with the customer to validate output, walk through an exhaustive list of business cases, and define usage models. His team started coding when everyone else had already begun unit testing.
>
> "But his team's coding went quickly because of their

thorough analysis, and they began system tests around the same time the rest of the teams went to quality assurance and customer acceptance test. His team continued to accelerate through all the testing phases and finished ahead of the rest of the other projects—with a significantly lower bug rate and a more successful customer acceptance test than any of the other teams.

"At the project retrospective, we learned that his project team was *439 percent* more productive than any other team in the program. His team accomplished with ten people what similar teams would have needed more than forty people to do. The principal reasons were reduced rework, a clearer understanding of the business needs, a better customer relationship, and superior overall project management."

The results of this retrospective are a compelling basis for continuous improvement of the planning process.

Esteri uses this example to overcome resistance to thorough project planning. She observes, "Project teams want to get going, and planning never seems very much like 'real project work.' People need to feel that they are accomplishing something." She deals with this by employing a "plan for the plan" to guide her teams through the initial analysis and planning phases for her projects. "This approach fills several needs," she says. "First, it gives the team a sense of accomplishment as they complete the planning deliverables. Second, it shows that the planning process, which few enjoy but everyone understands is necessary, will in fact soon come to a close and we can begin project execution. I have found that with teams using this approach we can produce higher quality, more thorough plans, and have far more successful projects."

KEY IDEAS FOR PROJECT CLOSURE

- Finish your work and get formal acceptance for your deliverables.
- Complete final project documentation.
- Thank your team and celebrate what you accomplished.
- Capture and apply the lessons you learned.

CHAPTER 10

Conclusion

IF YOU ARE ASKED to lead a project, *someone* believes that you are capable of doing it. If you believe it too, then you are both probably correct.

There are many elements of project control, but control begins with an understanding of the overall process of project management, figuring out what your project requires to be done, and then gaining commitments from the team members to do the work. The rest of control involves work—keeping up with all the effort, analyzing the status you collect, developing responses to deal with variances, and communicating project status—but it is manageable if you set the right foundation.

The first half of this book outlines three essential elements for control:

1. *Process* for ensuring consistency and alignment
2. *Influence* for gaining cooperation and establishing teamwork
3. *Metrics* for assessing the state of your project and driving behavior

The second half explores using these elements to control your project, starting with initiation, through planning, execution, and tracking, and finally ending with closure. While there are many ideas and examples included in this book to consider, projects come in all shapes and sizes, so determining exactly what will help you control your project best is a judgment that you must make. Rather than becoming overwhelmed with every single detail, pick a few ideas that relate to aspects of your recent projects that should have gone better.

Select a few practices from the book that you believe will help and then tailor them to use in your project. Apply them as you proceed, and pick some additional ideas for your next project.

Managing a project with limited authority is difficult, and it can be discouraging. If some particular problem arises during your project, review the material here for possible responses and use them to help manage your way back into control. Involve your team in problem solving. Work with colleagues who can act as mentors and sounding boards to support you when things are not going well and help you deal with obstacles.

Teamwork always makes a difference, because a high-performing, close-knit project team tends to find a way around most project difficulties, even seemingly insurmountable ones. Whatever else you do, work to establish and maintain a solid relationship of trust and respect with each member of your project team.

No matter how thorough your plans and regardless of how proactive you are in detecting and dealing with problems, there will inevitably be situations that you can't manage within your team. Throughout your project, keep your sponsor aware of your progress and issues, and when you do encounter barriers or problems you are unable to resolve, escalate promptly. Make your sponsor's job in helping you as easy as possible by providing a clear summary of what you are facing, an outline of the consequences of failing to deal with the situation, and at least one credible option for resolution. A cooperative sponsor is your ultimate control tool. If you escalate only to deal with the most severe project obstacles and showstoppers, your tactic of last resort can restore your control.

This suggestion works effectively only when sponsors behave properly, and sometimes they don't. Sponsors who act badly create project problems that lead to failure, and they may be completely unaware of what they are doing. Patrick Schmid, managing director of PS Consulting in Germany, once presented his list of sure-fire methods for sponsors to ensure project failures at a project management conference. I call this useful list "Maximum Strength Projecticide." You have Patrick's full permission to use his list in any way that might encourage your sponsors to act in the best interests of their projects.

How to Guarantee That Every Project Will Fail

- Always select projects using only "gut feel."
- Never share project selection criteria with the project team; it's none of their business.
- Avoid accountability for the project by claiming you're not the only decision maker.
- Always demand "stretch goal" results that are unachievable.

- Enlist additional sponsors to provide the project leader with conflicting objectives.
- Hold back allocated resources for more important things until the project is in crisis.
- Never waste time talking with project leaders; you have important things to do.
- Ignore environment changes and focus only on your daily activities.
- Make changes to projects at least weekly to keep everybody on their toes.
- Never make even small decisions without demanding more information and a detailed investigation.
- Discourage any analysis of post-project lessons learned, because everything will be different next time, anyway.

Ultimately, succeeding with any project is all about gaining the cooperation of all the people involved. Marketing guru and motivational speaker Zig Ziglar says, "You can get everything in life you want if you help enough other people get what they want." Controlling projects when you have little authority comes down primarily to aligning your project activities and goals with those of your sponsor, your team, and your stakeholders, and getting by with a little help from your friends.

Appendix A: Example Project Infrastructure Decisions

THESE SAMPLE QUESTIONS may be useful in drafting your own list. There are many more questions here than any single project would ever find useful, so only select the critical few decisions that will really make a difference. After many projects, you will probably find that you have given attention to most of these questions.

Planning Questions

Project Initiation
- Who is the sponsor of this project? What is the stated business purpose of the project?
- How will the project charter be developed? Who will write it?
- Who will review and approve the project charter?
- How will the initial project scoping be defined and documented?
- Who is responsible for validating the proposed initial project scope?
- What departments, functions, and external organizations will be involved in this project?
- Who are the key stakeholders for this project? For the project, what is the interest or connection for each stakeholder?
- How will the project be staffed? Who is responsible for resolving all open staffing decisions? What is the timing for closure?
- If hiring is required, how will it be done? Who will be responsible?

- For project team members who report to other managers, how will staffing commitments be documented? What ongoing role in the project will the managers in the other organizations play?
- What are the roles and responsibilities of each team member?
- Who is responsible for defining and managing the development, training, and skill building (if any) needed for each contributor to the project?

Project Plan Development
- What life cycle applies to this project? Will any modifications be needed?
- What activities are mandated at life-cycle phase-exits, checkpoints, stage gates, or milestones?
- Will a project methodology be used? Will this project need to get any exceptions or changes approved?
- What process will you use to develop the plan?
- What level of planning detail is appropriate for this project?
- What are the agenda and timing for a project start-up workshop? Where and when will it be held? What approvals will you need for the meeting?
- How will you capture and document project assumptions and constraints?
- How will you identify, analyze, and plan for project risk?
- What planning meetings will you hold?
- When and how will you conduct the planning meetings?
- How will you identify, document, and manage dependencies between related projects?
- How will you and your team conduct a review of the plan documents?
- What is the process and timing for establishing the plan as a project baseline?
- What process will you use if you must make changes to the baseline plan?
- Who approves the decision to freeze the baseline plan?
- Do you plan to conduct periodic plan reviews for this project? How frequently?

Outsourced Work
- How will you determine if you will need to outsource project work? Who in your organization must be involved in the outsourcing process?
- Before outsourcing project work, what approvals will you require? What support will you need, and who will provide it?
- Who will thoroughly document all work that is to be outsourced to an

external supplier? Who will create the request for proposal or other document that will be distributed to potential suppliers?

- Who will manage communications with potential suppliers and collect their proposals? Who will evaluate each proposal? With what process?
- Who will select suppliers for outsourced work? Who will negotiate the terms for the contracts and obtain all needed signatures and approvals?
- Who on your project team will be responsible for managing the relationship with each supplier while the contracts are in force? In each case, will the same person track progress, approve payments, and serve as a liaison?

Planning Deliverables
- What format is required for each planning component?
- What information is needed in the project charter?
- What are your standards and format for the project scope documentation?
- At what level of detail will you document your work breakdown structure (WBS)?
- What information will you define for each project activity?
- How will you develop, verify, and capture duration and effort estimates?
- What cost budgeting information does your project require?
- What level of detail will you use in your resource and staffing plans?
- What quality planning is necessary?
- What contracts and documents will be needed for outsourced work?
- How will you document and track project risks?
- What will be in your communications plan?
- Will you require a formal quality plan?
- What additional project planning documents, if any, are mandated by your life cycle, methodology, or organization?
- Where will project documents be stored?
- How will project data be distributed? How will you manage any security considerations on access to project data?
- Will it be necessary to provide any project planning documents in more than one language? If so, who will be responsible for translation into each relevant language? How will you verify consistency between versions?

Planning Participants
- In addition to the project leader, who will plan the project?
- What are the roles for the participants in the planning process? What are their responsibilities?
- How will you involve remote team members in project planning?

- Who will review the overall project plan?
- Who will validate and sign off on each project document?
- What are the roles of the project sponsor and other stakeholders in project planning?
- Who will be responsible for representing the customers and users of the project deliverable in planning?
- Who is responsible for the final decision to set the project baseline?

Planning Tools
- What techniques will you use for project planning and scheduling?
- Will you use a software application for project scheduling and tracking? Which product and version? Are related projects using the same tools?
- Who will enter the information into and use any software tools for planning? Will the same person be responsible for tool use in tracking?
- Will you use an automated tool for issue management, change control, resource and budget tracking, risk analysis, project communications, or other purposes? If so, which products and versions?
- Will other software (such as programs for database management, spreadsheet analysis, word processing, presentations and graphics, or knowledge management) be needed? What applications and versions will you use?
- Do you have all the equipment, capacity, and performance to operate the software you will use? When will all needed hardware and upgrades be available?
- If you need to share information with others who are using different software products or versions, how will you resolve compatibility issues?
- What tool training will be needed?
- What support will you need? Who will support your planning tools?

Planning Measures
- What plan-based predictive metrics will you define for this project?
- Who will document and evaluate the plans to determine the measures?
- How will you use these measures for your project?

Execution Questions

Project Status
- What status information will you collect for the project? What level of planning detail will you use as a basis for status requests?
- How frequently will you collect project status? On what day (or days)?

- What method will you use to collect project status from team members? Will you use different methods for remote contributors?
- How will you validate status data?
- Who will compare the status with the project baseline plan and assess project impact?

Status Metrics
- What status-based diagnostic measures will you use for this project?
- Are all metrics clearly defined and documented?
- Does each measure have a validated baseline or other realistically defined control limits?
- Are all measures understood by the people who will collect and report them? Have all people involved willingly agreed to participate?
- How will you minimize "gaming" of the project metrics?
- Will all metrics be collected in each status cycle? Who will collect any measures that are collected on a different frequency? How will these measures be collected?
- What process will you use to evaluate the measures?
- How will you use diagnostic measures on your project?
- What trends will you track for the diagnostic metrics? Are responses defined for metrics that drift outside defined control limits? Who will take action?
- In addition to routine project status reports, what other reporting will you do using diagnostic project metrics? How frequently?

Project Management Information System (PMIS)
- Where will status data and other diagnostic metrics data be stored?
- Who is responsible for establishing the PMIS? How will information be organized?
- Who will maintain and have change access to the PMIS? If multiple people can update the PMIS, who has authority to resolve any inconsistencies or information conflicts?
- Which project contributors and stakeholders, if any, will be restricted to read-only access to the PMIS?
- For project data stored online, how will you manage access security?
- What specific documents and other information will be in the PMIS?
- Will all documents in the PMIS be in the same language? For any documents in a different language, how will you handle translation? If some documents will be translated into one or more additional languages, how will you check the content for consistency?

- How long will project data in the PMIS be archived following the project?

Project Meetings
- What regular meetings will be held for this project? What are the stated objectives for the meetings?
- On what day and time will regular meetings be held? Where?
- If relevant, how will remote team members participate in the meetings? Will multiple meetings or periodic time shifts be necessary?
- Does each routine meeting have a well-defined standard agenda?
- Who is responsible for managing any changes or additions to the agenda for specific meetings, and who will distribute a reminder, including the current agenda, before each meeting?
- Is the length of each meeting as short as practical considering the agenda?
- Who will lead the meetings? Will the same person facilitate all of the meetings?
- Who is responsible for keeping notes during the meeting? Who will document the meeting and distribute meeting minutes to all attendees, appropriate stakeholders, and others?
- What documented ground rules do you use for project meetings?
- What other meetings, if any, will be required for this project? Where and when will they be scheduled? What are the purpose and agenda for these meetings, and who will lead them?

Team Concerns
- How will you and your project team make collaborative decisions? If you are unable to reach consensus, how do you come to closure?
- What process will you use to track project issues and problems?
- Where will issues and action items be logged and managed?
- How frequently will you update and communicate issue status?
- How will you manage conflicts between team members?
- How long will you spend trying to resolve decisions, issues, or conflicts within your team before escalating the situation? What other criteria will you use before escalating a team problem to someone with more authority?
- Who will you escalate problems to, as a last resort? Does that person have sufficient authority to make final decisions?
- What team activities unrelated to project work will you schedule? What else will you do to enhance team building?
- What training and development for team members is necessary and

appropriate on this project? How will you obtain the necessary approvals and support for this training?
- For this project, what periodic rewards and recognition will be available for team members? What will you do to ensure that you take advantage of all appropriate opportunities? Does your recognition process include notification of the managers of team members who report to others?
- How frequently will you meet one-on-one with each team member? Do you plan to provide specific feedback on performance and results at least monthly? Typically, how much of your discussions with individuals will be about nonproject matters?
- How frequently is the job performance of each team member formally evaluated? What will you do to ensure that your inputs are included in each project contributor's performance appraisal?

Informal Communications
- What will you do to encourage frequent interactions and informal conversations among project team members?
- What will you do to enhance relationships and trust between yourself and remote team members?
- What communication methods will you use for the project?

Life Cycles, Methodologies, and Other Organizational Requirements
- What specific deliverables are mandated by your organization at phase-exits, stage gates, or other project transition points?
- When are the deliverables due, and how much lead time should you allow normally for preparation of these documents, reports, and other items?
- Who will be responsible for preparation of the information needed?
- What other deliverables, if any, must you supply to your organization (or others) to comply with a project methodology, published standards, laws, regulations, or other requirements? When are they due? Who will be responsible for creating these deliverables?

Process Management and Quality Assurance
- Are key processes relating to consistent execution of project work and ensuring the quality of your deliverable well documented, understood, and routinely used?
- How frequently do you conduct process audits or reviews to ensure that the processes continue to serve their need? Alternatively, what diagnostic metrics with control limits will you monitor for these processes to trigger a review?
- What is your procedure for evaluating a process and proposing process

improvements? If the process affects other projects or teams, how do you manage modifications?

- What reporting or other communications, if any, are you required to provide during this project on your project processes?

Control Questions

Project Reporting

- What routine project reporting will be required?
- What format will be used for regular project status reporting?
- Who is responsible for creating reports? How often?
- Who will distribute the reports? Who will receive the reports?
- Will status reports in more than one language be necessary? If so, who is responsible for translation?
- Will summary or specialized reporting be needed for the project sponsor or key stakeholders? Who will create it? How frequently?
- In addition to periodic status, will separate reports for issue tracking, scope changes, risk management, or other project aspects be required for this project? Who will create them? How frequently?
- What criteria will be used to determine if problem or exception reports need to be generated? What distribution list will you use for nonroutine reporting?

Scope and Specification Control

- What is the process for project scope freeze? Will project scope be frozen to coincide with setting the project baseline? Who approves scope freeze? How is the accepted project scope documented?
- What scope change management process will you use? Where is it documented? Have all team members, your sponsor, and all relevant stakeholders (especially customers) agreed to the process?
- How will you document, log, and track all proposed changes?
- What criteria will you use to separate routine changes from urgent requests that must be dealt with as soon as possible?
- What process will you use to analyze each submitted change? How will you verify expected benefits or results? How will you estimate the cost, resource, timing, and other impact to the project? How will you assess potential risks and unintended consequences associated with each proposed change?
- Who needs to be involved in analyzing proposed changes?
- How frequently will you consider nonurgent changes?
- How quickly will decisions on routine changes be made?
- What process will be used to determine the disposition of each change?
- Which individuals are involved in making decisions to accept or reject

requested changes for your project? What is the role of each person? If the group fails to reach consensus on a particular change, who makes the final decision?

- How will you communicate change decisions?
- For each accepted change, who is responsible for updating the plans and other project documents? How will you obtain commitment from a team member to follow through and implement each accepted change?
- For major changes that impact the project baseline, what is the process for making a change? Who needs to approve project baseline modifications?

Overall Control

- Who in addition to the project leader is involved in assessing project progress? What is each person's role?
- How will you assess schedule progress?
- How much deviation from the baseline schedule will you accept before involving your project team in planning for a response?
- How much time slippage will you accept before escalating to management, either to get more assistance for recovery than your team can provide or to reset the project objective and modify the project baseline?
- How will you assess cost and resource usage?
- How much deviation from the planned project effort and expense estimates will you accept before exploring response options with your project team? Is overtime (particularly unpaid overtime) acceptable on this project? How much?
- How much effort or financial overrun can you tolerate before escalating to management to change the project baseline and approve more funding or obtain more staff?
- What metrics related to deliverable quality are relevant for this project? When the measures are outside acceptable ranges, how will you respond?
- How will you determine progress for outsourced work? What interim deliverables, early tests or inspections, or other evidence of progress are available? What remedies and responses do you have for addressing inadequate performance? If necessary, is there anyone to whom you can escalate? What alternatives, if any, are available that could substitute for the outsourced effort?
- How frequently will you reassess project risks? How do you document and communicate newly uncovered potential problems?
- How do you monitor for trigger events associated with identified risks? How often do you monitor the overall risk profile for the project? How

much risk will you and your sponsor and stakeholders accept before considering changes to the project or cancellation?

- What will you do if you lose your sponsor because of reorganization, resignation, health problems, or just loss of interest in your project? How will you reacquire adequate sponsorship to sustain progress?

Individual Performance Problems

- If analysis of a project performance problem appears to be due to inadequate performance by a project contributor, how will you investigate the situation and determine the cause?
- How will you confront the individual and work together to resolve the performance problem?
- If the individual reports to another manager, how will you involve this manager in your discussions?
- How will you renew the team member's commitment, document agreement, and work to resolve the project problem? What criteria will you use to determine when a situation cannot be resolved and you need to find other alternatives?

Project Reviews and Baseline Management

- How often will this project require plan reviews?
- Who will schedule and plan the reviews?
- Which project team members need to participate in the review?
- Will the sponsor or other stakeholders participate in the review?
- What is your project review agenda?
- Who will lead the review? Will the same person facilitate the review meeting?
- If all necessary people are unable to meet in the same location, how will you involve the remote participants?
- Who will take notes during the project review?
- How will the results of the review be documented? Who will the results be distributed to?
- Who will add the data to the PMIS?
- How will any changes, proposals, or other results of the review be presented to the project sponsor and other stakeholders?
- Who will follow up and ensure that all actions assigned in the review are closed promptly?

Project Cancellation

- What criteria will be used to determine whether to stop this project?
- Who has ultimate responsibility to decide whether to change the project baseline or to cancel the project?

- What process will you use to close a canceled project? What activities and deliverables are required?

Project Closure
- What process will you use for testing and scope verification?
- What sign-offs and approvals are required? Who must validate successful project completion?
- When will you conduct the post-project retrospective analysis to determine lessons learned? Who will participate?
- What end-of-project reports are required? Who will write them? Who will receive them?
- What process will you use to close out the contracts used for outsourced project work?
- How will you commemorate the conclusion of the project with your project team (for example, with a celebration or party)?
- What rewards and recognition are possible for individuals and teams who contributed to the project? What will you do to ensure that all appropriate rewards are used and that you personally thank each contributor?

Retrospective Metrics
- What post-project measures will you collect on this project?
- Are all retrospective metrics unambiguously defined and documented?
- Who will collect post-project measures for this project? How will these measures be collected and validated?
- What process will you use to evaluate the measures?
- How will you use retrospective measures to improve your next project?

Appendix B:
Selected References

WHILE THERE ARE HUNDREDS OF BOOKS on project management, influence, and metrics, the few listed here are a good starting point for further exploration of the topics covered in this book.

▪ Books on Project Management

Cagle, Ron. *Your Successful Project Management Career*. New York: AMACOM, 2004. This book provides a structured view of project management that is particularly useful for new project leaders. It offers extensive pointers to additional PM references.

Kendrick, Tom. *The Project Management Tool Kit: 100 Tips and Techniques for Getting the Job Done Right*. New York, AMACOM, 2004. Short process descriptions of essential project management processes.

Kerzner, Harold. *Project Management: A Systems Approach to Planning, Scheduling, and Controlling (Ninth Edition)*. New York: John Wiley & Sons, 2005. This sizable volume is thought by many to be the bible on project management.

Newell, Michael W. *Preparing for the Project Management Professional (PMP) Certification Exam*. New York: AMACOM, 2005. A detailed tour of the Project Management Institute (PMI) and PMBOK, with solid explanations of key concepts.

Project Management Institute. *A Guide to the Project Management Body of Knowledge (Third Edition)*. Newtown Square, PA: Project Management Institute, 2004. The PMBOK Guide is an overview of a wide range of project management topics. It provides a vocabulary and high-level descriptions, but lacks specifics on what to do and how to do it.

▪ Books on Influence

Cialdini, Robert B. *Influence: Science and Practice (Fourth Edition)*. Boston: Allyn & Bacon, 2000. A systematic exploration of how influence operates.

Cohen, Allan R., and David L. Bradford. *Influence Without Authority (Second Edition)*. New York: John Wiley & Sons, 2005. A very complete and thorough book on the topic of exchange and reciprocity.

DeMarco, Tom, and Tim Lister. *Peopleware: Productive Projects and Teams*. New York: Dorset House, 1999. Insightful essays on the human side of project management.

Fisher, Roger, and Alan Sharp. *Getting It Done: How to Lead When You're Not in Charge*. New York: HarperBusiness, 1999. A useful book on influencing others that builds on Fisher's *Getting to Yes* and focuses on principled negotiation.

Englund, Randall, Bob Graham, and Paul Dinsmore. *Creating the Project Office: A Manager's Guide to Leading Organizational Change*. San Francisco: Jossey-Bass, 2003. Thoroughly explores the process of effecting organizational changes using project management.

▪ Books on Metrics

Austin, Robert D. *Measuring and Managing Performance in Organizations*. New York: Dorset House, 1996. A useful book that explains why measurement so often leads to organizational dysfunction.

Grady, Robert B. *Successful Software Process Improvement*. Upper Saddle River, NJ: Prentice Hall PTR, 1997. Describes using metrics for sustainable process improvements.

Index